Pharmacokinetics and Pharmacodynamics of Abused Drugs

Pharmacokinetics and Pharmacodynamics of Abused Drugs

Edited by
Steven B. Karch, MD, FFFLM

Consultant Pathologist and Toxicologist
Berkeley, California

CRC Press
Taylor & Francis Group
Boca Raton London New York

CRC Press is an imprint of the
Taylor & Francis Group, an informa business

CRC Press
Taylor & Francis Group
6000 Broken Sound Parkway NW, Suite 300
Boca Raton, FL 33487-2742

10 9 8 7 6 5 4 3 2 1

International Standard Book Number-13: 978-1-4200-5458-3 (Hardcover)

Visit the Taylor & Francis Web site at
http://www.taylorandfrancis.com

and the CRC Press Web site at
http://www.crcpress.com

Contents

Preface

This volume discusses pharmacokinetics and pharmacodynamics. Chapters 1 through 4 discuss aspects of pharmacokinetics. Chapters 5 through 8 discuss aspects of pharmacodynamics.

Pharmacokinetics is defined as the study of the quantitative relationship between administered doses of a drug and the observed plasma/blood or tissue concentrations. The field of pharmacokinetics is concerned with drug absorption, distribution, biotransformation, and excretion or elimination. These processes, in addition to the dose, determine the concentration of drug at the effector or active site and, therefore, the intensity and duration of drug effect.

The practice of pharmacokinetics has been used in clinical medicine for many years in order to optimize the efficacy of medications administered to treat disease. Through a consideration of pharmacokinetics, physicians are able to determine the drug of choice, dose, route, frequency of administration, and duration of therapy in order to achieve a specific therapeutic objective. In the same manner, study of the pharmacokinetics of abused drugs aids investigators in addiction medicine, forensic toxicology, and clinical pharmacology in understanding why particular drugs are abused, factors that affect their potential for abuse, how their use can be detected and monitored over time, and also provides a rational, scientific basis for treatment therapies.

Pharmacodynamics is the study of the physiological and behavioral mechanisms by which a drug exerts its effects in living organisms. An effect is initiated by the drug binding to receptor sites in a cell's membrane, setting in motion a series of molecular and cellular reactions culminating in some physiological (e.g., opioid-induced analgesia) or behavioral (e.g., alcohol-induced impairment) effect. Drugs typically have multiple effects. For example, a benzodiazepine will produce its primary anxiolytic effect, but may also cause side effects of sedation and impaired performance.

The question of the behavioral effects of abused drugs has been the focus of research by behavioral pharmacologists for many decades. Because of the widespread use of psychoactive drugs throughout society, employers have become increasingly concerned about drugs in the workplace and the potential for impaired job performance and onsite drug-related accidents. There are now computerized tests that employers can use to aid in the detection of impaired employees. Some drugs of abuse also produce characteristic effects on the visual system, and for this reason, devices that detect eye movement and function are also being tested for their ability to predict drug ingestion and potential impairment in the workplace.

Knowledge of both pharmacokinetics and pharmacodynamics is central to an understanding of drug abuse and its treatment.

The Editor

Steven B. Karch, M.D., FFFLM, received his undergraduate degree from Brown University. He attended graduate school in anatomy and cell biology at Stanford University. He received his medical degree from Tulane University School of Medicine. Dr. Karch did postgraduate training in neuropathology at the Royal London Hospital and in cardiac pathology at Stanford University. For many years he was a consultant cardiac pathologist to San Francisco's Chief Medical Examiner.

In the U.K., Dr. Karch served as a consultant to the Crown and helped prepare the cases against serial murderer Dr. Harold Shipman, who was subsequently convicted of murdering 248 of his patients. He has testified on drug abuse–related matters in courts around the world. He has a special interest in cases of alleged euthanasia, and in episodes where mothers are accused of murdering their children by the transference of drugs, either *in utero* or by breast feeding.

Dr. Karch is the author of nearly 100 papers and book chapters, most of which are concerned with the effects of drug abuse on the heart. He has published seven books. He is currently completing the fourth edition of *Pathology of Drug Abuse*, a widely used textbook. He is also working on a popular history of Napoleon and his doctors.

Dr. Karch is forensic science editor for Humana Press, and he serves on the editorial boards of the *Journal of Cardiovascular Toxicology*, the *Journal of Clinical Forensic Medicine* (London), *Forensic Science, Medicine and Pathology*, and *Clarke's Analysis of Drugs and Poisons*.

Dr. Karch was elected a fellow of the Faculty of Legal and Forensic Medicine, Royal College of Physicians (London) in 2006. He is also a fellow of the American Academy of Forensic Sciences, the Society of Forensic Toxicologists (SOFT), the National Association of Medical Examiners (NAME), the Royal Society of Medicine in London, and the Forensic Science Society of the U.K. He is a member of The International Association of Forensic Toxicologists (TIAFT).

Contributors

David H. Epstein, Ph.D.
Clinical Pharmacology and Therapeutics Branch
National Institute on Drug Abuse
National Institutes of Health
Department of Health and Human Services
Baltimore, Maryland

Stephen J. Heishman, Ph.D.
Clinical Pharmacology and Therapeutics Branch
National Institute on Drug Abuse
National Institutes of Health
Department of Health and Human Services
Baltimore, Maryland

Jonathan Howland, Ph.D.
Social and Behavioral Sciences Department
Boston University School of Public Health
Boston, Massachusetts

Amanda J. Jenkins, Ph.D.
The Office of the Cuyahoga County Coroner
Cleveland, Ohio

Thomas H. Kelly, Ph.D.
Department of Behavioral Science
University of Kentucky College of Medicine
Lexington, Kentucky

Rudy Murillo, B.A.
Clinical Pharmacology and Therapeutics Branch
National Institute on Drug Abuse
National Institutes of Health
Department of Health and Human Services
Baltimore, Maryland

Carol S. Myers, Ph.D.
Clinical Pharmacology and Therapeutics Branch
National Institute on Drug Abuse
National Institute of Health
Department of Health and Human Services
Baltimore, Maryland

Wallace B. Pickworth, Ph.D.
Battelle Centers for Public Health Research and Evaluation
Baltimore, Maryland

Kenzie L. Preston, Ph.D.
Clinical Pharmacology and Therapeutics Branch
National Institute on Drug Abuse
National Institutes of Health
Department of Health and Human Services
Baltimore, Maryland

John P. Schmittner, M.D.
Clinical Pharmacology and Therapeutics Branch
National Institute on Drug Abuse
National Institutes of Health
Department of Health and Human Services
Baltimore, Maryland

Richard C. Taylor, M.A.
Clinical Pharmacology and Therapeutics Branch
National Institute on Drug Abuse
National Institutes of Health
Department of Health and Human Services
Baltimore, Maryland

Sharon L. Walsh, Ph.D.
Department of Behavioral Science
Center on Drug and Alcohol Research
University of Kentucky College of Medicine
Lexington, Kentucky

CHAPTER 1

Pharmacokinetics: Basic Concepts and Models

Amanda J. Jenkins, Ph.D.
The Office of the Cuyahoga County Coroner, Cleveland, Ohio

CONTENTS

1.1 INTRODUCTION

Pharmacokinetics is defined as the study of the quantitative relationship between administered doses of a drug and the observed plasma/blood or tissue concentrations.[1] The pharmacokinetic model is a mathematical description of this relationship. Models provide estimates of certain parameters, such as elimination half-life, which provide information about basic drug properties. The models may be used to predict concentration vs. time profiles for different dosing patterns.

The field of pharmacokinetics is concerned with drug absorption, distribution, biotransformation, and excretion or elimination. These processes, in addition to the dose, determine the concentration of drug at the effector or active site and, therefore, the intensity and duration of drug effect. The practice of pharmacokinetics has been used in clinical medicine for many years in order to optimize the efficacy of medications administered to treat disease. Through a consideration of pharmacokinetics, physicians are able to determine the drug of choice, dose, route, frequency of administration, and duration of therapy in order to achieve a specific therapeutic objective. In the same manner, study of the pharmacokinetics of abused drugs aids investigators in addiction medicine, forensic toxicology, and clinical pharmacology in understanding why particular drugs are abused, factors that affect their potential for abuse, and how their use can be detected and monitored over time, and also provides a rational, scientific basis for treatment therapies.

1.2 TRANSFER ACROSS BIOLOGICAL MEMBRANES

The processes of absorption, distribution, biotransformation, and elimination of a particular substance involve the transfer or movement of a drug across biological membranes. Therefore, it is important to understand those properties of cell membranes and the intrinsic properties of drugs that affect movement. Although drugs may gain entry into the body by passage through a single layer of cells, such as the intestinal epithelium, or through multiple layers of cells, such as the skin, the blood cell membrane is a common barrier to all drug entry and therefore is the most appropriate membrane for general discussion of cellular membrane structure. The cellular blood membrane consists of a phospholipid bilayer of 7- to 9-nm thickness with hydrocarbon chains oriented inward and polar head groups oriented outward. Interspersed between the lipid bilayer are proteins, which may span the entire width of the membrane permitting the formation of aqueous pores.[2] These proteins act as receptors in chemical and electrical signaling pathways and also as specific targets for drug actions.[3] The lipids in the cell membrane may move laterally, conferring fluidity at physiological temperatures and relative impermeability to highly polar molecules. The fluidity of plasma membranes is largely determined by the relative abundance of unsaturated fatty acids. Between cell membranes are pores that may permit bulk flow of substances. This is considered to be the main mechanism by which drugs cross the capillary endothelial membranes, except in the central nervous system (CNS), which possesses tight junctions that limit intercellular diffusion.[3]

Physicochemical properties of a drug also affect its movement across cell membranes. These include its molecular size and shape, solubility, degree of ionization, and relative lipid solubility of its ionized and non-ionized forms. Another factor to consider is the extent of protein binding to plasma and tissue components. Although such binding is reversible and usually rapid, only the free unbound form is considered capable of passing through biological membranes.

Drugs cross cell membranes through passive and active or specialized processes. Passive movement across biological membranes is the dominant process in the absorption and distribution of drugs. In passive transfer, hydrophobic molecules cross the cell membrane by simple diffusion along a concentration gradient. In this process there is no expenditure of cellular energy. The magnitude of drug transfer in this manner is dependent on the magnitude of the concentration gradient across the membrane and the lipid:water partition coefficient. Once steady state has been reached, the concentration of free (unbound) drug will be the same on both sides of the membrane. The exception to this situation is if the drug is capable of ionization under physiological conditions. In this case, concentrations on either side of the cell membrane will be influenced by pH differences across the membrane. Small hydrophilic molecules are thought to cross cell membranes through the aqueous pores.[4] Generally, only unionized forms of a drug cross biological membranes due to their relatively high lipid solubility. The movement of ionized forms is dependent on the pKa of the drug and the pH gradient. The partitioning of weak acids and bases across pH gradients may be predicted by the Henderson–Hasselbalch equation. For example, an orally ingested weakly acidic drug may be largely unionized in the acidic environs of the stomach but ionized to some degree at the neutral pH of the plasma. The pH gradient and difference in the proportions of ionized/non-ionized forms of the drug promote the diffusion of the weak acid through the lipid barrier of the stomach into the plasma.

Water moves across cell membranes either by the simple diffusion described above or as the result of osmotic differences across membranes. In the latter case, when water moves in bulk through aqueous pores in cellular membranes due to osmotic forces, any molecule that is small enough to pass through the pores will also be transferred. This movement of solutes is called filtration. Cell membranes throughout the body possess pores of different sizes; for example, the pores in the kidney glomerulus are typically 70 nm, but the channels in most cells are <4 nm.[2]

The movement of some compounds across membranes cannot be explained by simple diffusion or filtration. These are usually high-molecular-weight or very lipid soluble substances. Therefore, specialized processes have been postulated to account for the movement. Active processes typically involve the expenditure of cellular energy to move molecules across biological membranes. Characteristics of active transport include selectivity, competitive inhibition, saturability, and movement across an electrochemical or concentration gradient. The drug complexes with a macromolecular carrier on one side of the membrane, traverses the membrane, and is released on the other side. The carrier then returns to the original surface. Active transport processes are important in the elimination of xenobiotics. They are involved in the movement of drugs in hepatocytes, renal tubular cells, and neuronal membranes. For example, the liver has four known active transport systems, two for organic acids, one for organic bases, and one for neutral organic compounds.[2] A different specialized transport process is termed "facilitated diffusion." This transport is similar to the carrier-mediated transport described above except that no active processes are involved. The drug is not moved against an electrochemical or concentration gradient and there is no expenditure of energy. A biochemical example of such transport is the movement of glucose from the gastrointestinal tract through the intestinal epithelium.

1.2.1 Absorption

In order for a drug to exert its pharmacological effect, it must first gain entry into the body, be absorbed into the bloodstream, and transported or distributed to its site of action. This is true except in the case of drugs that exert their effect locally or at the absorption site. The absorption site, or port of entry, is determined by the route of drug administration.

Routes of administration are either enteral or parenteral. The former term denotes all routes pertaining to the alimentary canal. Therefore, sublingual, oral, and rectal are enteral routes of administration. All other routes, such as intravenous, intramuscular, subcutaneous, dermal, vaginal, and intraperitoneal, are parenteral routes.

Absorption describes the rate and extent to which a drug leaves its site of administration and enters the general circulation. Factors that, therefore, affect absorption include the physicochemical properties of the drug that determine transfer across cell membranes as described earlier; formulation or physical state of the drug; site of absorption; concentration of drug; circulation at absorption site; and area of absorbing surface.

1.2.1.1 Gastrointestinal

Absorption of drug may occur at any point along the tract including the mouth, stomach, intestine, and rectum. Because the majority of drugs are absorbed by passive diffusion, the non-ionized, lipid soluble form of the drug is favored for rapid action. Therefore, according to the Henderson–Hasselbalch equation, the absorption of weak acids should be favored in the stomach and the absorption of weak bases in the alkaline environment of the small intestine. However, other factors such as relative surface area will influence absorption. The stomach is lined by a relatively thick mucus-covered membrane to facilitate its primary function of digestion. In comparison, the epithelium of the small intestine is thin, with villi and microvilli providing a large surface area to facilitate its primary function of absorption of nutrients. Therefore, any factor that increases gastric emptying will tend to increase the rate of drug absorption, regardless of the ionization state of the drug.

The gastrointestinal (GI) tract possesses carrier-mediated transport systems for the transfer of nutrients and electrolytes across the gastric wall. These systems may also carry drugs and other xenobiotics into the organism. For example, lead is absorbed by the calcium transporter.[5] Absorption also depends on the physical characteristics of a drug. For example, a highly lipid soluble drug will not dissolve in the stomach. In addition, solid dosage forms will have little contact with gastric mucosa and the drug will not be absorbed until the solid is dissolved. Further, the particle size affects absorption, since dissolution rate is proportional to particle size.[6] Compounds that increase intestinal permeability or increase the residence time in the intestine by altering intestinal motility will thereby increase absorption of other drugs through that segment of the alimentary canal.

Once a drug has been absorbed through the GI tract, the amount of the compound that reaches the systemic circulation depends on several factors. The drug may be biotransformed by the GI cells or removed by the liver through which it must pass. This loss of drug before gaining access to the systemic circulation is known as the first pass effect.

Although oral ingestion is the most common route of GI absorption, drugs may be administered sublingually. Despite the small surface area for absorption, certain drugs that are non-ionic and highly lipid soluble are effectively absorbed by this route. The drugs nitroglycerin and buprenorphine are administered by this route. The blood supply in the mouth drains into the superior vena cava and, because of this anatomic characteristic, drugs are protected from first pass metabolism by the liver.

Although an uncommon route by which abused drugs are self-administered, rectal administration is used in medical practice when vomiting or other circumstances preclude oral administration. Approximately 50% of the drug that is absorbed will bypass the liver.[3] The disadvantage of this route for drug absorption is that the process is often incomplete and irregular and some drugs irritate the mucosal lining of the rectum.

1.2.1.2 Pulmonary

Gases, volatile liquids, and aerosols may be absorbed through the lungs. Access to the circulation by this route is rapid because of the large surface area of the lungs and extensive capillary network in close association with the alveoli. In the case of absorption of gases and volatilizable liquids, the ionization state and lipid solubility of the substance are less important than in GI absorption. This is because diffusion through cell membranes is not the rate-limiting step in the absorption process. The reasons include low volatility of ionized molecules, the extensive capillary network in close association with the alveoli resulting in a short distance for diffusion, and the rapid removal of absorbed substances by the blood. Some substances may not reach the lungs because they are deposited and absorbed in the mucosal lining of the nose.

Drugs may be atomized or volatilized and inhaled as droplets or particulates in air; a common example is the smoking of drugs. The advantages of this route include rapid transport into the blood, avoidance of first pass hepatic metabolism, and avoidance of the medical problems associated with other routes of illicit drug administration. Disadvantages include local irritant effect on the tissues of the nasopharynx and absorption of particulate matter in the nasopharynx and bronchial tree. For a drug to be effectively absorbed it should reach the alveoli. However, absorption of particulate matter is governed by particulate size and water solubility. Particles with diameters >5 µm are usually deposited in the nasopharyngeal region;[2] particles in the 2- to 5-µm range are deposited in the tracheobronchiolar region and particles 1 µm and smaller reach the alveolar sacs.

1.2.1.3 Dermal

The skin is impermeable to most chemicals. For a drug to be absorbed it must pass first through the epidermal layers or specialized tissue such as hair follicles or sweat and sebaceous glands. Absorption through the outer layer of skin, the stratum corneum, is the rate-limiting step in the dermal absorption of drugs. This outer layer consists of densely packed keratinized cells and is commonly referred to as the "dead" layer of skin because the cells comprising this layer are without nuclei. Drug substances may be absorbed by simple diffusion through this layer. The lower layers of the epidermis, and the dermis, consist of porous nonselective cells that pose little barrier to absorption by passive diffusion. Once a chemical reaches this level, it is then rapidly absorbed into the systemic circulation because of the extensive network of venous and lymphatic capillaries located in the dermis. Drug absorption through the skin depends on the characteristics of the drug and on the condition of the skin. Since the stratum corneum is the main barrier to absorption, damage to this area by sloughing of cells due to abrasion or burning enhances absorption, as does any mechanism that increases cutaneous blood flow. Hydration of the stratum corneum also increases its permeability and therefore enhances absorption of chemicals.

1.2.1.4 Parenteral Injection

Drugs are often absorbed through the GI tract, lungs, and skin but many illicit drugs have historically been self-administered by injection. These routes typically include intravenous, intramuscular, and subcutaneous administration. The intravenous route of administration introduces the drug directly into the venous bloodstream, thereby eliminating the process of absorption altogether. Substances that are locally irritating may be administered intravenously since the blood vessel walls are relatively insensitive. This route permits the rapid introduction of the drug to the systemic circulation and allows high concentrations to be quickly achieved. Intravenous administration may result in unfavorable physiological responses because, once introduced, the drug cannot be removed. This route of administration is dependent on maintaining patent veins and can result in extensive scar tissue formation due to chronic drug administration. Insoluble particulate matter deposited in the blood vessels is another medical problem associated with the intravenous route.

Intramuscular and subcutaneous administration involves absorption from the injection site into the circulation by passive diffusion. The rate of absorption is limited by the size of the capillary bed at the injection site and by the solubility of the drug in the interstitial fluid.[3] If blood flow is increased at the administration site, absorption will be increased. Conversely, if blood pressure is decreased for any reason (such as cardiogenic shock) absorption will be prolonged.

1.2.2 Distribution

After entering circulation, drugs are distributed throughout the body. The extent of distribution is dependent on the physicochemical properties of the drug and physiological factors. Drugs cross cell membranes throughout the body by passive diffusion or specialized transport processes. Small water-soluble molecules and ions cross cell membranes through aqueous pores, whereas lipid-soluble substances diffuse through the membrane lipid bilayer. The rate of distribution of a drug is dependent on blood flow and the rate of diffusion across cell membranes of various tissues and organs. The affinity of a substance for certain tissues also affects the rate of distribution.

Because only unbound drug (the free fraction) is in equilibrium throughout the body, disposition is affected by binding to or dissolving in cellular constituents. While circulating in blood, drugs may be reversibly bound to several plasma proteins. For example, basic compounds often bind to α1-acid glycoprotein; acidic compounds bind to albumin. The extent of plasma protein binding varies among drugs: nicotine is 5% bound, whereas the barbiturate, secobarbital, is 50% bound; and the benzodiazepine, diazepam, is 96% bound.[7] The fraction of drug that is bound is governed by the drug concentration, the drug's affinity for binding sites, and the number of binding sites available for binding. At low drug concentrations, the fraction bound is a function of the number of binding sites and the dissociation constant, a measure of binding affinity. When drug concentrations exceed the dissociation constant, concentration also governs the amount of protein binding. Therefore, published protein binding fractions for drugs only apply over a certain concentration range, usually the therapeutic concentration. Plasma protein binding limits the amount of drug entering tissues. Because plasma protein binding of drugs is relatively non-selective, drugs and endogenous substances compete for binding sites, and drug displacement from binding sites by another substance can contribute to toxicity by increasing the free fraction.

1.2.2.1 Binding to Tissue Constituents

In addition to binding to plasma proteins, drugs may bind to tissue constituents. The liver and kidney have a large capacity to act as storage depots for drugs. The mechanisms responsible for transfer of many drugs from the blood appear to be active transport processes.[2] Ligandin, a cytoplasmic liver protein, has a high affinity for many organic acids while metallothionein binds metals in the kidney and liver.

Lipid-soluble drugs are stored in neutral fat by dissolution. Since the fat content of an obese individual may be 50% body weight, it follows that large amounts of drug can be stored in this tissue. Once stored in fat, the concentration of drug is lowered throughout the body, in the blood, and also in target organs. Any activity, such as dieting or starvation, that serves to mobilize fat could potentially increase blood concentrations and hence contribute to an increase in the risk of drug toxicity.

Drugs may also be stored in bone. Drugs diffuse from the extracellular fluid through the hydration shell of the hydroxyapatite crystals of the bone mineral. Lead, fluoride, and other compounds may be deposited and stored in bone. Deposition may not necessarily be detrimental. For example, lead is not toxic to bone tissue. However, chronic fluoride deposition results in the condition known as skeletal fluorosis. Generally, storage of compounds in bone is a reversible process. Toxicants may be released from the bone by ion exchange at the crystal surface or by dissolution of the bone during osteoclastic activity. If osteolytic activity is increased, the hydroxyapatite lattice is mobilized, resulting in an increase in blood concentrations of any stored xenobiotics.

1.2.2.2 Blood–Brain Barrier

The blood–brain barrier is often viewed as an impenetrable barrier to xenobiotics. However, this is not true and a more realistic representation is as a site that is less permeable to ionized substances and high-molecular-weight compounds than other membranes. Many toxicants do not enter the brain because the capillary endothelial cells are joined by tight junctions with few pores between cells; the capillaries of the CNS are surrounded by glial processes; and the interstitial fluid of the CNS has a low protein concentration. The first two anatomical processes limit the entry of small- to medium-sized water-soluble molecules, whereas the entry of lipid-soluble compounds is limited by the low protein content, which restricts paracellular transport. It is interesting to note that the permeability of the brain to toxicants varies from area to area. For example, the cortex, area postrema, and pineal body are more permeable than other regions.[2] This may be due to differences in blood supply or the nature of the barrier itself. Entrance of drugs into the brain is governed by the same factors that determine transfer across membranes in other parts of the body. Only the unbound fraction is available for transfer, and lipid solubility and the degree of ionization dictate the rate of entry of drugs into the brain. It should be noted that the blood–brain barrier is not fully developed at birth. In animal studies, morphine has been found to be three to ten times more toxic to newborns than adults.[8]

1.2.2.3 Pregnancy

During pregnancy, drugs may also be distributed from the mother to the fetus by simple diffusion across the placenta. The placenta comprises several cell layers between the maternal and fetal circulations. The number of layers varies between species and state of gestation. The same factors govern placental drug transfer as movement by passive diffusion across other membranes. The placenta plays an additional role in preventing transfer of xenobiotics to the fetus by possessing biotransformation capabilities.

1.3 BIOTRANSFORMATION

Lipophilicity, a desirable drug characteristic for absorption and distribution across biological membranes, is a hindrance to elimination. To prevent accumulation of xenobiotics, the body chemically alters lipophilic compounds to more water-soluble products. The sum of all the processes that convert lipophilic substances to more hydrophilic metabolites is termed biotransformation. These biochemical processes are usually enzymatic and are commonly divided into Phase I and Phase II reactions.[9] Phase I reactions generally expose or introduce a polar group to the parent drug, thereby increasing its water solubility. These reactions are oxidative or hydrolytic in nature and include *N*- and *O*-dealkylation, aliphatic and aromatic hydroxylation, *N*- and *S*-oxidation, and deamination. These reactions usually result in loss of pharmacological activity, although there are numerous examples of enhanced activity. Indeed, formation of a Phase I product is desirable in the case of administration of prodrugs.

Phase II reactions are conjugation reactions and involve covalent bonding of functional groups with endogenous compounds. Highly water-soluble conjugates are formed by combination of the drug or metabolite with glucuronic acid, sulfate, glutathione, amino acids, or acetate. Again, these products are generally pharmacologically inactive or less active than the parent compound. An exception is the metabolite morphine-6-glucuronide. In this case, glucuronidation at the 6-position increases the affinity of morphine for binding at the mu receptor and results in equivalent or enhanced pharmacological activity.[10]

The enzymes that catalyze the biotransformation of drugs are found mainly in the liver. This is not surprising considering the primary function of the liver is to handle compounds absorbed from the GI tract. In addition, the liver receives all the blood perfusing the splanchnic area. Therefore, this organ has developed a high capacity to remove substances from blood, and store, transform, and/or release substances into the general circulation. In its primary role of biotransformation, the liver acts as a homogeneous unit, with all parenchymal cells or hepatocytes exhibiting enzymatic activity. In tissues involved in extrahepatic biotransformation processes, typically only one or two cell types are used. Many organs have demonstrated activity toward foreign compounds but the major extrahepatic tissues are those involved in the absorption or excretion of chemicals. These include the kidney, lung, intestine, skin, and testes. The main cells containing biotransformation enzymes in these organs are the proximal tubular cells, clara cells, mucosa lining cells, epithelial cells, and seminiferous tubules, respectively.

1.3.1 Phase I Enzymes

Phase I enzymes are located primarily in the endoplasmic reticulum of cells. These enzymes are membrane bound within a lipoprotein matrix and are referred to as microsomal enzymes. This is in reference to the subcellular fraction isolated by differential centrifugation of a liver homogenate. The two most important enzyme systems involved in Phase I biotransformation reactions are the cytochrome P450 system and the mixed function amine oxidase.

With the advances in recombinant DNA technology, eight major mammalian gene families of hepatic and extrahepatic cytochrome P450 have been identified.[2] A comprehensive discussion of the cytochrome P450 system is beyond the scope of this chapter and the reader is referred to a number of reviews.[11–13] Briefly, this system comprises two coupled enzymes: NADPH-cytochrome P450 reductase and a heme-containing enzyme, cytochrome P450. Numerous oxidative pathways for xenobiotics exist, both in humans and other animals. Much drug oxidation is performed by a group of enzymes known as CYPs (from *CY*tochrome *P*450, the 450 being derived from the cytochrome's maximal absorbance of light at 450 nm). The cytochrome P450s or CYPs are categorized according to amino acid sequence homology. CYPs that have less than 40% homology are placed in a different family (e.g., 1, 2, 3, and so on). CYPs that are 40 to 55% identical are assigned to different subfamilies (e.g., 1A, 1B, 1C, and so on). P450 enzymes that are more than 55% identical are classified as members of the same subfamily (e.g., 2B1, 2B2, 2B3). The P450 enzymes are expressed in numerous tissues, but are especially prevalent in the liver. This complex is associated with another cytochrome, cytochrome b_5 with a reductase enzyme. In reactions catalyzed by cytochrome P450, the substrate combines with the oxidized form of cytochrome P450 (Fe^{3+}) to form a complex. This complex accepts an electron from NADPH, which reduces the iron in the cytochrome P450 heme moiety to Fe^{2+}. This reduced substrate–cytochrome P450 complex then combines with molecular oxygen, which in turn accepts another electron from NADPH. In some cases, the second electron is provided by NADH via cytochrome b_5. Both electrons are transferred to molecular oxygen, resulting in a highly reactive and unstable species. One atom of the unstable oxygen molecule is transferred to the substrate and the other is reduced to water. The substrate then dissociates as a result, regenerating the oxidized form of cytochrome P450.

1.3.2 Phase II Enzymes

Many of the Phase II enzymes are located in the cytosol or supernatant fraction after differential centrifugation of a liver homogenate. These reactions are biosynthetic and therefore require energy. This is accomplished by transforming the substrate or cofactors to high-energy intermediates. One of the major Phase II reactions is glucuronidation. The resultant glucuronides are eliminated in the bile or urine. The enzyme uridine diphosphate (UDP) glucuronosyltransferase is located in the endoplasmic reticulum. This enzyme catalyzes the reaction between UDP–glucuronic acid and the functional group of the substrate. The location of this enzyme means that it has direct access to the products of Phase I enzymatic reactions. Another important conjugation reaction in humans is sulfation of hydroxyl groups. The sulfotransferases are a group of soluble enzymes, classified as aryl, hydroxysteroid, estrone, and bile salt sulfotransferases. Their primary function is the transfer of inorganic sulfate to the hydroxyl moiety of phenol or aliphatic alcohols.

Another important family of enzymes is the glutathione-*S*-transferases, which are located in both the cytoplasm and endoplasmic reticulum of cells. The activity of the cytosolic transferase is 5 to 40 times greater than the endoplasmic enzyme. These transferase enzymes catalyze the reaction between the sulfhydryl group of the tripeptide glutathione with substances containing electrophilic carbon atoms. The glutathione conjugates are cleaved to cysteine derivatives, primarily in the kidney. These derivatives are then acetylated resulting in mercapturic acid conjugates, which are excreted in the urine.

Many factors affect the rate at which a drug is biotransformed. One of the important factors is obviously the concentration of the drug at the site of action of biotransforming enzymes. Physicochemical properties of the drug, such as lipophilicity, are important, in addition to dose and route of administration. Certain physiological, pharmacological, and environmental factors may also affect the rate of biotransformation of a compound. Numerous variables affect biotransformation including sex, age, genetic polymorphisms, time of day or circadian rhythms, nutritional status, enzyme induction or inhibition, hepatic injury, and disease states.

1.4 ELIMINATION

Drugs are excreted or eliminated from the body as parent compounds or metabolites. The organs involved in excretion, with the exception of the lungs, eliminate water-soluble compounds more readily than lipophilic substances. The lungs are important for the elimination of anesthetic gases and vapors. The processes of biotransformation generally produce more polar compounds for excretion. The most important excretory organ is the kidney. Substances in the feces are mainly unabsorbed drugs administered orally or compounds excreted into the bile and not reabsorbed. Drugs may also be excreted in breast milk[14] and, even though the amounts are small, they represent an important pathway because the recipient of any drugs by this route is the nursing infant.

For a comprehensive discussion of renal excretion of drugs, the reader is referred to Weiner and Mudge.[15] Excretion of drugs and their metabolites involves three processes, namely, glomerular filtration, passive tubular reabsorption, and active tubular secretion. The amount of a drug that enters the tubular lumen of the kidney is dependent on the glomerular filtration rate and the fraction of drug that is plasma protein bound. In the proximal renal tubule organic anions and cations are added to the filtrate by active transport processes. Glucuronide drug metabolites are secreted in this way by the carrier-mediated system for naturally occurring organic acids. In the proximal and distal tubules of the kidney, the non-ionized forms of weak acids and bases are passively reabsorbed. The necessary concentration gradient is created by the reabsorption of water with sodium. The passive reabsorption of ionized forms is pH dependent because the tubular cells are less permeable to these moieties. Therefore, in the treatment of drug poisoning, the excretion of some drugs can be increased by alkalinization or acidification of the urine.

Under normal physiological conditions, excretion of drugs in the sweat, saliva, and by the lacrimal glands is quantitatively insignificant. Elimination by these routes is dependent on pH and diffusion of the unionized lipid-soluble form of the drug through the epithelial cells of the glands. Drugs excreted in saliva enter the mouth and may be reabsorbed and swallowed. Drugs have also been detected in hair and skin, and although quantitatively unimportant, these routes may be useful in drug detection and therefore have forensic significance.

1.5 PHARMACOKINETIC PARAMETERS

Pharmacokinetics assumes that a relationship exists between the concentration of drug in an accessible site, such as the blood, and the pharmacological or toxic response. The concentration of drug in the systemic circulation is related to the concentration of drug at the site of action. Pharmacokinetics attempts to quantify the relationship between dose and drug disposition and provide the framework, through modeling, to interpret measured concentrations in biological fluids.[3] Several pharmacokinetic parameters are utilized to explain various pharmacokinetic processes. It is often changes in these parameters, through disease, genetic abnormalities, or drug interactions, that necessitate modifications of dosage regimens for therapeutic agents. The most important parameters are clearance, the ability of the body to eliminate drug, volume of distribution, a measure of the apparent volume of the body available to occupy the drug, bioavailability, the proportion of drug absorbed into the systemic circulation, and half-life, a measure of the rate of drug elimination from the blood. These concepts are discussed below.

1.5.1 Clearance

Clearance is defined as the proportionality factor that relates the rate of drug elimination to the blood or plasma drug concentration:[16]

$$\text{Clearance} = \text{Rate of elimination/Concentration}$$

In the above equation, the concentration term refers to drug concentration at steady state. The units of clearance are volume per unit time and, therefore, this parameter measures the volume of biological fluid, such as blood, that would have to have drug removed to account for drug elimination. Therefore, clearance is not a measure of the amount of drug removed.

The concept of clearance is useful in pharmacokinetics because clearance is usually constant over a wide range of concentrations, provided that elimination processes are not saturated. Saturation of biotransformation and excretory processes may occur in overdose and toxicokinetic effects should be considered. If a constant fraction of drug is eliminated per unit time, the elimination follows first-order kinetics. However, if a constant amount of drug is eliminated per unit time, the elimination is described by zero-order kinetics. Some drugs, for example, ethanol, exhibit zero-order kinetics at "normal" or non-intoxicating concentrations. However, for any drug that exhibits first-order kinetics at therapeutic or nontoxic concentrations, once the mechanisms for elimination become saturated, the kinetics become zero order and clearance becomes variable.[3]

Clearance may also be viewed as the loss of drug from an organ of elimination such as the liver or kidney. This approach enables evaluation of the effects of a variety of physiological factors such as changes in blood flow, plasma protein binding, and enzyme activity. Therefore, total systemic clearance is determined by adding the clearance (CL) values for each elimination organ or tissue:

$$\mathrm{CL_{systemic}} = \mathrm{CL_{renal}} + \mathrm{CL_{hepatic}} + \mathrm{CL_{lung}} + \mathrm{CL_{other}}$$

Clearance from an individual organ is a product of blood flow and the extraction ratio. The extraction ratio is derived from the concentration of drug in the blood entering the organ and the concentration of drug in the blood leaving the organ. If the extraction ratio is 0, no drug is removed. If it is 1, then all the drug entering the organ is removed from the blood. Therefore, the clearance of an organ may be determined from the following equation:

$$\mathrm{CL_{organ}} = Q(C_A - C_V/C_A) = Q \times E$$

where

Q = blood flow
C_A = arterial drug concentration
C_V = venous drug concentration
E = extraction ratio

1.5.2 Volume of Distribution

The plasma drug concentration reached after distribution is complete is a result of the dose and the extent of uptake by tissues. The extent of distribution can be described by relating the amount of drug in the body to the concentration. This parameter is known as the volume of distribution. This volume does not indicate a defined physiological dimension but the volume of fluid required to contain all the drug in the body at the same concentration as in the plasma or blood. Therefore, it is often called the apparent volume of distribution (V) and is determined at steady state when distribution equilibrium has been reached between drug in plasma and tissues.

$$V = \text{Amount in body/Plasma drug concentration}$$

The volume of distribution depends on the pKa of the drug, the degree of plasma protein and tissue binding, and the lipophilicity of the drug. As would be expected, drugs that distribute widely throughout the body have large volumes of distribution (for example, the V_d of fluphenazine, which is a widely distributed drug, is 11; the V_d for ketoconozole is only 0.7, indicating that very little drug leaves the circulation). In the equation above, the body is considered one homogeneous unit and therefore exhibits a one-compartment model. In this model, drug administration occurs in the central compartment, and distribution is instantaneous throughout the body. For most drugs, the simple one-compartment model does not describe the time course of drug in the body adequately and drug distribution and elimination are more completely described in multiple exponential terms using multicompartmental models. In these models, the volume of distribution, V_{area}, is calculated as the ratio of clearance to the rate of decline of the concentration during the elimination phase:

$$V_{area} = CL/k$$

where k = rate constant.

1.5.3 Bioavailability

The bioavailability of a drug refers to the fraction of the dose that reaches the systemic circulation. This parameter is dependent on the rate and extent of absorption at the site of drug administration. Obviously, it follows that drugs administered intravenously do not undergo absorption, but immediately gain access to the systemic circulation and are considered 100% bioavailable. In the case of oral administration, if the hepatic extraction ratio is known, it is possible to predict the maximum bioavailability of drug by this route assuming first-order processes, according to the following equation:[3]

$$F_{max} = 1 - E = 1 - (CL_{hepatic}/Q_{hepatic})$$

The bioavailability of a drug by various routes may also be determined by comparing the area under the curve (AUC) obtained from the plasma concentration vs. time curve after intravenous and other routes of administration:[9]

$$\text{Bioavailability} = AUC_{oral}/AUC_{IV}$$

1.5.4 Half-Life

The half-life is the time it takes for the plasma drug concentration to decrease by 50%. Half-life is usually determined from the log-terminal phase of the elimination curve. However, it is important to remember that this parameter is a derived term and is dependent on the clearance and volume of distribution of the drug. Therefore, as CL and V change with disease, drug interactions, and age, so a change in the half-life should be expected. The half-life is typically calculated from the following equation:

$$t_{1/2} = 0.693/k$$

where $t_{1/2}$ = half life and k = elimination rate constant.

Because $k = CL/V$, the interrelationship between these parameters is clearly evident.

1.6 DOSAGE REGIMENS

Pharmacokinetic principles, in addition to clinical factors such as the state of the patient, are utilized in determining dosage regimens. Factors that relate to the safety and efficacy of the drug, such as activity–toxicity relationships (therapeutic window and side effects), and pharmaceutical factors, such as dosage form and route of administration, must be considered.[16]

The goal of a therapeutic regimen is to achieve therapeutic concentrations of a drug continuously or intermittently. The latter is useful if tolerance to the drug develops, or if the therapeutic effects of the drug persist and increase in intensity even with rapid drug disappearance. Adjustments to the dosage regimen are made to maintain therapeutically effective drug concentrations and minimize undesirable effects. Optimization of drug therapy is typically determined empirically, that is, changing the dose based on response of the individual. However, there is often better correlation between blood or plasma concentration or amount of drug in the body than the dose administered. Therefore, pharmacokinetic data are useful in the design of dosage regimens. In theory, data following a single dose may be used to estimate plasma concentrations following any dosing design.

For drugs whose effects are difficult to measure, or whose therapeutic index is low, a target-level or steady-state plasma concentration is desirable. A dose is computed to achieve this level, drug concentrations are measured, and the dose is adjusted accordingly. To apply this strategy, the therapeutic range should be determined. For many drugs the lower limit of this range appears to be the concentration that produces 50% maximal response. The upper limit is determined by drug toxicity and is commonly determined by the concentration at which 5 to 10% of patients experience a toxic effect.[3] The target concentration is then chosen at the middle of the therapeutic range.

1.6.1 Loading Doses

The loading dose is one or a series of doses that are administered at the beginning of therapy. The objective is to reach the target concentration rapidly. The loading dose can be estimated using the following formula:

$$\text{Loading Dose} = \text{Target } C_p \times V_{ss}/F$$

where C_p = concentration in plasma, V_{ss} = volume of distribution at steady state, and F = fractional bioavailability of the dose.

A loading dose is desirable if the time to achieve steady state is long compared to the need for the condition being treated. One disadvantage of a loading dose is the acute exposure to high concentrations of the drug, which may result in toxic effects in sensitive individuals.

1.6.2 Dosing Rate

In the majority of clinical situations, drugs are administered as a series of repeated doses or as a continuous infusion in order to maintain a steady-state concentration. Therefore, a maintenance dose must be calculated such that the rate of input is equal to the rate of drug loss. This may be determined using the following formula:

$$\text{Dosing Rate} = \text{Target} \times \text{CL}/F$$

where CL = clearance and F = fractional bioavailability of the dose.

It is obvious from the above that in order to design an appropriate dosage regimen, several pharmacokinetic factors, including CL, F, V_{ss}, and half-life, must be known in addition to an understanding of the principles of absorption and distribution of the drug in question. The clinician must also be aware of variations in these factors in a particular patient. One should note that even "normal" individuals exhibit variations in these parameters. For example, one standard deviation on clearance values may be 50%. These unpredicted variations in pharmacokinetic parameters may result in a wide range of drug concentrations. This is unacceptable in most cases especially for those drugs with a low therapeutic index. Therefore, C_p should be measured and estimates of CL, F, and V_{ss} calculated directly.

1.7 THERAPEUTIC DRUG MONITORING

Blood or plasma drug concentrations at steady state are typically measured to refine estimates of CL/*F* for the individual. Updated estimates are then used to adjust maintenance doses to reach the desired target concentration. Drug concentrations can be misleading if the relevant pharmacokinetics (and toxicokinetics; see Chapter 3) are not considered. In addition, individual variability in drug response, due to multiple drug use, disease, genetic differences, and tolerance, must be considered. Pharmacokinetic characteristics of drugs may differ with development and age. Therefore, drug effects may vary considerably among infants, children, and adults. For example, water constitutes 80% of the weight of a newborn, whereas in adults it constitutes approximately 60%. These differences affect distribution of drugs throughout the body.

1.7.1 Plasma

Measurement of drug concentrations in plasma is the cornerstone of therapeutic drug monitoring (TDM), but it is not without pitfalls. In many instances, clinical response does not correlate with plasma drug concentrations. Other considerations may be as follows.

1.7.1.1 Time Delays

It often takes time for a response to reflect a given plasma concentration due to the individual kinetics of the drug. Until this equilibrium is reached, correlation between response and concentration is difficult and may lead to misinterpretation of the clinical picture. Delay may be due to lack of equilibration between plasma and target organ as the drug distributes throughout the body. In addition, delay may be because the response measured is an indirect measure of drug effect, e.g., a change in blood pressure is an indirect measure of either change in peripheral resistance or cardiac output or both.

1.7.1.2 Active Metabolites

Poor correlation may be found between response and plasma concentration of parent drug if active metabolites are present and not measured. Formation of active metabolites may be a function of the route of drug administration because oral ingestion generally produces an initial surge of metabolites due to the first-pass effect of the liver compared with drugs administered intravenously.

1.7.1.3 Exposure Duration

Some drugs exhibit unusual concentration/response relationships, which minimizes the utility of TDM. In these cases, clinical response correlates more with duration of dosing than the actual dose or resultant plasma concentrations.

1.7.1.4 Tolerance

The effectiveness of a drug may diminish with continual use. Tolerance denotes a decreased pharmacological responsiveness to a drug. This is demonstrated by several drugs of abuse including ethanol and heroin. The degree of tolerance varies but is never complete. For example, tolerance to the effects of morphine quickly develops, but the user is not totally unresponsive to the pharmacological effects. To compensate for the development of tolerance, the dose is increased. Tolerance may develop slowly, such as in the case of tolerance to the CNS effects of ethanol, or can occur acutely (tachyphylaxis) as in the case of nicotine. In these cases, a correlation may be found between plasma drug concentration and the intensity of response at a given moment, but the relationship is not consistent and varies with time.[16]

1.7.2 Saliva

In recent years, saliva has been utilized for TDM. The advantage is that collection is noninvasive and painless and so it has been used as a specimen of choice in pediatric TDM. Due to the low protein content of saliva, it is considered to represent the unbound or free fraction of drug in plasma. Since this is the fraction considered available for transfer across membranes and therefore responsible for pharmacological activity, its usefulness is easy to understand. Saliva collection methods are known to influence drug concentrations, but if these are compensated for and a standardized procedure utilized, correlation between plasma and saliva drug concentrations may be demonstrated for several drugs (e.g., phenytoin). Inconsistent results have been found for some drugs such as phenobarbital, so additional studies are needed to clearly define the limitations of testing saliva for TDM.

REFERENCES

1. Derendorf, H. and Hochhaus, G., Eds., *Handbook of Pharmacokinetic/Pharmacodynamic Correlation,* CRC Press, Boca Raton, FL, 1995.
2. Amdur, M.O., Doull, J., and Klaassen, C.D., Eds., *Casarett and Doull's Toxicology: The Basic Science of Poisons,* Pergamon Press, Elmsford, NY, 1991.
3. Hardman, J.G. and Limbird, L.E., Eds., *Goodman & Gilman's The Pharmacological Basis of Therapeutics,* McGraw-Hill, New York, 1996.
4. Benz, R., Janko, K., and Langer, P., Pore formation by the matrix protein (porin) to *Escherichia coli* in planar bilayer membranes, *Ann. N.Y. Acad. Sci.,* 358, 13–24, 1980.
5. Sobel, A.E., Gawron, O., and Kramer, B., Influence of vitamin D in experimental lead poisoning, *Proc. Soc. Exp. Biol. Med.,* 38, 433–435, 1938.
6. Bates, T.R. and Gibaldi, M., Gastrointestinal absorption of drugs. In Swarbuck, J., Ed.: *Current Concepts in the Pharmaceutical Sciences: Biopharmaceutics,* Lea & Febiger, Philadelphia, 1970.
7. Baselt, R.C. and Cravey, R.H., *Disposition of Toxic Drugs and Chemicals in Man,* Chemical Toxicology Institute, Foster City, CA, 1995.
8. Kupferberg, H.J. and Way, E.L., Pharmacologic basis for the increased sensitivity of the newborn rat to morphine, *J. Pharmacol. Exp. Ther.,* 141, 105–112, 1963.
9. Pratt, W.B. and Taylor, P., Eds., *Principles of Drug Action: The Basis of Pharmacology,* Churchill Livingstone, New York, 1990.
10. Mulder, G.J., Ed., *Sulfation of Drugs and Related Compounds,* CRC Press, Boca Raton, FL, 1981.
11. Schenkman, J.B. and Kupfer, D., Eds., *Hepatic Cytochrome P-450 Monooxygenase System,* Pergamon Press, Oxford, 1982.
12. Gonzalez, F.J., The molecular biology of cytochrome P450s, *Pharmacol. Rev.,* 40, 243, 1988.
13. Conney, A.H., Induction of microsomal cytochrome P-450 enzymes, *Life Sci.,* 39, 2493, 1986.
14. Stowe, C.M. and Plaa, G.L., Extrarenal excretion of drugs and chemicals, *Annu. Rev. Pharmacol.,* 8, 337–356, 1968.
15. Weiner, I.M. and Mudge, G.H., Renal tubular mechanisms for excretion of organic acids and bases, *Am. J. Med.,* 36, 743–762, 1964.
16. Rowland, M. and Tozer, T.N., *Clinical Pharmacokinetics Concepts and Applications,* Lea & Febiger, Philadelphia, 1989.

CHAPTER 2

Pharmacokinetic Modeling and Pharmacokinetic–Pharmacodynamic Correlations

Amanda J. Jenkins, Ph.D.
The Office of the Cuyahoga County Coroner, Cleveland, Ohio

CONTENTS

2.1 COMPARTMENTAL MODELING

The pharmacokinetic profile of a drug is described by the processes of absorption, distribution, metabolism, and excretion. The disposition of a drug in the body may be further delineated by mathematical modeling. These models are based on the concept that the body may be viewed as a series of compartments in which the drug is distributed. If the compartmental concept is considered literally, then each tissue and organ become an individual compartment. However, in pharmacokinetic modeling, several organs or tissues exhibit similar characteristics in drug deposition and are often considered the same compartment. The pharmacokinetic profiles of many drugs may be explained using one- or two-compartment models, but more complex models exist and, with advances in computer software, the ability to describe drug disposition has increased. The use of models does not mean that the drug distributes into distinct physiological compartments, but that these mathematical models adequately describe the fate of the drug in the human body.

2.1.1 One-Compartment Models

In the one-compartment model the entire body is considered as one unit (Figure 2.1A). The drug is administered into the compartment and distributed throughout the compartment (the body) instantaneously.[1] Similarly, the drug is eliminated directly from the one compartment at a rate measured by k_{el}, the elimination rate constant. The time course of the drug, as measured in the

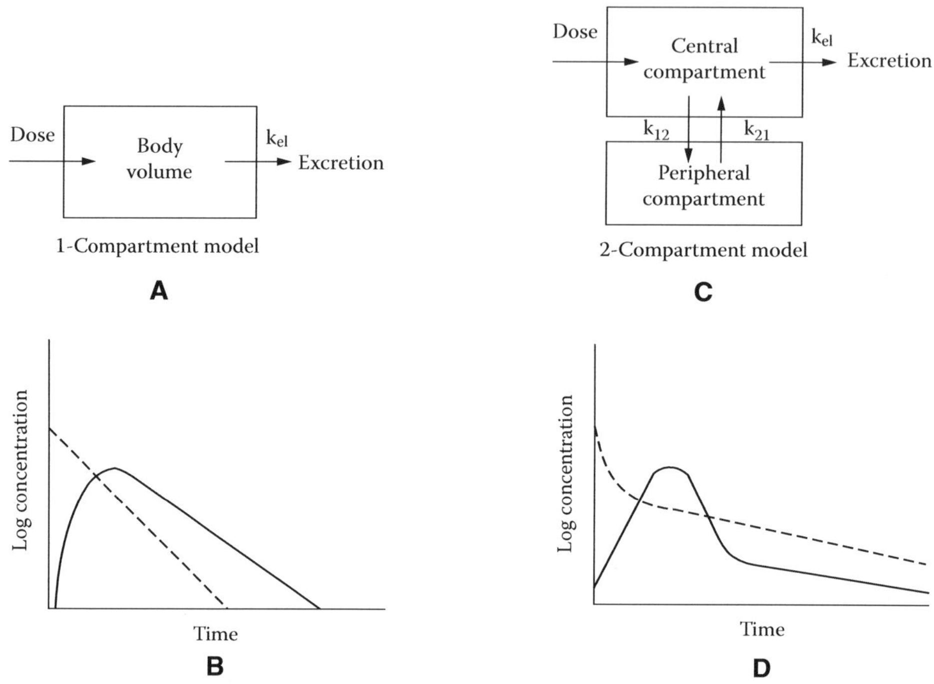

Figure 2.1 (A) Schematic representation of a one-compartment model. (B) Log plasma concentration vs. time curve after intravenous (---) and oral (—) administration. (C) Schematic representation of a two-compartment model. (D) Log plasma concentration vs. time curve after intravenous (---) and oral (—) administration. (Adapted from Hagan, R.L., Basic Pharmacokinetics. In-Service Training and Continuing Education AACC/TDM, American Association for Clinical Chemistry, Inc., Washington, D.C., 17(9), 231–247, 1996.)

readily accessible blood or plasma, is typically graphed as a log concentration vs. time profile. Figure 2.1B shows the log plasma concentration vs. time plot for a drug that distributes according to a one-compartment model. The dotted line demonstrates the time course after intravenous administration and the solid line demonstrates the time course after oral administration. Since intravenous administration does not have an absorption phase, the time course of drug in the plasma is linear. For oral administration, the drug concentration on the blood is slower to reach a peak due to absorptive processes of the GI tract.

2.1.2 Two-Compartment Models

Figure 2.1C illustrates the concept of the two-compartment model. In this model, the drug is administered into the central compartment and then there is a time lag due to slower distribution into other tissues and organs. These other organs are represented by the peripheral compartment(s). More complex models may be developed if distribution to other organs occurs at different rates that can be mathematically differentiated. In the two-compartment model, equilibrium is reached between the central and peripheral compartments and this marks the end of the distribution phase. The beginning of the distribution phase may be observed graphically by an initial rapid decline after peaking in the drug concentration in the central compartment (represented by the plasma/blood) as shown in Figure 2.1D. Rate constants may be estimated for drug movement between the central and peripheral compartments, but drug elimination from the body is assumed to occur from the central compartment.[1] As mentioned previously, more complex models may be developed including models in which the number of compartments into which the drug distributes is not assumed in the initial modeling.

2.1.3 Elimination Kinetics

The concept of zero- or first-order kinetics may be utilized to describe any rate process in pharmacokinetics. Therefore, if we are discussing drug absorption, a drug exhibits zero-order kinetics if a constant amount of drug is absorbed regardless of dose.[2] Conversely, a drug exhibits first-order absorption kinetics if the amount absorbed is dependent on dose, i.e., is a fraction of the dose. Similarly, when considering drug excretion, ethanol exhibits zero-order elimination kinetics because a constant amount of drug is excreted per unit time regardless of the drug concentration (unless processes become saturated). Most drugs exhibit first-order elimination kinetics in which a constant fraction of drug is eliminated per unit time.

Zero-order elimination kinetics are described by the following equation:[1]

$$C = C_0 - kt$$

where C = drug concentration at time t, C_0 = the concentration at time zero or the initial concentration, and k = the elimination rate constant.

A plot of this equation is linear with a slope, $-k$, and a y-intercept, C_0. The elimination half-life may be calculated from this equation for a drug that exhibits zero-order elimination. When $t = t_{1/2}$, then $C = 1/2\ C_0$, the initial or peak concentration. This results in the following equation:

$$t_{1/2} = 1/2\ C_0/k$$

This equation has a concentration term, C_0, indicating that the half-life is variable and dependent on drug concentration. Changes in pharmacokinetic parameters that occur as a function of dose or drug concentration are referred to as nonlinear pharmacokinetic processes. Nonlinearity is usually due to saturation of protein binding, hepatic metabolism, or active renal transport of the drug.[3]

First-order elimination kinetics are described by the equation:[1]

$$C = C_0 e^{-kt}$$

Taking the natural logarithm of this equation and plotting it semilogarithmically results in a linear graph with a slope of $-k$, and a y-intercept of ln C_0. Again, to determine the half-life, $1/2\ C_0$ is substituted into the equation to give:

$$1/2\ C_0 = C_0 e^{-kt1/2}$$

Taking natural logs and solving for $t_{1/2}$:

$$t_{1/2} = 0.693/k$$

It is important to note that the elimination half-life is a derived term, and any process that changes k will change the half-life of the drug. Factors that may affect pharmacokinetic parameters are discussed elsewhere, but in this example may include disease states, changes in urinary pH, changes in plasma protein binding, and coadministration of other drugs.

2.2 PHYSIOLOGICAL MODELS

An alternative method of building a pharmacokinetic profile of a drug in the body is to utilize anatomic and physiological information. Such a model does not make assumptions about body compartments or first-order processes for drug absorption and elimination.[4] The first step in such modeling is to decide whether drug distribution into a particular tissue is perfusion rate or membrane transport limited.[5] These decisions are based on the physicochemical characteristics of the drug and physiological conditions in addition to reference to any experimental data. In order to write a mass balance equation, blood flow, Q, and the volume, V, of the organ or tissue of interest is needed and may be obtained from the literature. The other parameters, venous drug concentration, C_v, and the partition coefficient, R, are determined experimentally.[5] A simple mass balance equation may be written as:[2]

$$V_t \times dC_t/dt = Q_t \times [C_v - C_t/R_t]$$

where t = tissue.

Mass balance equations may be constructed for each organ or tissue considered and algebraic equations added to account for growth, changes in tissue weight ratios, and other physiological parameters. The advantage of this modeling over the more traditional compartmental method is provision of a time course of drug distribution to any organ or tissue, and this model allows estimation of the effects of changing physiological parameters on tissue concentrations. Disadvantages include the need for complex mathematical equations and the lack of data on the physiological parameters necessary to construct the differential equations.[5]

2.3 PHARMACOKINETIC–PHARMACODYNAMIC CORRELATIONS

Pharmacodynamics (PD) may be defined as the quantitative relationship between the measured plasma or tissue concentration of the active moiety and the magnitude of the observed pharmacological effect(s).[6] The study of pharmacokinetics (PK) has been defined previously. A PK/PD model is a mathematical description of the relationship. Knowledge of the model and model parameter estimates permits prediction of concentration vs. time and effect vs. time profiles for different dosing regimens.[6] Different drugs are characterized by different PK and PD models and by differences in model parameters such as volume of distribution and receptor affinity. Understanding the PK/PD model permits comparison of the pharmacological properties for different drugs. For a specific compound, there may be significant variation in model parameters between individuals. PK/PD modeling allows assessment of the contribution of the variability in model parameters to the overall variability in drug response.[6]

To fully understand the significance of PK/PD modeling, it is important to note that the observed effect vs. time profile for a particular individual is determined by several factors. These include (1) drug input dose, rate, and route of administration; (2) intrinsic PK drug properties; and (3) intrinsic PD drug properties. Modeling allows estimation of PK/PD parameters. Further, PK/PD modeling provides dose–response curves for the onset, magnitude, and duration of effects that can be utilized to optimize dose and dosing regimens. Models have been described for reversible and irreversible drug effects and for a range of drug classes including analgesics, benzodiazepines, and anticonvulsants. For a more detailed explanation of PK/PD modeling and correlations and description of computer applications, the reader is referred elsewhere.[6]

REFERENCES

1. Hagan, R.L., Basic pharmacokinetics: in-service training and continuing education AACC/TDM, American Association for Clinical Chemistry, Inc., Washington, D.C., 17(9), 231–247, 1996.
2. Pratt, W.B. and Taylor, P., Eds., *Principles of Drug Action: The Basis of Pharmacology,* Churchill Livingstone, New York, 1990.

3. Hardman, J.G. and Limbird, L.E., Eds., *Goodman & Gilman's The Pharmacological Basis of Therapeutics,* McGraw-Hill, New York, 1996.
4. Rowland, M. and Tozer, T.N., *Clinical Pharmacokinetics Concepts and Applications,* Lea & Febiger, Philadelphia, 1989.
5. Amdur, M.O., Doull, J., and Klaassen, C.D., Eds., *Casarett and Doull's Toxicology: The Basic Science of Poisons,* Pergamon Press, Elmsford, NY, 1991.
6. Derendorf, H. and Hochhaus, G., Eds., *Handbook of Pharmacokinetic/Pharmacodynamic Correlation,* CRC Press, Boca Raton, FL, 1995.

CHAPTER 3

Toxicokinetics and Factors Affecting Pharmacokinetic Parameters

Amanda J. Jenkins, Ph.D.
The Office of the Cuyahoga County Coroner, Cleveland, Ohio

CONTENTS

3.1 TOXICOKINETICS

Toxicokinetics is the study of drug disposition in overdose. The biochemical processes that constitute the science of pharmacokinetics may be altered when drugs are administered in high concentrations.[1] GI absorption may be altered in overdose due to delayed gastric emptying, changes in intestinal motility, and therapy with activated charcoal.[2] Drugs such as morphine, ethanol, and barbiturates delay gastric emptying and as a consequence slow drug movement into the small intestine. In addition, morphine decreases intestinal motility, resulting in increased transit time through the intestine and increased absorption. Little is known about changes in drug distribution throughout the body after overdose. Several mechanisms may be at work in overdose to cause changes in drug disposition. For example, the bioavailability of a drug with a high first pass metabolism may be increased when the hepatic metabolizing enzymes become saturated. In a similar manner, the concentration of free drug in the plasma may be increased when protein binding becomes saturated. This may result in significant toxicity for those drugs that are highly plasma protein bound. Also, changes in peripheral blood flow due to the cardiac effects of some drugs may result in prolonged drug distribution and higher blood drug concentrations.

Drug metabolism may be altered in overdose when those enzymes responsible for metabolism become saturated. In this event, clearance is decreased, half-life is prolonged, and therefore high drug concentrations exist for a longer time. If multiple drugs are co-ingested, competitive inhibition of metabolism may occur. In addition, if hepatic blood flow is decreased, due to impaired liver function or cardiovascular drug effects, biotransformation of xenobiotics may be decreased.

Renal excretion may or may not be altered in drug overdose. Alteration of renal drug clearance may be utilized therapeutically to enhance drug elimination. Urinary pH is adjusted to increase the clearance of acidic and basic drugs. For example, administration of sodium bicarbonate will raise the urine pH above 7.5, concentrating the ionized form in the renal tubule and, therefore, enhancing elimination of salicylate. Conversely, acidification of the urine may be utilized to enhance renal excretion of basic drugs. However, with some drugs, such as phencyclidine, there is controversy about the role of urinary acidification in enhanced excretion and whether this procedure improves clinical outcome. Acidification is contraindicated with myoglobinuria and may also increase the risk of metabolic complications.[3]

3.2 FACTORS AFFECTING PHARMACOKINETIC PARAMETERS

Toxicokinetics is utilized to describe the changes in pharmacokinetic processes as a result of drug overdose. Other factors may contribute to changes in pharmacokinetic parameters when nontoxic doses are therapeutically or illicitly administered. Besides species differences in the variability in drug response, which are not discussed here, other factors that contribute to changes in parameters include drug formulation and route of administration, gender differences, age, weight or body composition, disease, genetic abnormalities, and drug interactions.

3.2.1 Genetic Factors

When a distinguishable difference between individuals is under genetic control, it is known as genetic polymorphism. Some drug responses have been found to be genetically determined. For example, the activity of the liver enzyme *N*-acetyltransferase differs between individuals such that the population may be divided into slow and fast acetylators. Approximately 60% of the U.S. population are slow acetylators and may show toxicity unless doses of drugs requiring acetylation for metabolism are reduced. Other inherited variations in pharmacokinetics include deficiency of one or more hepatic cytochrome-P450 isozymes or plasma cholinesterase.[2]

3.2.2 Sex Differences

Examples of sex differences in drug pharmacokinetics have also been identified. These differences may be due to variations in body composition, hepatic metabolism, renal elimination, protein binding, or absorption. Differences in weight may influence muscle mass, organ blood flow, body water spaces, and hence affect the pharmacokinetic parameters of many drugs. In addition, women tend to have a higher percentage of body fat than men, which will affect the volume of distribution of lipophilic drugs. The clinical significance of differences in body composition is unclear but there are some important examples: women have a lower volume of distribution (V) of ethanol[4] and a higher V for diazepam than men.

A number of studies have examined the effect of gender on hepatic metabolism and drug elimination. Greenblatt et al.[5] found that young women have a significantly higher CL for diazepam than young men. In contrast, clearances of oxazepam[6] and chlordiazepoxide[7] are higher in men than in women and no sex difference has been observed in the metabolism of nitrazepam or lorazepam.[4] Differences can be explained by differences in metabolic pathways because oxazepam is metabolized primarily through conjugation, nitrazepam is metabolized by reduction of the nitro group, and most of the other benzodiazepines are metabolized by various cytochrome P450 isozymes. It has been found that the isozyme cytochrome 3A4, responsible for the metabolism of many drugs, is approximately 1.4 times more active in women than men. The isozymes P2D6 and P2C19 display genetic polymorphism that is not influenced by gender. The isozyme P1A2 may be influenced by sex although the data are inconclusive. The work of Relling et al.[8] suggests that the activity of this isozyme is lower in women than men. As mentioned above, gender differences have been demonstrated in the elimination of drugs that are metabolized solely by conjugation. The male:female clearance ratio for oxazepam is approximately 1.5:1.

When considering renal elimination, the glomerular filtration rate (GFR) is on average higher in men than women,[4] but this may be a weight rather than a gender effect as GFR is directly proportional to weight. The effects of gender on tubular secretion and reabsorption have not been well characterized. The influence of gender on plasma protein binding appears to be minimal. Albumin levels are not altered by gender in contrast to the protein α1-acid glycoprotein, which is reduced by estrogen.[9] Other plasma constituents whose levels are influenced by gender include cortico-steroid binding globulin and various lipoproteins.[10] Gender differences in the binding of diazepam and chlordiazepoxide have been demonstrated.

Some studies have suggested that gender influences gastric emptying rate and intestinal transit time.[11] Women empty solids from the stomach more slowly than men and the activity of a stomach enzyme, alcohol dehydrogenase, may be much lower in women. The GI tract also contains large concentrations of the isozyme cytochrome P3A4, so gender differences in the activity of this enzyme could affect the bioavailability of certain drugs. Gender differences observed after intramuscular drug administration may be due to differences in blood flow or incorrect injection into fat in women. Drug absorption in the lung may differ according to gender. Knight et al.[12] found significantly less deposition of an aerosolized drug in women than men, which the authors attributed to differences in breathing characteristics.

It should be noted that female-specific issues may have significant effects on drug distribution and metabolism. For example, pregnancy may increase the elimination of certain drugs, reducing their efficacy. In addition, oral contraceptive use can affect the metabolism of drugs. The effects of menopause, menstruation, and hormone replacement on the pharmacokinetics of drugs are largely unknown.

3.2.3 Age

Changes in the rate but not the extent of drug absorption are usually observed with age.[13] Factors that affect drug absorption, such as gastric pH and emptying, intestinal motility, and blood flow, change with age. Gastric acid secretion does not approach adult levels until the age of 3 and gastric emptying and peristalsis is slow during the first few months of life. Because skeletal muscle mass is limited, muscle contractions, which aid blood flow, are minimal, and therefore will limit the distribution of intramuscularly administered drug. Higher gastric pH, delayed gastric emptying, and decreased intestinal motility and blood flow are observed in elderly individuals.

3.2.4 Drug and Disease Interactions

The pharmacokinetics of several drugs have been shown to be influenced by concurrent disease processes.[13] The clearance of many drugs decreases in those individuals with chronic hepatic disease such as cirrhosis. In contrast, in acute reversible liver conditions, such as acute viral hepatitis, the clearance of some drugs is decreased or the half-life increased, and for others no change is detected. The volumes of distribution of some drugs are unaltered in hepatic disease while an increase is observed for other drugs, especially those bound to albumin in individuals with cirrhosis. This phenomenon is due to the decreased synthesis of albumin and other proteins. The influence of liver disease on drug absorption is unclear. It is probable, however, that the oral bioavailability of drugs highly extracted from the liver is increased in cirrhosis. The reasons are decreased first pass hepatic metabolism and the development of portal bypass in which blood enters the superior vena cava directly via esophageal varices.

Renal diseases such as uremia may result in decreased renal clearance of certain drugs.[13] Gastrointestinal diseases, such as Crohn's disease, result in increased plasma protein binding of several drugs due to increased levels of binding proteins. Further, respiratory diseases such as cystic fibrosis increase the renal clearance of some drugs.

Patients commonly receive two or more drugs concurrently and most individuals who abuse drugs are polydrug users. Multiple drug use may result in drug interactions. This occurs when the pharmacokinetics or pharmacodynamics of one drug is altered by another. This concept is important to consider because interaction may result in decreased therapeutic efficacy or an increased risk of toxicity. The degree of drug interaction depends on the relative concentrations and therefore dose and time.[13] Changes in absorption rate, competition for binding sites on plasma proteins, oral bioavailability, volume of distribution, and hepatic and renal clearance have been demonstrated for therapeutic drugs. Few studies have systematically documented pharmacokinetic interactions between illicit drugs.

REFERENCES

1. Derendorf, H. and Hochhaus, G., Eds., *Handbook of Pharmacokinetic/Pharmacodynamic Correlation,* CRC Press, Boca Raton, FL, 1995.
2. Amdur, M.O., Doull, J., and Klaassen, C.D., Eds., *Casarett and Doull's Toxicology: The Basic Science of Poisons,* Pergamon Press, Elmsford, NY, 1991.
3. Ellenhorn, M.J., and Barceloux, D.G., *Medical Toxicology, Diagnosis and Treatment of Human Poisoning,* Elsevier, New York, 1988.
4. Harris, R.Z., Benet, L.Z., and Schwartz, J.B., Gender effects in pharmacokinetics and pharmacodynamics, *Drugs,* 50(2), 222–239, 1995.
5. Greenblatt, D.J., Allen, M.D., and Harmatz, J.S., Diazepam disposition determinants, *Clin. Pharmacol. Ther.,* 27, 301–312, 1980.
6. Greenblatt, D.J., Divoll, M., and Harmatz, J.S., Oxazepam kinetics: effects of age and sex, *J. Pharmacol. Exp. Ther.,* 215, 86–91, 1980.
7. Greenblatt, D.J., Divoll, M., and Abernathy, D.R., Age and gender effects on chlordiazepoxide kinetics: relation to antipyrine disposition, *Pharmacology,* 38, 327–334, 1989.
8. Relling, M.V., Lin, J.S., and Ayers, G.D., Racial and gender differences in *N*-acetyltransferase, xanthine oxidase, and CYP1A2 activities, *Clin. Pharmacol. Ther.,* 52, 643–658, 1992.
9. Routledge, P.A., Stargel, W.W., and Kitchell, B.B., Sex-related differences in the plasma protein binding of lignocaine and diazepam, *Br. J. Clin. Pharmacol.,* 11, 245–250, 1981.
10. Wilson, K., Sex-related differences in drug disposition in man, *Clin. Pharmacokinet.,* 9, 189–202, 1984.
11. Yonkers, K.A., Kando, J.C., and Cole, J.O., Gender differences in pharmacokinetics and pharmacodynamics of psychotropic medication, *Am. J. Psychiatry,* 149, 587–595, 1992.
12. Knight, V., Yu, C.P., and Gilbert, B.E., Estimating the dosage of ribavirin aerosol according to age and other variables, *J. Infect. Dis.,* 158, 443–447, 1988.
13. Rowland, M. and Tozer, T.N., *Clinical Pharmacokinetics Concepts and Applications,* Lea & Febiger, Philadelphia, 1989.

CHAPTER 4

Pharmacokinetics of Specific Drugs

Amanda J. Jenkins, Ph.D.
The Office of the Cuyahoga County Coroner, Cleveland, Ohio

CONTENTS

4.1 AMPHETAMINE

The term *amphetamine* refers to the group of stimulants that includes amphetamine, methamphetamine, methylenedioxyamphetamine, and methylenedioxymethamphetamine. These low-molecular-weight basic drugs are sympathomimetic phenethylamine derivatives possessing central and peripheral stimulant activity. Amphetamines suppress appetite and produce CNS and cardiovascular stimulation. These effects are mediated by increasing synaptic concentrations of norepinephrine and dopamine either by stimulating neurotransmitter release or inhibiting uptake, or both. Clinical uses of amphetamine and methamphetamine include chronic administration for the treatment of narcolepsy in adults and attention-deficit/hyperactivity disorder in children.[1]

These drugs are abused for their stimulant effect. The effects are usually longer lasting than those of cocaine and may prevent fatigue. The latter factor has led to their study in athletes and in military field situations. It is postulated that the disturbances in perception and psychotic behavior, which may occur at high doses, may be due to dopamine release from dopaminergic neurons and also serotonin release from tryptaminergic neurons located in the mesolimbic area of the brain.

Amphetamine and methamphetamine occur as structural isomers and stereoisomers. Structural isomers are compounds with the same empirical formula but a different atomic arrangement, e.g., methamphetamine and phentermine. Stereoisomers differ in the three-dimensional arrangement of the atoms attached to at least one asymmetric carbon and are nonsuperimposable mirror images. Therefore, amphetamine and methamphetamine occur as both D- and L-isomeric forms. The two isomers together form a racemic mixture. The D-amphetamine form has significant stimulant activity, and possesses approximately three to four times the central activity of the L-form. It is also important to note that the D- and L-enantiomers may have not only different pharmacological activity but also varying pharmacokinetic characteristics.

When indicated for therapeutic use, 5 to 60 mg or 5 to 20 mg of amphetamine or methamphetamine, respectively, are administered orally. An oral dose of amphetamine typically results in a peak plasma concentration of 110 ng/ml.[2] When abused, amphetamines may be self-administered by the oral, intravenous, or smoked route. The last route of administration is common for methamphetamine. With heavy use, addicts may ingest up to 2000 mg per day.

4.1.1 Absorption

Limited data are available on the GI absorption of amphetamine in humans. Beckett and Rowland[3] reported serum concentrations of amphetamine in two healthy volunteers after a 15-mg oral dose of the D-isomer. Peak serum concentrations of 48 and 40 ng/ml were achieved at 1.25 h when the volunteers' urine was acidified. Slightly higher serum concentrations were observed (52 and 47 ng/ml) if the urine pH conditions were not controlled. Rowland[4] observed a peak blood concentration of 35 ng/ml, 2 h after a 10-mg oral dose of D-amphetamine to a healthy 66-kg adult. The half-life for the D-isomer was 11 to 13 h compared with a 39% longer half-life for the L-isomer. If the urine were acidified, excretion was enhanced and the half-lives of both isomers were reduced to approximately 7 h.[5] Amphetamine demonstrates a linear one-compartment open model over the dose range 20 to 200 mg.

4.1.2 Distribution

The plasma protein binding of amphetamine in humans is approximately 16 to 20% and is similar in drug-dependent and naive subjects.[6] Research by Rowland[4] and Franksson and Anggard[6] indicated that there was a difference in the volume of distribution between non-users (3.5 to 4.6 L/kg) and drug-dependent individuals (6.1 L/kg). It has been suggested that the larger V_d observed in drug-dependent subjects may be due to a higher tissue affinity for amphetamine in these individuals. Evidence to support this suggestion is found in studies with amphetamine-dependent animals in which higher tissue concentrations of amphetamine were found.[7]

4.1.3 Metabolism and Excretion

Amphetamine is metabolized by deamination, oxidation, and hydroxylation. Figure 4.1 illustrates the metabolic scheme for amphetamine. Deamination produces an inactive metabolite, phenylacetone, which is further oxidized to benzoic acid and then excreted in urine as hippuric acid and glucuronide conjugates. In addition, amphetamine is also converted to norephedrine by oxidation and then this metabolite and the parent compound are *p*-hydroxylated. Several metabolites, including norephedrine, its hydroxy metabolite, and hydroxyamphetamine, are pharmacologically active. The excretion of amphetamine depends on urinary pH. In healthy men who were administered 5 mg of isotopically labeled D,L-amphetamine, approximately 90% of the dose was excreted

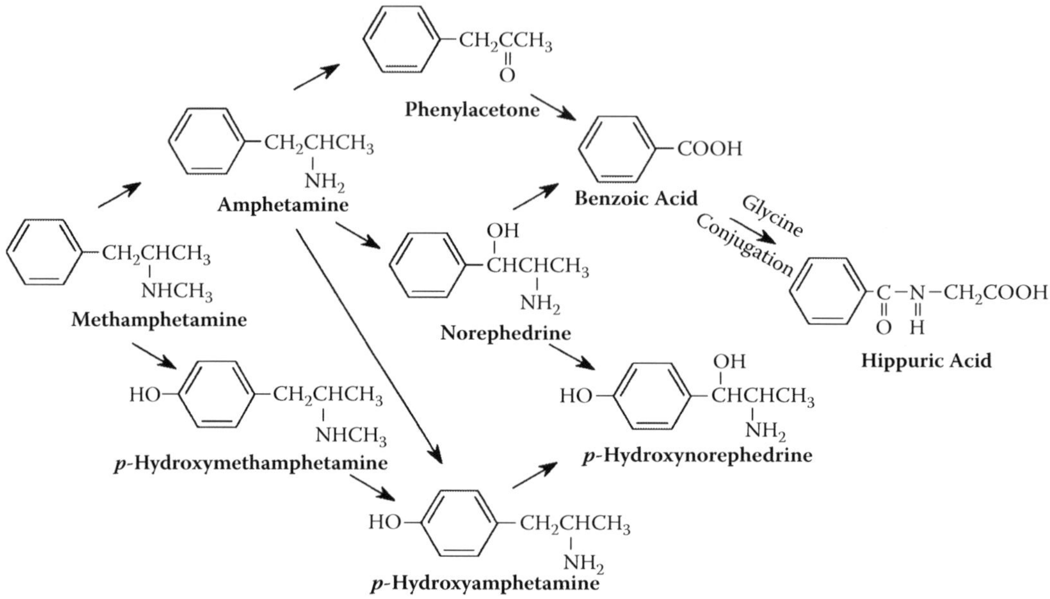

Figure 4.1 Metabolic pathway of amphetamine and methamphetamine.

in the urine within 3 to 4 days.[8] Approximately 70% of the dose was excreted in the 24-h urine with 30% as unchanged drug. This was increased to 74% under acidic conditions and reduced to 1% in alkaline urine. Under normal conditions, <1% is excreted as phenylacetone, 16 to 28% as hippuric acid, 4% as benzoylglucuronide, 2% as norephedrine, <0.5% as *p*-hydroxynorephedrine, and 2 to 4% as *p*-hydroxyamphetamine.[9] L-Amphetamine is not as extensively metabolized as the D-isomer. When volunteers were orally administered 5 to 15 mg of D- or L-amphetamine, the mean excretion of unchanged D-amphetamine was 33% of the dose and that of the L-isomer was 49% of the dose.[2]

The metabolism of amphetamine has been studied in those presenting with amphetamine psychosis. In the presence of acidified urine, the renal elimination of amphetamine increased significantly. The intensity of the psychosis was found to correlate with the amount of basic polar metabolites excreted in the urine, such as norephedrine and *p*-hydroxyamphetamine, and not with the plasma amphetamine concentration. This suggests that these metabolites may play an important role in the development of paranoid psychosis in chronic amphetamine users.[6]

4.2 METHAMPHETAMINE

D-Methamphetamine, the *N*-methyl derivative of amphetamine, was first synthesized in 1919. Methamphetamine is available in the D- and L-forms. The D-form has reportedly greater central stimulant activity than the L-isomer, which has greater peripheral sympathomimetic activity. The D-form is the commonly abused form while the L-isomer is typically found in nonprescription inhalers as a decongestant.

Although initially available as an injectable solution for the treatment of obesity, D-methamphetamine hydrochloride is currently available as conventional and prolonged release tablets. Illicit methamphetamine is synthesized from the precursors phenylacetone and *N*-methylformamide (DL mixture) or alternatively from ephedrine or pseudoephedrine by red phosphorus/acid reduction.

4.2.1 Absorption

Doses of 5 to 10 mg methamphetamine typically result in blood concentrations between 20 and 60 ng/ml. In one study,[10] six healthy adults were orally administered a single dose of 0.125 mg/kg methamphetamine. Peak plasma concentrations were achieved at 3.6 h with a mean concentration of 20 ng/ml. In a second study, Lebish et al.[11] observed a peak blood concentration of 30 ng/ml, 1 h after a single oral dose of 10 mg methamphetamine to one subject. In a study by Schepers et al.,[12] eight subjects were administered four oral doses of 10 mg methamphetamine hydrochloride as sustained release tablets within 7 days. Three weeks later five subjects received four oral 20-mg doses. After the first dose, methamphetamine was detected in plasma between 0.25 and 2 h; the c_{max} was 14.5 to 33.8 ng/ml (10-mg dose) and 26.2 to 44.3 ng/ml (20-mg) and occurred within 2 to 12 h. Methamphetamine was first detected in oral fluid in this study 0.08 to 2 h post dose, with a c_{max} of 24.7 to 312.2 and 75.3 to 321.7 ng/ml after the 10- and 20-mg doses, respectively. Peak methamphetamine concentrations in oral fluid occurred at 2 to 12 h and the median oral fluid-plasma concentration ratio was 2.0 for 24 h. In general, the detection window for drug in oral fluid exceeded that in plasma.

4.2.2 Metabolism and Excretion

In humans, both the D- and L-forms undergo hydroxylation and *N*-demethylation to their respective *p*-hydroxymethamphetamine and amphetamine metabolites. Amphetamine is the major active metabolite of methamphetamine. Under normal conditions, up to 43% of a D-methamphetamine dose is excreted unchanged in the urine in the first 24 h and 4 to 7% will be present as amphetamine. In acidic urine, up to 76% is present as parent drug[10] compared with 2% under alkaline conditions. Approximately 15% of the dose was present as *p*-hydroxymethamphetamine and the remaining minor metabolites were similar to those found after amphetamine administration. Urine concentrations of methamphetamine are typically 0.5 to 4 mg/L after an oral dose of 10 mg. However, methamphetamine and amphetamine urine concentrations vary widely among abusers. Lebish et al.[11] reported urine methamphetamine concentrations of 24 to 333 mg/L and amphetamine concentrations of 1 to 90 mg/L in the urine of methamphetamine abusers.

L-Methamphetamine is biotransformed in a similar manner to the D-isomer but at a slower rate. Following a 13.7-mg oral dose, the 24-h urine contained an average of 34% of the dose as L-methamphetamine and 1.7% of the dose as L-amphetamine.[3] Oyler et al.[13] described the appearance of methamphetamine and amphetamine in urine after volunteers (n = 8) ingested 4 × 10-mg doses of methamphetamine hydrochloride daily for 7 days followed by 4 × 20 mg daily several weeks later. Parent and metabolite were generally detected in the first or second void post dose in a concentration range of 82 to 1827 and 12 to 180 ng/ml, respectively. Peak methamphetamine urine concentrations (1871 to 6004 ng/ml) occurred within 1.5 to 60 h after a single dose.

D-Methamphetamine is commonly self-administered by the smoked route. Both the free-base and hydrochloride salt of methamphetamine are volatile and >90% of parent drug can be recovered intact when heated to temperatures of 300°C. When cigarettes containing tobacco mixed with methamphetamine were pyrolyzed, amphetamine, phenylacetone, dimethylamphetamine, and *N*-cyanomethyl methamphetamine were the major resulting products.[14] Cook[15] conducted a study in which six volunteers were administered 30 mg D-methamphetamine from a pipe that was heated to approximately 300°C. Blood samples and physiological and subjective measures were collected after drug administration. Plasma methamphetamine concentrations rose rapidly after the start of smoking. However, concentrations plateaued (40 to 44 ng/ml) after 1 h with a slight increase in concentration over the next 1 h. Thereafter, concentrations in plasma declined slowly, reaching the same concentration at 8 h on the downward side of the curve as reached at 30 min on the upward side. The authors used a noncompartmental model to determine an average elimination half-life of

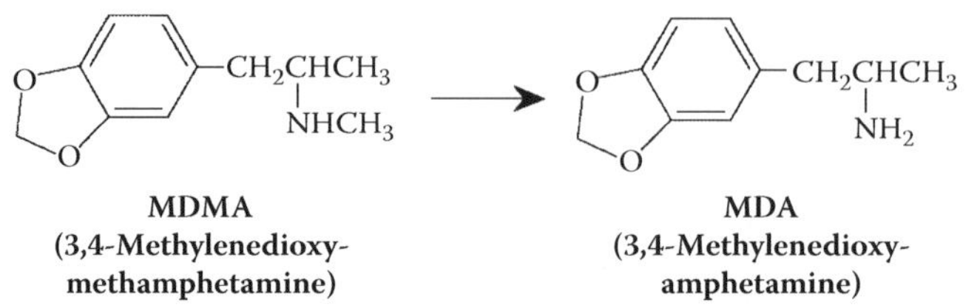

Figure 4.2 Structures of MDA and MDMA.

11.7 h with a range of 8 to 17 h. These authors also administered methamphetamine (0.250 mg/kg) orally and the resulting plasma data were fit to a one-compartment model with first-order elimination and a lag time. A maximum plasma concentration of 35 to 38 ng/ml was achieved at 3.1 h with a terminal elimination half-life of 10 h. Although the plasma concentration time curves for smoked and oral methamphetamine appeared similar, the subjective effects were markedly different, with a greater "high" being reported after smoked methamphetamine. This indicates that it may be the rate of change of plasma drug concentrations that is a significant factor in determining subjective effects. Other investigators[16] have reported the bioavailability of methamphetamine after intranasal and smoked drug to be 79 and 67% (of estimated delivered dose), respectively. Maximum blood concentrations of parent drug occurred at 2.7 and 2.5 h after intranasal and smoked doses ($n = 8$).

4.3 3,4-METHYLENEDIOXYAMPHETAMINE

3,4-Methylenedioxyamphetamine (MDA) is a potent psychotropic amphetamine derivative first synthesized in 1910 (Figure 4.2). It has no accepted medical use but is self-administered orally or intravenously in doses of 50 to 250 mg for illicit use.[10] Blood concentrations following normal use have not been reported and, to date, there are no reported clinical studies delineating the pharmacokinetic or pharmacodynamic characteristics of this drug. Blood concentrations in humans have been reported following overdose. The average blood concentration in 12 fatal cases was 9.3 mg/L (range 1.8 to 26).[10] The metabolism of MDA in humans has not been studied, but in other animals MDA is metabolized by *O*-dealkylation, deamination, and conjugation.[17] Polymorphically expressed CYP2D6 is the major isozyme catalyzing the metabolic steps in the metabolism of MDA and MDMA.[18]

4.4 3,4-METHYLENEDIOXYMETHAMPHETAMINE

3,4-Methylenedioxymethamphetamine (MDMA) is a ring-substituted derivative of methamphetamine (Figure 4.2) that has widespread use as a recreational drug. Self-administration is typically by the oral route in doses of 100 to 150 mg. Helmlin et al.[19] reported a mean peak plasma MDMA concentration of 300 ng/ml at 2.3 h after an oral dose of 1.5 mg/kg to adult subjects; de la Torre et al. studied eight healthy volunteers and reported a peak MDMA concentration of 180 ng/m occurring 1.8 h after a 75-mg oral dose, with an MDA peak of 78 ng/ml 5 h after administration. MDMA presents nonlinear pharmacokinetics. In a randomized double-blind crossover placebo-controlled study with nine healthy male subjects, Farre et al.[20] reported increased plasma MDMA concentrations after a second dose of 100 mg, 24 h after the initial dose, were greater than expected by accumulation. The authors suspected the reason to be due to metabolic inhibition. Parameters such as blood pressure, heart rate, and subjective effects were higher after the second dose than after the first.

MDMA is metabolized to MDA with 65% of the dose excreted as parent drug within 3 days. Both MDMA and MDA are hydroxylated to mono- and di-hydroxy derivatives and subsequently conjugated before elimination. The plasma half-life has been reported to be 7.6 h.[10]

If MDMA is co-administered with ethanol, as 100 mg plus 0.8 g/kg ethanol, plasma concentrations of the former demonstrate a 13% increase compared with MDMA administered alone.[21] Plasma concentrations of ethanol decreased 9 to 15% after MDMA administration ($n = 9$).

MDMA has also been reported in alternative biological specimens. After a single oral dose of 75 mg in human volunteers, MDMA concentrations in oral fluid exceeded those in plasma with a mean peak concentration of 1215 ng/ml ($n = 12$) and a range of 50 to 6982 ng/ml compared with an average peak plasma concentration of 178 ng/ml (range 21 to 295 ng/ml).[22] In sweat the average concentration was 25 ng/wipe when measured 4 to 5 h after ingestion of a similar dose.[23] When MDMA and MDA concentrations measured in ante-mortem samples have been compared, consistent and significant increases in the postmortem concentrations have been observed.[24]

REFERENCES

1. *Physicians Desk Reference 2005*. Medical Economics Data, a division of Medical Economics Company, Inc., p. 1315, Montvale, NJ.
2. Baylor, M.R. and Crouch, D.J., Sympathomimetic amines: pharmacology, toxicology, and analysis. In-service training and continuing education AACC/TDM, American Association for Clinical Chemistry, Inc., Washington, D.C., 14(5), 101–111, 1993.
3. Beckett, A.H. and Rowland, M., Urinary excretion kinetics of amphetamine in man, *J. Pharm. Pharmacol.*, 17, 628–639, 1965.
4. Rowland, M., Amphetamine blood and urine levels in man, *J. Pharm. Sci.*, 58, 508–509, 1969.
5. Matin, S.B., Wan, S.H., and Knight, J.B., Quantitative determination of enantiomeric compounds, *Biomed. Mass Spectrosc.*, 4, 118–121, 1977.
6. Franksson, G. and Anggard, E., The plasma protein binding of amphetamine, catecholamines and related compounds, *Acta Pharmacol. Toxicol.*, 28, 209–214, 1970.
7. Ellison, T., Siegel, M., Silverman, A.G., and Okun, R., Comparative metabolism of D,L H3-amphetamine hydrochloride in tolerant and non tolerant cats, *Proc. Western Pharmacol. Soc.*, 11, 75–77, 1968.
8. Dring, L.G., Smith, R.L., and Williams, R.T., The metabolic fate of amphetamine in man and other species, *Biochem. J.*, 116, 425–435, 1970.
9. Sever, P.S., Caldwell, J., Dring, L.G., and Williams, R.T., The metabolism of amphetamine in dependent subjects, *Eur. J. Clin. Pharm.*, 6, 177–180, 1973.
10. Baselt, R.C. and Cravey, R.H., *Disposition of Toxic Drugs and Chemicals in Man,* 4th ed., Chemical Toxicology Institute, Foster City, CA, 1995.
11. Lebish, P., Finkle, B.S., and Brackett, J.W., Jr., Determination of amphetamine, methamphetamine, and related amines in blood and urine by gas chromatography by hydrogen-flame ionization detector, *Clin. Chem.*, 16, 195–200, 1970.
12. Schepers, R.J.F., Oyler, J.M., Joseph, R.E., Cone, E.J., Moolchan, E.T., and Huestis, M.A., Methamphetamine and amphetamine pharmacokinetics in oral fluid and plasma after controlled oral methamphetamine administration to human volunteers, *Clin. Chem.*, 49(1), 121–132, 2003.
13. Oyler, J.M., Cone, E.J., Joseph, R.E., Moolchan, E.T., and Huestis, M.A., Duration of detectable methamphetamine and amphetamine excretion in urine after controlled oral administration of methamphetamine to humans, *Clin. Chem.*, 48(10), 1703–1714, 2002.
14. Sekine, H. and Nakahara, Y., Abuse of smoking methamphetamine mixed with tobacco: I. Inhalation efficiency and pyrolysis products of methamphetamine, *J. Forensic Sci.*, 32(5), 1271–1280, 1987.
15. Cook, C.E., Pyrolytic characteristics, pharmacokinetics, and bioavailability of smoked heroin, cocaine, phencyclidine and methamphetamine, NIDA Research Monograph 99, 6–23. DHHS Pub. No. 1990.
16. Harris, D.S., Boxenbaum, H., Everhart, E.T., Sequeira, G., Mendelson, J.E., and Jones, R.T., The bioavailability of intranasal and smoked methamphetamine, *Clin. Pharmacol. Ther.*, 74(5), 475–486, 2003.

17. Midha, K.K., McGilveray, I.J., Bhatnager, S.P., and Cooper, J.K., GLC identification and determination of 3,4-methylenedioxyamphetamine *in vivo* in dog and monkey, *Drug Met. Disp.*, 6, 623–630, 1978.
18. Maurer, H.H., Kraemer, T., Springer, D., and Staack, R.F., Chemistry, pharmacology, toxicology, and hepatic metabolism of designer drugs of the amphetamine (ecstasy), piperazine, and pyrrolidinophenone types: a synopsis, *Ther. Drug Monit.*, 26(2), 127–131, 2004.
19. Helmlin, H.J., Bracher, K., Salamone, S.J., and Brenneisen, R., Analysis of 3,4-methylenedioxymethamphetamine (MDMA) and its metabolites in human plasma and urine, Society of Forensic Toxicologists, Inc., Phoenix, AZ, October 1993 [Abstract].
20. Farre, M., de la Torre, R., Mathuna, B.O., Roset, P.N., Peiro, A.M., Torrens, M., Ortuno, J., Pujadas, M., and Cami, J., Repeated doses administration of MDMA in humans: pharmacological effects and pharmacokinetics, *Psychopharmacology* (Berlin), 173(3–4), 364–375, 2004.
21. Hernandez-Lopez, C., Farre, M., Roset, P.N., Menoyo, E., Pizarro, N., Ortuno, J., Torrens, M., Cami, J., and de la Torre, R., 3,4-Methylenedioxymethamphetamine (ecstasy) and alcohol interactions in humans: psychomotor performance, subjective effects, and pharmacokinetics, *J. Pharmacol. Exp. Ther.*, 300(1), 236–244, 2002.
22. Samyn, N., De Boeck, G., Wood, M., Lamers, C.T., De Waard, D., Brookhuis, K.A., Verstraete, A.G., and Riedel, W.J., Plasma, oral fluid and sweat wipe ecstasy concentrations in controlled and real life conditions, *Forensic Sci. Int.*, 128(1–2), 90–97, 2002.
23. de la Torre, R., Farre, M., Ortuno, J., Mas, M., Brenneisen, R., Roset, P.N., Segura, J., and Cami, J., Non-linear pharmacokinetics of MDMA ("ecstasy") in humans, *Br. J. Clin. Pharmacol.*, 49(2), 104–109, 2000.
24. Elliott, S.P., MDMA and MDA concentrations in antemortem and postmortem specimens in fatalities following hospital admission, *J. Anal. Toxicol.*, 29(5), 296–300, 2005.

4.5 BARBITURATES

Barbituric acid, 2,4,6-trioxohexahydropyrimidine, was first synthesized in 1864.[1] In 1903 it was marketed for use as an antianxiety and sedative hypnotic medication. Barbituric acid is without CNS depressant activity but by substituting an aryl or alkyl group on C-5, anxiolytic and sedative properties may be conferred. Substitution of sulfur on C-2 produces the thiobarbituates, which have characteristically greater lipophilicity. Generally, structural changes that increase lipophilicity result in decreased duration of action, decreased latency to onset of action, increased biotransformation, and increased hypnotic potency.[2] Although the use of barbiturates as sedative-hypnotic agents has largely been replaced by the benzodiazepines, the barbiturates maintain an important role as anticonvulsant and anesthetic drugs.

4.5.1 Pharmacology

As a class of drugs, barbiturates exert hypnotic, sedative, anxiolytic, anticonvulsant, and anesthetic properties. The clinical use of these drugs is based on their shared properties and also unique properties of individual drugs within this class.[1] As CNS depressants, barbiturates exert effects on excitatory and inhibitory synaptic neurotransmission. Barbiturates are known to decrease excitatory amino acid release and post-synaptic response in experimental animals by blocking the excitatory glutamate response. This may be due to a direct effect on the glutamate-sensitive channel, or an indirect effect on calcium channels.[1] The ultrashort-acting barbiturates used for anesthesia, such as thiopental, depress excitatory neuronal transmission to a greater extent than the anticonvulsant barbiturates.[3]

Barbiturates also exert an effect on gamma-amino butyric acid (GABA) neurotransmission. Barbiturates, such as pentobarbital, enhance the binding of GABA to $GABA_A$ receptors. This effect occurs both in the CNS and the spinal cord. The enhanced action of GABA depresses both normal physiological processes, such as post-synaptic potential evocation, and pathophysiological processes such as seizures.[1] Barbiturates also enlarge GABA-induced chloride currents by extending the time for chloride channel opening.[3] It is important to note that some barbiturates such as 5-(1,3-dimethylbutyl)-5-ethyl barbituric acid (DMBB) promote convulsions by directly depolarizing the neuronal membrane and increasing transmitter release.

4.5.2 Absorption

When utilized as sedative hypnotics, barbiturates are administered orally. They are rapidly and completely absorbed by this route with nearly 100% bioavailability and an onset of action ranging from 10 to 60 min.[3] Sodium salts are more rapidly absorbed than free acids. Intramuscular injections of sodium salts should be made deep into the muscle to prevent pain and tissue damage. Some barbiturates are also administered rectally; barbiturates utilized for the induction and maintenance of anesthesia (thiopental) or for treating status epilepticus (phenobarbital) are administered intravenously.

Pentobarbital is a short-acting barbiturate available for oral, intramuscular, rectal, and intravenous administration. After a single oral dose of 100 mg, peak serum concentrations of 1.2 to 3.1 mg/L were achieved at 0.5 to 2.0 h.[4] These concentrations diminished slowly to an average of 0.3 mg/L at 48 h. When administered intravenously, in a 5-min continuous infusion of 50 mg, plasma concentrations averaged 1.18 mg/L ($n = 5$) at 0.08 h, declining to 0.54 mg/L after 1 h and reaching 0.27 mg/L after 24 h.[5] Repeated intravenous doses of pentobarbital, typically 100 to 200 mg every 30 to 60 min, are administered to reduce intracranial pressure and decrease cerebral oxygen demand in patients with severe head trauma or anoxic brain damage.[6] Doses are adjusted to maintain plasma concentrations between 25 to 40 mg/L.

Amobarbital is a barbituric acid derivative of intermediate duration of action. It is administered orally in doses of 15 to 200 mg as a sedative hypnotic and in ampoules of 65 to 500 mg for intravenous and intramuscular injection for the seizure control.[6] Following a single oral dose of 120 mg, peak serum concentrations averaged 1.8 mg/L after 2 h.[7] After an oral dose of 600 mg distributed over a 3-h period, the peak blood concentration was achieved after 30 min, averaging 8.7 mg/L, with a decline to 4.1 mg/L by 18 h.[6]

Phenobarbital is utilized as a daytime sedative and anticonvulsant. It also induces several cytochrome P450 isozymes. Compared to other barbiturates, phenobarbital has a low oil/water partition coefficient, which results in slow distribution into the brain. It is available for oral, intravenous, or intramuscular administration. Doses for epileptic patients range from 60 to 200 mg per day. After a single oral dose of 30 mg, peak serum concentrations averaged 0.7 mg/L ($n = 3$). Repeated doses over a period of 7 days resulted in an average peak concentration of 8.1 mg/L.[6] Chronic administration of 200 mg per day as anticonvulsant medication resulted in an average blood concentration of 29 mg/L (range = 16 to 48 mg/L).[8]

4.5.3 Distribution

Barbiturates are generally widely distributed throughout the body. The highly lipophilic barbiturates, especially those used to induce anesthesia, undergo redistribution when administered intravenously. Barbiturates enter less vascular tissues over time, such as muscle and adipose tissue, and this redistribution decreases concentrations in the blood and brain. With drugs such as thiopental, this redistribution results in patients waking up within 5 to 15 min after injection of a anesthetic dose.

Pentobarbital is 65% plasma protein bound with a volume of distribution of 0.5 to 1.0 L/kg.[6] After intravenous administration, estimates of the plasma half-life have averaged between 20 and 30 h. Amobarbital is similar to pentobarbital in the degree of plasma protein binding (59%) with a slightly larger volume of distribution (0.9 to 1.4 L/kg). The plasma half-life, however, is dose dependent, with a range of 15 to 40 h.[6] Phenobarbital is approximately 50% plasma protein bound with a volume of distribution of 0.5 to 0.6 L/kg. The plasma half-life averages 4 days with a range of 2 to 6 days.

4.5.4 Metabolism and Elimination

Generally, barbiturates are metabolized by oxidation and conjugation in the liver prior to renal excretion. The oxidation of substituents at the C-5 position is the most important factor in terminating pharmacological activity.[2] Oxidation of barbiturates results in the formation of alcohols, phenols, ketones, or carboxylic acids with subsequent conjugation with glucuronic acid. Other metabolic transformations include *N*-hydroxylation, desulfuration of thiobarbiturates to oxybarbiturates, opening of the barbituric acid ring, and *N*-dealkylation of *N*-alkylbarbiturates to active metabolites, e.g., mephobarbital to phenobarbital.[2]

Pentobarbital is biotransformed by oxidation of the penultimate carbon of the methyl butyl side-chain to produce a mixture of alcohols, and by *N*-hydroxylation. The alcoholic metabolites of pentobarbital are pharmacologically inactive. Approximately 86% of a radioactive dose is excreted in the urine in 6 days, about 1% as unchanged drug and up to 73% as the L- and D-diastereoisomers of 3´-hydroxypentobarbital in a 5.4:1 ratio, and up to 15% as *N*-hydroxypentobarbital.[9] None of these metabolites is eliminated as a conjugate.

Amobarbital is extensively metabolized to polar metabolites in a process that is saturable and best described by zero-order kinetics at therapeutic doses.[10] Two major metabolites are produced by hydroxylation and *N*-glycosylation. 3´-Hydroxyamobarbital possesses pharmacological activity. Approximately 92% of a single dose is excreted in the urine with 5% excreted in the feces over a 6-day period. Approximately 2% is excreted unchanged in the urine, 30 to 40% is excreted as free 3´-hydroxyamobarbital, 29% as *N*-glycosylamobarbital, and 5% as the minor metabolite, 3´-carboxyamobarbital.

Phenobarbital is primarily metabolized via *N*-glycosylation and by oxidation to form *p*-hydroxyphenobarbital followed by conjugation with glucuronic acid (Figure 4.3). A dihydrohydroxy metabolite has been identified in minor amounts, thought to arise from an epoxide intermediate.[11] Approximately 80% of a single labeled dose is excreted in the urine within 16 days. Unchanged drug accounts for 25 to 33% of the dose, *N*-glucosyl-phenobarbital for 24 to 30%, and free or conjugated *p*-hydroxyphenobarbital for 18 to 19%.[12] When administered chronically, approximately 25% of the dose is excreted unchanged in the 24-h urine with 8% free and 9% conjugated *p*-hydroxyphenobarbital.

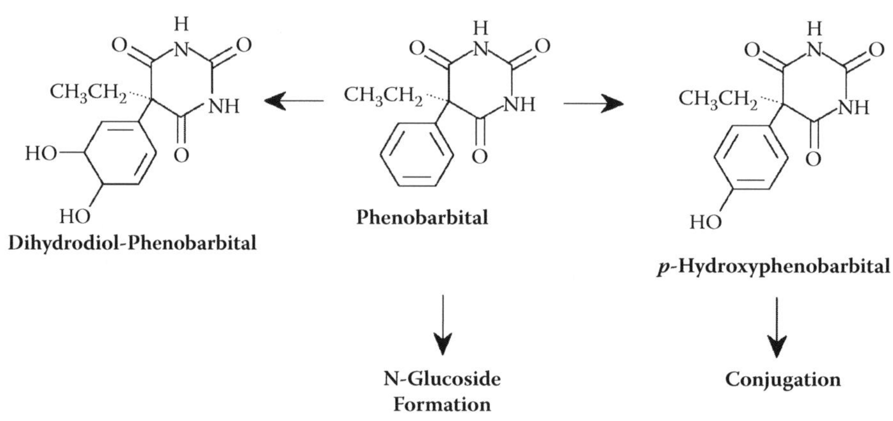

Figure 4.3 Metabolic pathway of phenobarbital.

REFERENCES

1. Smith, M.C. and Riskin, B.J., The clinical use of barbiturates in neurological disorders, *Drugs,* 42(3), 365–378, 1991.
2. Hardman, J.G. and Limbird, L.E., Eds., *Goodman & Gilman's The Pharmacological Basis of Therapeutics,* McGraw-Hill, New York, 1996.
3. MacDonald, R.L. and Barker, J.L., Anticonvulsant and anesthetic barbiturates: different postsynaptic action in cultured mammalian neurons, *Neurology,* 29, 432–477, 1979.
4. Sun, S. and Chun, A.H.C., Determination of pentobarbital in serum by electron capture GLC, *J. Pharm. Sci.,* 66, 477–480, 1977.
5. Smith, R.B., Dittert, L.W., Griffen, W.O., Jr., and Doluisio, J.T., Pharmacokinetics of pentobarbital after intravenous and oral administration, *J. Pharm. Biopharm.,* 1, 5–16, 1973.
6. Baselt, R.C. and Cravey, R.H., *Disposition of Toxic Drugs and Chemicals in Man,* Chemical Toxicology Institute, Foster City, CA, 1995.
7. Tang, B.K., Inaba, T., Endrenyi, L., and Kalow, W., Amobarbital — a probe of hepatic drug oxidation on man, *Clin. Pharmacol. Ther.,* 20, 439–444, 1976.
8. Plaa, G.L. and Hine, C.H., Hydantoin and barbiturate blood levels observed in epileptics, *Arch. Int. Pharm. Ther.,* 128, 375–383, 1960.
9. Tang, B.K., Inaba, T., and Kalow, W., *N*-Hydroxylation of pentobarbital in man, *Drug Met. Disp.,* 5, 71–74, 1977.
10. Garrett, E.R., Bres, J., Schnelle, K., and Rolf, L.L., Jr., Pharmacokinetics of saturably metabolized amobarbital, *J. Pharm. Biopharm.,* 2, 43–103, 1974.
11. Harvey, D.L., Glazener, L., and Stratton, L., Detection of a 5-(3,4-dihydroxy-1,5-cyclohexadien-1-yl)-metabolite of phenobarbital and mephobarbital in rat, guinea pig and human, *Res. Comm. Chem. Pathol. Pharm.,* 3, 557–565, 1972.
12. Tang, B.K., Kalow, W., and Grey, A.A., Metabolic fate of phenobarbital in man, *Drug Met. Disp.,* 7, 315–318, 1979.

4.6 BENZODIAZEPINES

The benzodiazepines are among the most commonly encountered prescribed drugs in forensic analysis. It has been estimated that between 10 and 20% of the adult population in the Western world has ingested these drugs within any year.[1] They are prescribed for the treatment of anxiety or panic disorder, and as a sleeping aid, anticonvulsant, or muscle relaxant. Abuse of this family of drugs is observed primarily in two forms: persistent therapeutic use, i.e., use longer than generally recommended; and illicit use, in which the drug is self-administered without physician approval or supervision. The former type of abuse is common and typically involves use at low doses compared to the rarely encountered illicit use that may involve high doses and clear indications of acute intoxication and impairment.[2]

4.6.1 Pharmacology

Benzodiazepines exert central depressant effects on spinal reflexes, in part mediated by the brainstem reticular system.[3] For example, chlordiazepoxide depresses the duration of electrical after-discharge in the limbic system. Most benzodiazepines elevate the seizure threshold and therefore may be used as anticonvulsant medications. Diazepam, clonazepam, and clorazepate may be prescribed for this therapeutic purpose.

Benzodiazepines potentiate the inhibitory effects of GABA and neurophysiological studies have identified specific benzodiazepine binding sites in the cerebellum, cerebral cortex, and limbic system.[4] These sites are located in a complex protein macromolecule that includes $GABA_A$ receptors and a chloride channel. Binding of benzodiazepines is modulated by both GABA and chloride.

Several benzodiazepine antagonists, such as flumazenil, and inverse agonists (compounds with opposite physiological effects to benzodiazepines), such as ethyl-β-carboline-3-carboxylate, competitively inhibit the binding of benzodiazepines.

Benzodiazepines are used as hypnotics because they have the ability to increase total sleep time. They demonstrate minimal cardiovascular effects, but do have the ability to increase heart rate and decrease cardiac output. Most CNS depressants, including the benzodiazepines, exhibit the ability to relax skeletal muscles. Clozapine, a dibenzodiazepine, is used in the treatment of schizophrenia. It has both sedative and antipsychotic actions, and is the only FDA-approved medication indicated for treatment-resistant schizophrenia, and for reducing the risk of suicidal behavior in patients with schizophrenia. This drug can have potentially life-threatening side effects, but appears to have no abuse potential and will not be considered further.

4.6.2 Absorption

The benzodiazepines comprise a large family of lipophilic acids (diazepam pKa = 3.4) with high octanol/water coefficients. They demonstrate a wide range of absorption rates when orally administered. Diazepam is absorbed rapidly, with peak concentrations occurring in 1 h in adults and as rapidly as 15 to 30 min in children. Following a single oral dose of 10 mg, peak blood diazepam concentrations averaged 148 ng/ml at 1 h, declining to 37 ng/ml by 24 h.[5] Bioavailability is dependent on drug formulation and route of administration, with approximately 100% bioavailability of diazepam when administered orally as tablets or in suspension, decreasing to 50 to 60% when administered intramuscularly or as suppositories. The rapid rate of absorption may be explained in part by the lipophilicity of diazepam. In contrast, less lipophilic benzodiazepines, such as lorazepam, exhibit slower rates of absorption, with an average time to peak blood concentration of 2 h. Prazepam and clorazepate act as prodrugs and are decarboxylated in the stomach to nordiazepam. Consequently, absorption is slowed and a delay occurs to the onset of action of these drugs.

4.6.3 Distribution

The benzodiazepines exhibit a two-compartment pharmacokinetic model.[6] Central compartment distribution is rapid and a slower distribution occurs into less perfused tissues, such as adipose. One-compartment pharmacokinetic models have been described for some benzodiazepines, such as lorazepam.[5] It is obvious that the more lipophilic benzodiazepines distribute more rapidly than less lipophilic drugs. Therefore, after a single dose, diazepam, a highly lipophilic drug, will have a shorter duration of action than lorazepam because it will be rapidly redistributed throughout the body. This may not be easily understood when considering the half-life because diazepam has a longer half-life (approximately 30 h) than lorazepam (12 to 15 h). Therefore, a long elimination half-life does not necessarily imply long duration of action after a single dose.

The majority of benzodiazepines are highly bound to plasma proteins (85 to 95%) with apparent volumes of distribution ranging from 1 to 3 L/kg[3] due to rapid removal from plasma to brain, lungs, and adipose tissue.

4.6.4 Metabolism and Elimination

The benzodiazepines are extensively metabolized producing multiple metabolites, many of which share common pathways (Figure 4.4). Metabolic processes include hydroxylation, demethylation, and glucuronidation.

Diazepam undergoes *N*-demethylation to an active metabolite, nordiazepam. Both of these compounds are then hydroxylated to temazepam and oxazepam, respectively. These metabolites are also active, but are usually rapidly excreted and do not accumulate in plasma. Only small

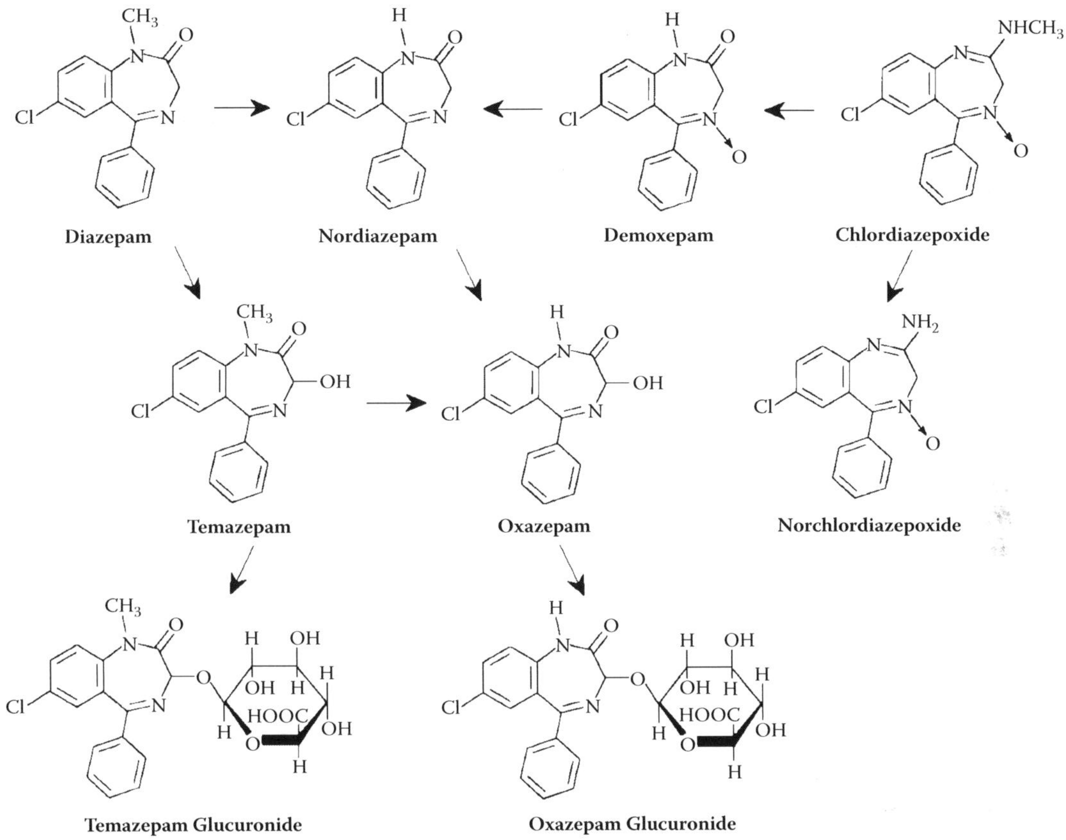

Figure 4.4 Metabolic pathway of the benzodiazepines.

amounts of diazepam and nordiazepam are detected in urine, with 33% of a dose excreted as oxazepam glucuronide and another 20% excreted as various conjugates.[5] Oxazepam, the 3-hydroxy metabolite of nordiazepam, is rapidly conjugated with glucuronic acid to form an inactive metabolite. This conjugate accounts for 61% of an oral dose in the 48-h urine. Trace amounts of free drug are detected in the urine and other hydroxylation products account for less than 5% of a dose.[7] Lorazepam is also rapidly conjugated, forming the inactive product, lorazepam glucuronide. This conjugate is not rapidly excreted but may achieve plasma concentrations exceeding the parent drug, with an elimination half-life of approximately 16 h.[5] Approximately 75% of a dose is eliminated in the urine as the conjugate over 5 days. Minor metabolites, such as ring hydroxylation products and quinazoline derivatives, constitute another 14% of the dose. Trace amounts of free drug are found in urine.

Chlordiazepoxide is metabolized to four active metabolites. The drug is *N*-demethylated to norchlordiazepoxide, then deaminated to form demoxepam. These metabolites demonstrate pharmacological activity similar to the parent drug. Demoxepam is reduced to form nordiazepam, which accumulates in plasma with multiple dosing. Nordiazepam is then hydroxylated to produce oxazepam. Less than 1% of the dose is excreted unchanged in the urine with approximately 6% excreted as demoxepam and the rest as glucuronide conjugates.[8] Temazepam undergoes *N*-demethylation to form the active metabolite oxazepam. Both parent and metabolite are subsequently conjugated. An average of 82% of a dose is excreted in urine and 12% in the feces.[5]

Alprazolam, a triazolobenzodiazepine, is also extensively metabolized by oxidation and conjugation. Metabolites include a-hydroxyalprazolam, 4-hydroxyalprazolam, and a,4-dihydroxyalprazolam. The first two metabolites possess approximately 66 and 19% of the pharmacological activity of the parent, respectively. 3-Hydroxy-5-methyltriazolyl, an analogue of chlorobenzophenone, is also formed. Approximately 94% of a dose is excreted within 72 h with 80% excreted in the urine.[9] Flunitrazepam, the *N*-methyl-2′-fluoro analogue of nitrazepam, undergoes biotransformation via *N*-demethylation, 3-hydroxylation, and glucuronidation. In addition, the nitro group is reduced to an amine and is subsequently acetylated. Approximately 84% of a labeled dose is excreted in the urine over 1 week, and 11% is excreted in the feces.[5] Less than 0.5% is excreted unchanged. Norflunitrazepam and 7-aminoflunitrazepam may be detected in plasma for 1 day after a single dose of 2 mg. Triazolam is extensively metabolized by hydroxylation and subsequent conjugation. The major metabolite, 1-hydroxymethyltriazolam, possesses pharmacological activity. Only trace amounts of unchanged drug are excreted in the urine, with approximately 80% of a dose appearing in the urine in 72 h, mainly as glucuronide conjugates.

Since benzodiazepines are metabolized by the cytochrome P450 family of isozymes,[1] potential inhibitors of these may produce significant increases in blood concentrations of benzodiazepines. An example of this inhibition is the drug midazolam, administered as a presurgical anesthetic. Lam et al.[11] reported a mean increase in the area under the curve of midazolam by ketoconazole (772%) and nefazodone (444%) in a group of 40 healthy human subjects administered 200 mg ketoconazole per day and 400 mg nefazodone per day. The authors concluded that caution should be exercised when use of midazolam is warranted with potent CYP3A4 inhibitors.[11]

REFERENCES

1. Balter, M.B., Manheimer, D.I., Mellinger, G.D., and Uhlenhuth, E.H., A cross-national comparison of anti-anxiety/sedative drug use, *Curr. Med. Res. Opin.,* 8(Suppl. 4), 5–20, 1984.
2. Busto, U., Bendayan, R., and Sellers, E.M., Clinical pharmacokinetics of non-opiate abused drugs, *Clin. Pharmacokinet.,* 16, 1–26, 1989.
3. Hardman, J.G. and Limbird, L.E., Eds., *Goodman & Gilman's The Pharmacological Basis of Therapeutics,* McGraw-Hill, New York, 1996.
4. Potokar, J. and Nutt, D.J., Anxiolytic potential of benzodiazepines receptor partial agonists, *CNS Drugs,* 1, 305–315, 1994.
5. Baselt, R.C. and Cravey, R.H., *Disposition of Toxic Drugs and Chemicals in Man*, Chemical Toxicology Institute, Foster City, CA, 1995.
6. Bailey, L., Ward., M., and Musa, M.N., Clinical pharmacokinetics of benzodiazepines, *J. Clin. Pharmacol.,* 34, 804–811, 1994.
7. Knowles, J.A. and Ruelius, H.W., Absorption and excretion of 7-chloro-1,3-dihydro-3-hydroxy-5-phenyl-2H-1,4-benzodiazepin-2-one (oxazepam) in humans, *Arz. Forsch.,* 22, 687–692, 1972.
8. Schwartz, M.A., Pathways of metabolism of benzodiazepines. In *The Benzodiazepines*, Garattini, S., Mussini, E., and Randall, L.O., Eds., Raven Press, New York, 1973, 53–74.
9. Dawson, G.W., Jue, S.G., and Brogden, R.N., Alprazolam. A review of its pharmacodynamic properties and efficacy in the treatment of anxiety and depression, *Drugs,* 27, 132–147, 1984.
10. Moody, D.E., Drug interactions with benzodiazepines. In *Handbook of Drug Interactions: A Clinical and Forensic Guide,* Mozayani, A. and Raymon, L.P., Eds., Humana Press, Totowa, NJ, 2004.
11. Lam, Y.W., Alfaro, C.L., Ereshefsky, L., and Miller, M., Pharmacokinetic and pharmacodynamic interactions of oral midazolam with ketoconazole, fluoxetine, fluvoxamine, and nefazodone, *J. Clin. Pharmacol.*, 43(11), 1274–1282, 2003.

4.7 COCAINE

Cocaine is a naturally occurring alkaloid obtained from the plant *Erythroxylon coca* L. This plant grows in the Andes region of South America, ideally at elevations between 1500 and 5000 ft.[1] A second closely related species has been identified, *Erythroxylon novogranatense* H., and each species has one variety known as *E. coca* var. *ipadu* Plowman and *E. coca novogranatense* var.

truxillense, respectively. Cocaine may also be chemically synthesized with cold aqueous succinaldehyde and cold aqueous methylamine, methylamine hydrochloride, and the potassium salt of acetone-dicarboxylic acid monomethyl ester.[2]

Cocaine is used medically by otorhinolaryngologists and plastic surgeons as an epinephrine cocaine mixture. Solutions for topical application are typically less than 4% cocaine hydrochloride. In the U.S. cocaine is a scheduled drug under the federal Controlled Substances Act of 1970. Refined cocaine, in the form of the base or hydrochloride salt, is self-administered by many routes, including snorting, smoking, genital application, and by injection.

4.7.1 Pharmacology

Cocaine inhibits the presynaptic reuptake of the neurotransmitters norepinehrine, serotonin, and dopamine at synaptic junctions. This results in increased concentrations in the synaptic cleft. Since norepinephrine acts within the sympathetic nervous system, increased sympathetic stimulation is produced. Physiological effects of this stimulation include tachycardia, vasoconstriction, mydriasis, and hyperthermia.[3] CNS stimulation results in increased alertness, diminished appetite, and increased energy. The euphoria or psychological stimulation produced by cocaine is thought to be related to the inhibition of serotonin and dopamine reuptake. Cocaine also acts as a local anesthetic due to its ability to block sodium channels in neuronal cells.[3]

4.7.2 Absorption

Cocaine is rapidly absorbed from mucous membranes and the pulmonary vasculature. However, the rate at which cocaine appears in the blood is dependent on the route of administration. Coca leaves have been chewed by native South Americans for more than 3000 years. Recent studies of the oral route of administration found that chewing powdered coca leaves containing between 17 and 48 mg of cocaine produced peak plasma concentrations of 11 to 149 ng/ml ($n = 6$) at 0.4 to 2 h after administration.[4] In another study, healthy male volunteers were administered cocaine hydrochloride (2 mg/kg) in gelatin capsules. Peak plasma concentrations of 104 to 424 ng/ml were achieved at 50 to 90 min. One of the most common routes of self-administration of cocaine in North America is the intranasal route. Wilkinson et al.[5] found that peak plasma concentrations of cocaine were reached 35 to 90 min after "snorting," but another study using equivalent doses found that peak plasma concentrations were achieved between 120 and 160 min.[6] Intravenous administration of 32-mg cocaine hydrochloride resulted in an average peak plasma concentration of 308 ng/ml at 5 min.[6] Cocaine may also be self-administered by the smoked route in the form of cocaine base, commonly called "crack," or by a process known as "free-basing" in which powdered cocaine hydrochloride is converted into its base form. In a study of six subjects who each smoked 50 mg of cocaine, the average peak plasma cocaine concentration of 203 ng/ml was achieved at 5 min.[7] The bioavailability of cocaine after smoking depends on several factors including the temperature of volatilization and drug loss in main- and sidestream smoke.

Perez-Reyes et al.[8] estimated that only 32% of a dose of cocaine base placed in a pipe is actually inhaled by the smoker. Cone[9] compared the pharmacokinetics and pharmacodynamics of cocaine by the intravenous, intranasal, and smoked routes of administration in the same subjects. Venous plasma cocaine concentrations peaked within 5 min by the intravenous and smoked routes. Estimated peak cocaine concentrations ranged from 98 to 349 ng/ml and 154 to 345 ng/ml after intravenous administration of 25-mg cocaine hydrochloride and 42-mg cocaine base by the smoked route, respectively. After dosing by the intranasal route (32 mg cocaine hydrochloride) estimated peak plasma cocaine concentrations ranged from 40 to 88 ng/ml after 0.39 to 0.85 h.[9] In this study, the average bioavailability of cocaine was 70.1% by the smoked route and 93.7% by the intranasal route. Jenkins et al.[10] described the correlation between pharmacological effects and plasma cocaine concentrations in seven volunteers after they had smoked 10 to 40 mg cocaine. The mean plasma cocaine concentration 2 min after smoking 40 mg cocaine was 153 ± 107.5 ng/ml. Peak concentrations ranged from 160.8 ± 99.1 ng/ml. Increases in pupil diameter, systolic and diastolic blood pressure, heart rate, and subjective measures of drug effect occurred early after drug administration, with maximum effects observed at 2 min (first measure) for blood pressure and subjective measures, or after a brief delay (at 5 to 10 min post dose) for others, notably heart rate and pupil diameter.

4.7.3 Distribution

After an intravenous dose of radiolabeled cocaine to rats, the highest concentrations were found in the brain, spleen, kidney, and lung after 15 min, with the lowest concentrations in the blood, heart, and muscle.[11] Plasma protein binding in humans is approximately 91% at low concentrations.[11] Cocaine binds to the plasma protein, albumin, and also to α1-acid glycoprotein. The steady-state volume of distribution is large (1.6 to 2.7 L/kg), reflecting extensive extravascular distribution.[12] In 1991 Ambre et al.[13] studied the pharmacokinetics of benzoylecgonine in nine human volunteers. The metabolite is much more polar than the parent and liphophobic, explaining why the measured mean V_d was only 0.71.

A two-compartment open linear model has been described for the pharmacokinetic profile of cocaine after intravenous administration.[14] The distribution phase after cocaine administration is rapid and the elimination half-life estimated as 31 to 82 min.[14] Cone[9] fitted data to a two-compartment model with bolus input and first-order elimination for the intravenous and smoked routes. For the intranasal route, data were fitted to a two-compartment model with first-order absorption and first-order elimination. The average elimination half-life ($t_1/2\beta$) was 244 min after intravenous administration, 272 min after smoked administration, and 299 min after intranasal administration.

The disposition of cocaine in nontraditional testing matrices has been described. For example, Lester et al.[15] measured cocaine and benzoylecgonine (BE) concentrations in skin, interstitial fluid (IF), sebum, and stratum corneum in five volunteers after the intravenous 1-h infusion of 1 mg/kg cocaine d_5. Peak cocaine concentrations in the skin were achieved at 1.5 h and were undetectable after 6 h. No BE was measured in the skin. Peak cocaine concentrations were achieved at 5 h after administration in the IF and were nondetectable by 24 h. BE was found in the IF. In the sebum peak cocaine concentrations occurred between 3 to 24 h but in the stratum corneum cocaine was detected in only one subject.

4.7.4 Metabolism

In humans, the principal route of metabolism of cocaine is by hydrolysis of the ester linkages. Pseudocholinesterase and liver esterases produce the inactive metabolite, ecgonine methyl ester (EME) (Figure 4.5). The second major metabolite, BE, is formed spontaneously at physiological pH. In addition, there is evidence that BE may be formed enzymatically from cocaine by liver carboxylesterases. *N*-Demethylation of BE produces benzoylnorecgonine. Further metabolism of EME and BE produces ecgonine. Further hydrolysis of cocaine and BE produces minor metabolites, meta- and para-hydroxy-cocaine and -BE. The proportion of each metabolite produced and the activity of the individual metabolites have yet to be completely determined.

Cocaine may be *N*-demethylated by the cytochrome P450 system to produce an active metabolite, norcocaine. Further breakdown produces *N*-hydroxynorcocaine and norcocaine nitroxide. Further metabolism produces a highly reactive free radical that is thought to be responsible for the hepatotoxicity observed in cocaine users.[1]

When cocaine is coadministered with ethanol, cocaethylene (CE) is formed in the liver by transesterification by liver methylesterase. CE may also be formed by fatty acid ethyl synthase.[16] This lipophilic compound crosses the blood–brain barrier and is known to contribute to the psychological effects produced by cocaine.[1] Harris et al.[17] administered deuterium-labeled cocaine (0.3 to 1.2 mg/kg) intravenously 1 h after an oral dose of ethanol (1 g/kg) to ten volunteers. When

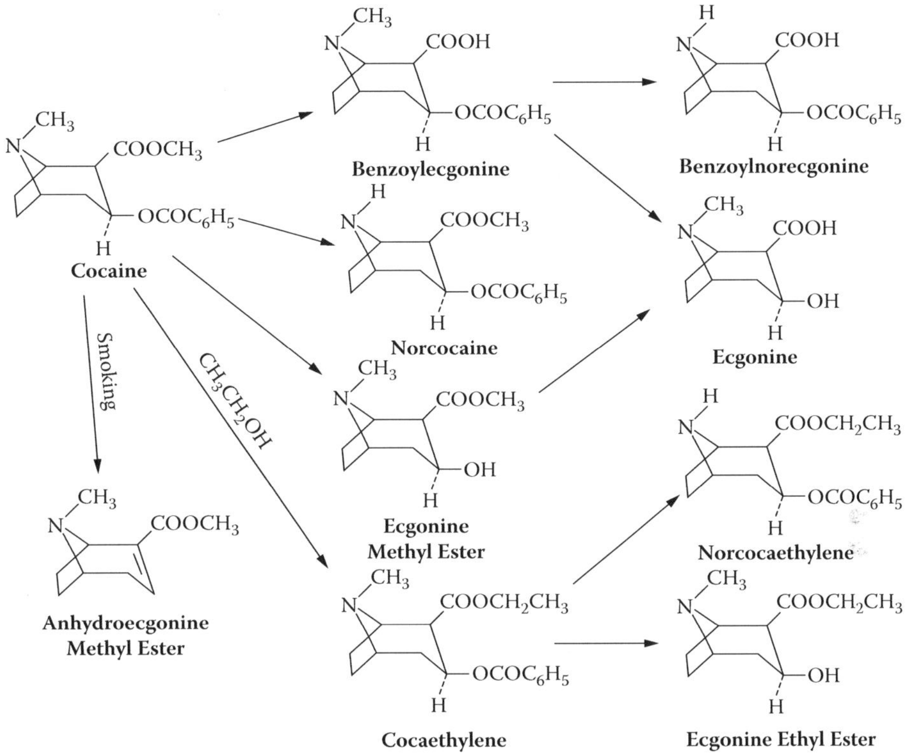

Figure 4.5 Metabolic pathway of cocaine.

coadministered with ethanol, 17 ± 6% (mean ± S.D.) of the cocaine was converted to cocaethylene. Ethanol ingestion prior to cocaine administration decreased urine BE levels by 48%. When cocaine is smoked, a pyrolysis product, anhydroecgonine methyl ester (AEME), is formed. Therefore, the presence of this compound indicates exposure to smoked cocaine. The pharmacological and toxicological properties of this compound have not been studied.

4.7.5 Elimination

Approximately 85 to 90% of a cocaine dose is recovered in the 24-h urine.[18] Unchanged drug accounts for 1 to 9% of the dose depending on urine pH, BE, 35 to 54%, and EME, 32 to 49%. In one study, excretion data were obtained from subjects administered a bolus intravenous injection of cocaine followed by an intravenous infusion, supplying total doses of 253, 444, and 700 mg cocaine.[19] Elimination half-lives averaged 0.8, 4.5, and 3.1 h for cocaine, BE, and EME, respectively. After intranasal application of 1.5 mg/kg, urine cocaine concentrations averaged 6.7 mg/L during the first hour, and BE concentrations peaked between 4 and 8 h at 35 mg/L.[11] Oral ingestion of 25 mg cocaine by a single individual resulted in a peak urine BE concentration of 7.9 mg/L in the 6- to 12-h collection period, with a decline to 0.4 mg/L by 48 h.[20] Oral consumption of coca tea of Peruvian origin containing approximately 4 mg of cocaine resulted in a peak urine BE concentration of 3.9 mg/L after 10 h in one individual.[21] The cumulative urinary excretion of BE after approximately 48 h was 3.1 mg. Consumption of coca tea of Bolivian origin by the same individual, containing a similar amount of cocaine, resulted in a peak urine BE level of 4.9 mg/L at 3.5 h.[21] The cumulative BE excreted in urine was 2.6 mg. The minor metabolites, including the *p*- and *m*-hydroxy metabolites, and also the pyrolysis product, AEME, have been detected in urine after cocaine administration.[22,23]

REFERENCES

1. Karch, S., *The Pathology of Drug Abuse,* CRC Press, Boca Raton, FL, 1993.
2. Saferstein, R., *Forensic Science Handbook,* Vol. II, Prentice Hall, Englewood Cliffs, NJ, 1988.
3. Warner, E.A., Cocaine abuse, *Ann. Int. Med.,* 119(3), 226–235, 1993.
4. Holmstedt, B., Lindgren, J., Rivier, L., and Plowman, T., Cocaine in blood of coca chewers, *J. Ethnopharm.,* 1, 69–78, 1979.
5. Wilkinson, P., Van Dyke, C., Jatlow, P., Barash, P., and Byck, R., Intranasal and oral cocaine kinetics, *Clin. Pharmacol. Ther.,* 27, 386–394, 1980.
6. Javaid, J.I., Musa, M.N., Fischman, M., Schuster, C.R., and Davis, J.M., Kinetics of cocaine in humans after intravenous and intranasal administration, *Biopharm. Drug Disp.,* 4, 9–18, 1983.
7. Jeffcoat, A.R., Perez-Reyes, M., and Hill, J.M., Cocaine disposition in humans after intravenous injection, nasal insufflation (snorting), or smoking, *Drug Met. Disp.,* 17, 153–159, 1989.
8. Perez-Reyes, M., DiGuiseppi, S., Ondrusek, G., Jeffcoat, A.R., and Cook, C.E., Free base cocaine smoking, *Clin. Pharmacol. Ther.,* 32, 459–465, 1982.
9. Cone, E.J., Pharmacokinetics and pharmacodynamics of cocaine, *J. Anal. Toxicol.,* 19, 459–478, 1995.
10. Jenkins, A.J., Keenan, R.M., Henningfield, J.E., and Cone, E.J., Correlation between pharmacological effects and plasma cocaine concentrations after smoked administration, *J. Anal. Toxicol.,* 26, 382–392, 2002.
11. Busto, U., Bendayan, R., and Sellers, E.M., Clinical pharmacokinetics of non-opiate abused drugs, *Clin. Pharmacokinet.,* 16, 1–26, 1989.
12. Baselt, R.C. and Cravey, R.H., *Disposition of Toxic Drugs and Chemicals in Man,* 4th ed., Chemical Toxicology Institute, Foster City, CA, 1995.
13. Ambre, J.J., Connelly, T.J., and Ruo, T.I., A kinetic model of benzoylecgonine disposition after cocaine administration in humans, *J. Anal. Toxicol.,* 15(1), 17–20, 1991.
14. Chow, M.J., Ambre, J.J., Ruo, T.I., Atkinson, A.J., and Bowsher, D.J., Kinetics of cocaine distribution, elimination and chronotropic effects, *Clin. Pharmacol. Ther.,* 38, 318–324, 1985.
15. Lester, L., Uemura, N., Ademola, J., Harkey, M.R., Nath, R.P., Kim, S.J., Jerschow, E., Henderson, G.L., Mendelson, J., and Jones, R.T., Disposition of cocaine in skin, interstitial fluid, sebum, and stratum corneum, *J. Anal. Toxicol.,* 26, 547–553, 2002.
16. Isenschmid, D.S., Cocaine. In *Principles of Forensic Toxicology,* 2nd ed., B.S. Levine, Ed., AACC Press, Washington, D.C., 2003.
17. Harris, D.S., Everhart, E.T., Mendelson, J., and Jones, R.T., The pharmacology of cocaethylene in humans following cocaine and ethanol administration, *Drug Alcohol Depend.,* 72(2), 169–182, 2003.
18. Jatlow, P., Cocaine: analysis, pharmacokinetics and disposition, *Yale J. Biol. Med.,* 61, 105–113, 1988.
19. Ambre, J., Ruo, T.I., Nelson, J., and Belknap, S., Urinary excretion of cocaine, benzoylecgonine, and ecgonine methyl ester in humans, *J. Anal. Toxicol.,* 12, 301–306, 1988.
20. Baselt, R. and Chang, R., Urinary excretion of cocaine and benzoylecgonine following oral ingestion in a single subject, *J. Anal. Toxicol.,* 11, 81–82, 1987.
21. Jenkins, A.J., Llosa, T., Montoya, I., and Cone, E.J., Identification and quantitation of alkaloids in coca tea, *Forensic Sci. Int.,* 77, 179–189, 1996.
22. Jacob, P., III, Lewis, E.R., Elias-Baker, B.A., and Jones, R., A pyrolysis product, anhydroecgonine methyl ester (methylecgonidine) is in the urine of cocaine smokers, *J. Anal. Toxicol.,* 14, 353–357, 1990.
23. Zhang, J.Y. and Foltz, R.L., Cocaine metabolism in man: identification of four previously unreported cocaine metabolites in human urine, *J. Anal. Toxicol.,* 14, 201–205, 1990.

4.8 LYSERGIC ACID DIETHYLAMIDE

Lysergic acid diethylamide (LSD) is an indolealkylamine discovered by Albert Hoffman of Sandoz Laboratories in 1943.[1] It may be synthesized from lysergic acid and diethylamine. Lysergic acid, a naturally occurring ergot alkaloid, is present in grain parasitized by the fungus *Claviceps purpurea.* A closely related alkaloid, lysergic acid amide, is present in morning glory seeds and the Hawaiian baby wood rose.[1] In the 1950s, LSD was used as an aid in the treatment of alcoholism, opioid addiction, psychoneurosis, and sexual disorders, but currently it is classified under Schedule I of the federal Controlled Substances Act with no accepted medical use in the U.S. It is available illicitly as a powder, tablet, or gelatin capsule, or impregnated in sugar cubes, gelatin squares, blotter paper, or postage stamps.

4.8.1 Pharmacology

LSD is a potent centrally acting drug. The D-isomer is pharmacologically active while the L-isomer is apparently inactive.[1] Neuropharmacological studies have shown that LSD exerts a selective inhibitory effect on the brain's raphe system by causing a cessation of the spontaneous firing of serotonin-containing neurons of the dorsal and median raphe nuclei. In this way, LSD acts as an indirect serotonin antagonist. However, inhibition of raphe firing is not sufficient to explain the psychotomimetic effects of LSD because the compound lisuride is a more potent inhibitor of the raphe system yet does not demonstrate hallucinogenic potential in humans. Therefore, other post-synaptic mechanisms such as action on glutamate or serotonin receptors may be involved.[2] Also, there is evidence that LSD indirectly exerts effects on the cytoskeleton by reducing the amount of serotonin released by the raphe system.[3] LSD produces sympathomimetic, parasympathomimetic, and neuromuscular effects, which include mydriasis, lacrimation, tachycardia, and tremor.

4.8.2 Absorption

LSD may be self-administered orally, nasally, or by parenteral ingestion; however, the oral route is the most common. Doses of 50 to 300 μg are ingested, with a minimum effective dose of 20 to 25 μg. Absorption is rapid and complete regardless of the route of administration. However, food in the stomach slows absorption when ingested. Effects are observed within 5 to 10 min, with psychosis evident after 15 to 20 min. Peak effects have been reported 30 to 90 min after dosing; effects decline after 4 to 6 h.[4] The duration of effects may be 8 to 12 h.

Pharmacokinetic studies in humans are limited with much of the data dating from the 1960s. Following intravenous administration of 2 μg/kg, a peak plasma LSD concentration of 5 ng/ml was observed after 1 h.[1] At 8 h, the plasma concentration had declined to 1 ng/ml.[1] In much more recent studies a method using liquid chromatography with electrospray ionization and tandem mass spectrometric detection has been developed and validated for LSD and iso-LSD. Using this technique the lower limit for quantitative determination was 0.02 μg/L for LSD and iso-LSD. Peak plasma levels were slightly higher than earlier reports (case 1 plasma LSD = 0.31 μg/L, iso-LSD = 0.27 μg/L and in a second case LSD = 0.24 μg/L, iso-LSD = 0.6 μg/L in urine).

4.8.3 Distribution

Plasma protein binding of LSD is >80%. As the drug penetrates the CNS, it is concentrated in the visual brain areas and the limbic and reticular activating systems, correlating with perceived effects. LSD is also found in the liver, spleen, and lungs.[5] The volume of distribution is reported to be low at 0.28 L/kg.[1] Wagner et al.[6] described a two-compartment open model for LSD with an elimination half-life of 3 h.

4.8.4 Metabolism and Excretion

LSD metabolism was investigated using MS-MS. Metabolites were determined using MS-MS. The main metabolite was 2-oxo-3-hydroxy-LSD (O-H-LSD) present in urine at concentrations of 2.5 and 6.6 μg/L, respectively, for case 1 and 2, but it was not detected at all in plasma. Nor-LSD was also found in urine at 0.15 and 0.01 μg/L levels. Nor-iso-LSD, lysergic acid ethylamide (LAE),

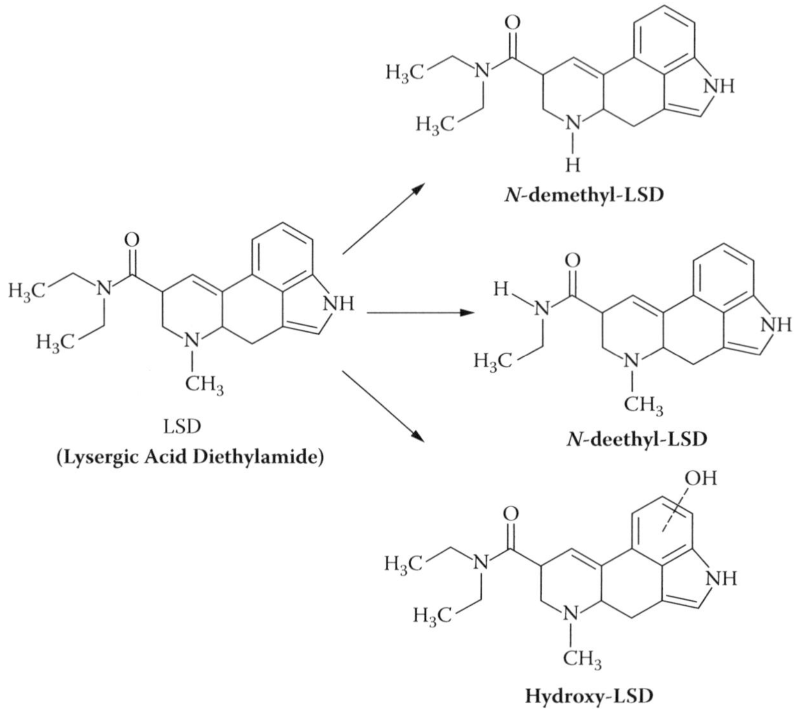

Figure 4.6 Metabolic pathway of LSD.

trioxylated-LSD, lysergic acid ethyl-2-hydroxyethylamide (LEO), and 13- and 14-hydroxy-LSD and their glucuronide conjugates were detected in urine using specific MS-MS transitions.[4]

The metabolism and elimination of LSD in humans has received limited study. Animal studies demonstrated extensive biotransformation via *N*-demethylation, *N*-deethylation, and hydroxylation to inactive metabolites (Figure 4.6).[7] In humans, demethylation and aromatic hydroxylation occur to produce *N*-desmethyl-LSD and 13- and 14-hydroxy-LSD. Hydroxylated metabolites undergo glucuronidation to form water-soluble conjugates. Excretion into the bile accounts for approximately 80% of a dose.[5] Concentrations of unchanged drug ranged from 1 to 55 ng/ml in the 24-h urine after ingestion of 200 to 400 μg LSD in humans.[8] LSD or its metabolites were detectable for 34 to 120 h following a 300-μg oral dose in seven human subjects.[9] The clearance of LSD in humans is unknown.

REFERENCES

1. Baselt, R.C. and Cravey, R.H., *Disposition of Toxic Drugs and Chemicals in Man,* 4th ed., Chemical Toxicology Institute, Foster City, CA, 1995.
2. Goldberger, B.A., Lysergic acid diethylamide. In-service training and continuing education AACC/TDM, American Association for Clinical Chemistry, Inc., Washington, D.C. 14(6), 99–100, 1993.
3. Van Woerkom, A.E., The major hallucinogens and the central cytoskeleton: an association beyond coincidence? Towards sub-cellular mechanisms in schizophrenia, *Med. Hypoth.,* 31, 7–15, 1990.
4. Leikin, J.B., Karantz, A.J., Zell-Kanter, M., Barkin, R.L., and Hryhorczuk, D.O., Clinical features and management of intoxication due to hallucinogenic drugs, *Med. Toxicol. Adverse Drug Exp.,* 4(5), 324–350, 1989.
5. Canezin, J., Cailleux, A., Turcant, A., Le Bouil, A., Harry, P., and Allain, P., Determination of LSD and its metabolites in human biological fluids by high-performance liquid chromatography with electrospray tandem mass spectrometry, *J. Chromatogr. B Biomed. Sci. Appl.,* 765(1), 15–27, 2001.

6. Wagner, J.G., Aghajanian, G.K., and Bing, O.H.L., Correlation of performance test scores with "tissue concentration" of lysergic acid diethylamide in human subjects, *Clin. Pharmacol. Ther.,* 9, 635–638, 1968.
7. Axelrod, J., Brady, R.O., Witkop, B., and Evarts, E.V., Metabolism of lysergic acid diethylamide, *Nature,* 178, 143–144, 1956.
8. Taunton-Rigby, A., Sher, S.E., and Kelley, P.R., Lysergic acid diethylamide: radioimmunoassay, *Science,* 181, 165–166, 1973.
9. Peel, H.W. and Boynton, A.L., Analysis of LSD in urine using radioimmunoassay — excretion and storage effects, *Can. Soc. For. Sci. J.,* 13, 23–28, 1980.

4.9 MARIJUANA

The term "marijuana" refers to all parts of the plant *Cannabis sativa* L., whether growing or not: the seeds; resin extracted from any part of such plant; and every compound, salt, derivative, or mixture; but does not include the mature stalks, fiber produced from the stalks, or oil or cake prepared from the seeds.[1] *Cannabis sativa* L. is an annual plant that grows in all parts of the world to a height of 16 to 18 ft. Commercially, it is cultivated for hemp production, with the bulk of the plant consisting of stalks with very little foliage, except at the apex. In contrast, the wild plant and those cultivated illegally possess numerous branches as the psychoactive ingredient is concentrated in the leaves and flowering tops. There may be significant differences in the gross appearance of marijuana plants due to climatic and soil conditions, the closeness of other plants during growth, and the origin of the seed. Marijuana is the crude drug derived from the plant *Cannabis sativa* L., a plant that is currently accepted as belonging to a family (Cannabaceae) that has only one genus (*Cannabis*) with only one species (*sativa*) that is highly variable.[2]

In 1980 the total number of natural compounds identified in *C. sativa* L. was 423.[3] By 1995 the number had risen to 483, and recently 6 new compounds, 4 new cannabinoids and 2 new flavonoids, have been described.[4]

The major psychoactive constituent of marijuana is delta-9-tetrahydrocannabinol, commonly referred to as THC. Different parts of the plant contain varying concentrations of THC, with leaves containing <1% to 10% THC by weight, and hashish, a resin prepared from the flowering tops, containing approximately 15% THC. THC may be synthesized using citral and olivetol in boron trifluoride and methylene chloride.[5] Although no reports have appeared within the published peer-reviewed literature, persistent reports from the enforcement community suggest that intensive cross-breeding has led to production of plants that have a THC content well over 20%. These "super" plants appear to be grown mainly along the Canadian–American border, primarily by Asian gangs.

4.9.1 Pharmacology

Marijuana is typically self-administered orally or by smoking in doses of 5 to 20 mg.[6] It may produce a variety of pharmacological effects including sedation, euphoria, hallucinations, and temporal distortion. In addition, THC possesses activity at benzodiazepine, opioid, and cannabinoid receptors and also exerts effects on prostaglandin synthesis, DNA, RNA, and protein metabolism.[7,8] Early workers thought that THC effects were nonspecific, but in the late 1980s a specific cannabinoid receptor was identified in the brains of rats. It is now apparent that there are two types of cannabinoid receptor — CB1 and CB2 — and these receptors are the primary targets of endogenous cannabinoids (endocannabinoids). THC binds to both cannabinoid receptors. The CB1 receptor is mostly found in the brain, while the CB2 receptor is found in immune tissues such as the spleen, thymus, and tonsils[8] but not in the brain. Specific antagonists exist for each of the CB1 and CB2 receptors.

Cannabinoid-coupled G protein–coupled receptors are involved in the control of many processes, including metabolic regulation, craving, pain, anxiety, bone growth, and immune function. The exogenous cannabinoids found in marijuana plants can also exert effects via G(i/o) proteins, negatively modulating cyclic AMP levels and activating the inward rectifying K(+) channels.[9] Manipulation at either receptor site may have important clinical consequences and therapies based on cannabinoid–receptor interactions are under development. Cannabinoids mediate a decrease in blood pressure and can suppress cardiac contractility in hypertension. Conversely, if the CB1-mediated cardiodepressor and vasodilator effects of anandamide are enhanced (by blocking its hydrolysis), blood pressure tends to normalize.[10] Many clinical developments taking advantage of these properties are likely to occur. By the time of publication of this book, rimonabant (Acompliat™), a C1 blocking agent, will have been approved for weight loss by the FDA.[11]

4.9.2 Absorption

Marijuana is commonly self-administered by the smoked route by rolling dried marijuana leaves in tobacco paper and smoking as a cigarette. Smoking results in rapid drug delivery from the lungs to the brain. However, loss of drug occurs during the smoking process due to pyrolysis and sidestream smoke. In an *in vitro* study in which loss due to sidestream smoke was minimized, Perez-Reyes et al.[12] reported a 30% loss of THC due to pyrolysis. Sidestream THC losses of 40 to 50% have been reported. Once THC reaches the lungs, it is rapidly absorbed. Peak plasma THC concentrations of 100 to 200 ng/ml occur after 3 to 8 min and THC is present in blood after the first puff from a marijuana cigarette. Mean ± SD THC concentrations of 7.0 ± 8.1 ng/ml and 18.1 ± 12.0 ng/ml were observed after the first inhalation of low- or high-dose marijuana cigarettes (1.75%, 3.55%), respectively.[13] Peak concentrations occurred at 9 min after the first puff. Lemberger et al.[14] demonstrated that physiological and subjective measures of drug effects occurred simultaneously with the rise in blood THC concentrations.

After oral administration, THC is 90 to 95% absorbed. However, the oral route results in lower peak plasma concentrations at a later time. Wall et al. reported a mean peak plasma THC concentration of 6 ng/ml after ingestion of 20 mg.[15] Wall et al. noted that peak plasma THC concentrations occurred 30 min after intravenous administration of 4 to 5 mg, with a mean concentration ($n = 7$) of 62 ng/ml.[16] Reported values for the bioavailability of THC after smoking have ranged from 18 to 50%.[14] This wide range reflects the large inter- and intrasubject variability that occurs in smoking dynamics.[18] Altering the number, duration, and spacing of puffs, the length of time the inhalation is held and the inhalation volume or depth of puff[19] may vary the amount of drug delivered. Measures to minimize the loss of side- and mainstream smoke as well as optimizing the temperature for drug volatilization will, in turn, increase the amount of drug available for delivery to the lungs. One facet of smoking that cannot be controlled by the smoker is drug deposition on non- or poorly absorbing surfaces within the body. Deposition outside of the lungs is usually a function of drug particle or vapor size. Drug may be deposited in the nasopharyngeal region or the upper bronchial tree. This reduces the amount of drug reaching the lung alveoli where rapid absorption into the blood and subsequent transport to the brain occur.

Ohlsson et al. compared the bioavailability of THC after intravenous, smoked, and oral administration. Eleven healthy subjects were administered 5 mg intravenously, 19 mg smoked, and 20 mg orally. Plasma concentrations rose rapidly after intravenous administration, reaching 161 to 316 ng/ml at 3 min and declining rapidly thereafter. Peak plasma concentrations also occurred at 3 min after smoking, with lower concentrations of THC ranging from 33 to 118 ng/ml. The plasma concentration time curve after smoking was similar to that obtained after intravenous administration but at lower concentrations. In contrast, low THC concentrations were found after oral administration, with much higher intersubject variability. The authors determined the bioavailability of THC to be 8 to 24% after smoking compared with 4 to 12% after oral ingestion.[20]

4.9.3 Distribution

THC is 97 to 99% plasma protein bound with little present in red blood cells. Due to its lipophilicity, THC distributes rapidly into tissues. Highly perfused organs, such as the brain, accumulate THC rapidly after administration, whereas THC distributes more slowly into poorly perfused tissues such as fat.[21] Harvey et al. reported finding maximum THC concentrations in the brains of mice 30 min after a single intravenous dose. The distribution of THC into various tissues and organs such as brain, liver, heart, kidney, salivary glands, breast milk, fat, and lung is reflected in the large volume of distribution (4 to 14 L/kg).[20,22] Hunt and Jones proposed a four-compartment model to describe four tissue composites into which THC distributes after intravenous injection.[23] They observed average half-lives of 1 min, 4 min, 1 h, and 19 h to describe these compartments. They concluded that a "pseudoequilibrium" is achieved between plasma and tissues 6 h after an intravenous dose. Thereafter, THC is slowly eliminated as THC diffuses from tissue to the blood. The terminal elimination half-life is approximately 1 day but has been reported to be 3 to 13 days in frequent users.[24,25]

4.9.4 Metabolism and Excretion

Metabolism is the major route of elimination of THC from the body as little is excreted unchanged. In humans, over 20 metabolites have been identified in urine and feces.[26] Metabolism in humans involves allylic oxidation, epoxidation, aliphatic oxidation, decarboxylation, and conjugation. The two monohydroxy metabolites (Figure 4.7) 11-hydroxy (OH)-THC and 8-beta-hydroxy THC are active, with the former exhibiting similar activity and disposition to THC, while the latter is less potent. Plasma concentrations of 11-OH-THC are typically <10% of the THC concentration after marijuana smoking. Two additional hydroxy compounds have been identified, namely, 8-alpha-hydroxy-THC and 8,11-dihydroxy-THC, and are believed to be devoid of THC-like activity. Oxidation of 11-OH-THC produces the inactive metabolite, 11-nor-9-carboxy-THC, or THC-COOH. This metabolite may be conjugated with glucuronic acid and is excreted in substantial amounts in the urine.

The average plasma clearance is 600 to 980 ml/min with a blood clearance of 1.0 to 1.6 L/min, which is close to hepatic blood flow. This indicates that the rate of metabolism of THC is dependent on hepatic blood flow. Approximately 70% of a dose of THC is excreted in the urine (30%) and

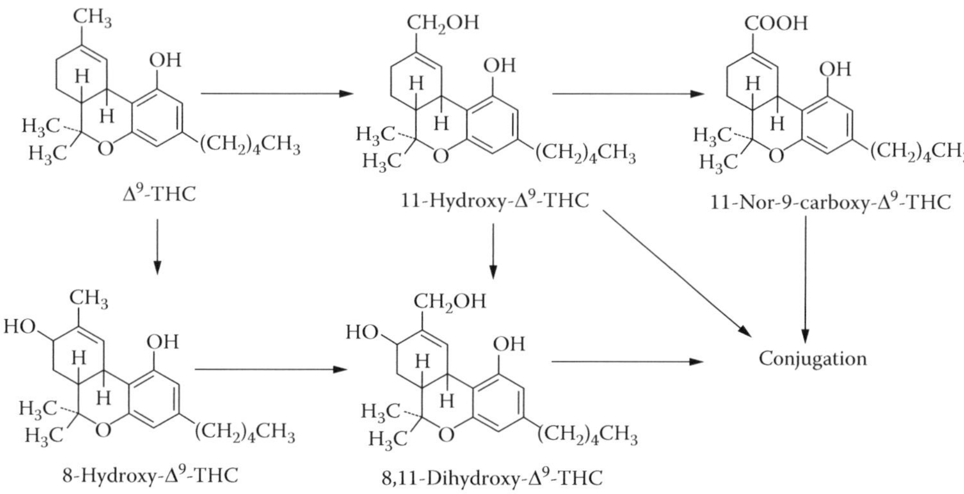

Figure 4.7 Metabolic pathway of delta-9-THC.

feces (40%) within 72 h.[26] Because a significant amount of the metabolites are excreted in the feces, enterohepatic recirculation of THC metabolites may occur. This would also contribute to the slow elimination and hence long plasma half-life of THC. Unchanged THC is present in low amounts in the urine and 11-OH-THC accounts for only 2% of a dose.

The remainder of the urinary metabolites consists of conjugates of THC-COOH and unidentified acidic products. Following a single smoked 10-mg dose of THC, urinary THC-COOH concentrations peaked within 16 h of smoking, at levels of 6 to 129 ng/ml (n = 10).[27] Huestis et al.[25] reported a mean (± SEM) urinary excretion half-life for THC-COOH of 31.5 ± 1 h and 28.6 ± 1.5 h for six healthy volunteers after administration of a single marijuana cigarette containing 1.75 or 3.55% THC, respectively. Passive exposure to marijuana smoke may also produce detectable urinary metabolite concentrations. Cone et al. exposed five volunteers to the smoke of 16 marijuana cigarettes (2.8% THC content) for 1 h each day for 6 consecutive days.[24] After the first session, THC-COOH concentrations in urine ranged from 0 to 39 ng/ml. A maximum THC-COOH concentration of 87 ng/ml was detected in one subject on day 4 of the study.

THC may be ingested orally by consuming food products containing the seeds or oil of the hemp plant. Ingestion of 0.6 mg/day (equivalent to 125 ml hemp oil containing 5 μg/g of THC or 300 g hulled seeds at 2 μg/g) for 10 days resulted in urine THC-COOH concentrations of <6 ng/ml.[28] The maximum urinary concentration of THC-COOH in another study after ingestion of hemp oil containing 0.39 to 0.47 mg THC/day for 5 days was 5.4 to 38.2 ng/ml (n = 7).[20] After oral administration of a higher dose (7.5 and 14.8 mg THC/day) peak concentrations of THC-COOH ranged from 19.0 to 436 ng/ml. Controlled studies have shown that at the federally mandated cannabinoid cutoffs, it is possible but unlikely for a urine specimen to test positive after ingestion of manufacturer-recommended doses of low-THC hemp oils.[29] On the other hand, patients taking Marinol®, the synthetic form of THC approved by the FDA for the control of nausea and vomiting in cancer patients, will almost certainly test positive. Dronabinol or synthetic THC is present in Marinol® capsules and ElSohly et al. found that within 24 h of administering a single 15-mg dose of dronabinol to four subjects, peak urine THC-COOH concentrations were between 189 and 362 ng/ml.[30]

REFERENCES

1. Farnsworth, N.R., Pharmacognosy and chemistry of "*Cannabis sativa*," *J. Am. Pharm. Assoc.*, 9(8), 410–414, 1969.
2. ElSohly, M.A. and Slade, D., Chemical constituents of marijuana: the complex mixture of natural cannabinoids, *Life Sci.*, 78(5), 539–548, 2005.
3. Turner, C.E., ElSohly, M.A., and Boeren, E.G., Constituents of *Cannabis sativa* L. XVII. A review of the natural constituents, *J. Nat. Prod.*, 43(2), 169–234, 1980.
4. Ross, S.A. et al., Flavonoid glycosides and cannabinoids from the pollen of *Cannabis sativa* L., *Phytochem. Anal.*, 16(1), 45–48, 2005.
5. Lander N. et al., Total synthesis of cannabidiol and delta1-tetrahydrocannabinol metabolites, *J. Chem. Soc.* (Perkin 1), 1, 8–16, 1976.
6. Kiplinger, G.F. and Manno, J.E., Dose-response relationships to cannabis in human subjects, *Pharmacol. Rev.*, 23(4), 339–347, 1971.
7. Cabral, G.A. and Staab, A., Effects on the immune system, *Handb. Exp. Pharmacol.*, 168, 385–423, 2005.
8. Vaughan, C.W. and Christie, M.J., An analgesic role for cannabinoids, *Med. J. Aust.*, 173(5), 270–272, 2000.
9. Petrzilka, T. and Demuth, L.M., Synthesis of (–)-11 hydroxy-delta8-6a,10a-transtetrahydrocannabinol, *Helv. Chim. Acta*, 57(1), 121–150, 1974.
10. Begg, M. et al., Evidence for novel cannabinoid receptors, *Pharmacol. Ther.*, 106(2), 133–145, 2005.
11. Heusser, K. et al., Influence of sibutramine treatment on sympathetic vasomotor tone in obese subjects, *Clin. Pharmacol. Ther.*, 79(5), 500–508, 2006.

12. Perez-Reyes, M. et al., Passive inhalation of marihuana smoke and urinary excretion of cannabinoids, *Clin. Pharmacol. Ther.*, 34(1), 36–41, 1983.
13. Huestis, M.A. et al., Characterization of the absorption phase of marijuana smoking, *J. Clin. Pharmacol. Ther.*, 52(1), 31–41, 1992.
14. Lemberger, L. et al., Marihuana: studies on the disposition and metabolism of delta-9-tetrahydrocannabinol in man, *Science*, 170(964), 1320–1322, 1970.
15. Perez-Reyes, M., Owens, S.M., and Di Guiseppi, S., The clinical pharmacology and dynamics of marihuana cigarette smoking, *J. Clin. Pharmacol.*, 21(8–9 Suppl.), 201S–207S, 1981.
16. Wall, M.E., Brine, D.R., and Perez-Reyes, M., Metabolism and disposition of naltrexone in man after oral and intravenous administration, *Drug Metab. Dispos.*, 9(4), 369–375, 1981.
17. Robinson, K., Beyond resinable doubt? *J. Clin. Forensic Med.*, 12(3), 164–166, 2005.
18. McGilveray, I.J., Pharmacokinetics of cannabinoids, *Pain Res. Manage.*, 10(A), 15A–22A, 2005.
19. Grotenhermen, F., Pharmacokinetics and pharmacodynamics of cannabinoids, *Clin. Pharmacokinet.*, 42(4), 327–360, 2003.
20. Ohlsson, A. et al., Plasma delta-9 tetrahydrocannabinol concentrations and clinical effects after oral and intravenous administration and smoking, *Clin. Pharmacol. Ther.*, 28(3), 409–416, 1980.
21. Babor, T.F. et al., Marijuana, affect and tolerance: a study of subchronic self-administration in women, *NIDA Res. Monogr.*, 49, 199–204, 1984.
22. Johansson, E. et al., Single-dose kinetics of deuterium-labelled cannabinol in man after intravenous administration and smoking, *Biomed. Environ. Mass Spectrom.*, 14(9), 495–499, 1987.
23. Hunt, C.A. and Jones, R.T., Tolerance and disposition of tetrahydrocannabinol in man, *J. Pharmacol. Exp. Ther.*, 215(1), 35–44, 1980.
24. Huestis, M.A., Mitchell, J.M., and Cone, E.J., Detection times of marijuana metabolites in urine by immunoassay and GC-MS, *J. Anal. Toxicol.*, 19(6), 443–449, 1995.
25. Huestis, M.A., Mitchell, J.M., and Cone, E.J., Urinary excretion profiles of 11-nor-9-carboxy-delta 9-tetrahydrocannabinol in humans after single smoked doses of marijuana, *J. Anal. Toxicol.*, 20(6), 441–452, 1996.
26. Widman, M. et al., Metabolism of delta1-tetrahydrocannabinol by the isolated perfused dog lung: comparison with in vitro liver metabolism, *J. Pharm. Pharmacol.*, 27(11), 842–848, 1975.
27. Manolis, A., McBurney, L.J., and Bobbie, B.A., The detection of delta 9-tetrahydrocannabinol in the breath of human subjects, *Clin. Biochem.*, 16(4), 229–233, 1983.
28. Leson, G. et al., Evaluating the impact of hemp food consumption on workplace drug tests, *J. Anal. Toxicol.*, 25(8), 691–698, 2001.
29. Gustafson, R.A. et al., Urinary cannabinoid detection times after controlled oral administration of delta9-tetrahydrocannabinol to humans, *Clin. Chem.*, 49(7), 1114–1124, 2003.
30. ElSohly, M.A. et al., Delta9-tetrahydrocannabivarin as a marker for the ingestion of marijuana versus Marinol®: results of a clinical study, *J. Anal. Toxicol.*, 25(7), 565–571, 2001.

4.10 OPIOIDS

Members of the group of natural, semisynthetic, or synthetic alkaloid compounds prepared from opium are referred to as "opioids." This group includes natural compounds usually denoted "opiates," such as morphine and codeine, and the synthetic and semisynthetic compounds such as oxycodone, buprenorphine, fentanyl, methadone, and tramadol. The pharmacological effects and pharmacokinetic parameters of these drugs share many common characteristics and are illustrated with the prototypic drug in this class, morphine.

Morphine is obtained from the latex of the opium poppy, *Papaver somniferum*. Morphine, codeine, and other opiates are extracted from a milky exudate that forms within 12 h when unripe seed capsules are incised. When dried, the material is called raw opium. The principal alkaloid in raw opium is morphine, constituting 8 to 19% of opium by dry weight. The actual percentage is highly dependent on growing conditions and location.[1] Morphine is the analgesic of choice for the treatment of both chronic pain syndromes and acute myocardial infarction. Whether it will remain so for long is not clear. The results of recently published observational studies strongly suggest that in patients with acute coronary syndrome, the use of morphine, either alone or in combination with nitroglycerin, is associated with an increased mortality rate.[2]

Morphine remains the prototypic mu-opioid analgesic. And, even though other opioids share similar structures, there is overwhelming proof that morphine is different from other similarly appearing agents. In the past, these differences had been explained by different pharmacokinetics, but now it appears that heroin and morphine act via different receptor mechanisms. As a result, the concept of multiple mu receptors has emerged. Multiple splice variants of the cloned mu-opioid receptor have been identified. Nonetheless, a relatively large volume of pharmacokinetic data exists describing morphine clinical applications, which are reviewed here.[3] It is becoming increasingly obvious that knowledge of the molecular mechanisms involved in causing drug dependence and in providing pain relief is mandatory if there are to be clinical advances.

4.10.1 Morphine

4.10.1.1 Pharmacology

Morphine and other related opioids produce their pharmacological effects by binding to opiate receptors located throughout the body. Three types of opiate receptors μ (mu), κ (kappa), and δ (delta) — are recognized; they are approximately 70% homologous. Differences between receptors occur mainly at the N- and C-terminal ends. The mu receptor is thought to be the most important because it is where morphine (and like drugs) exerts its effect. When a mu receptor binds with an agonist, such as morphine, heroin, or oxycodone, a G protein attached to the third intracellular loop of the receptor is activated (opiate receptors have seven loops, also called transmembrane domains).[4] The genes that determine the various receptor subtypes are located on different chromosomes. There are two mu, three kappa, and two delta subtypes. It is assumed that these receptors arise from post-translational modifications (i.e., they arise at a late stage in protein synthesis) because their genes have not been identified. A purported fourth opiate receptor, referred to as the sigma receptor, is now recognized as a completely unrelated entity.[5]

Mu receptors are almost always located proximally, on the presynaptic side of the synapse. The periaqueductal gray is the region containing the most mu receptors, but they are also found in the superficial dorsal horn of the spinal cord, the external plexiform layer of the olfactory bulb, the nucleus accumbens (an area deeply implicated in the process of addiction), in some parts of the cerebral cortex, and in some of the nuclei of the amygdala. Mu receptors avidly bind enkephalins and beta-endorphin, but they have a low affinity for dynorphins (primarily a kappa receptor agonist).[6]

The obvious clinical effects of morphine are papillary constriction due to its excitatory action on the parasympathetic nerves that supply the pupil. Respiratory depression also occurs because mu agonists exert a direct effect on brain stem respiratory centers, reducing their responsiveness to carbon dioxide. In addition, mu-stimulation depresses respiratory centers located in the pons. Small doses of morphine merely depress the respiratory rate, while large doses cause respiratory arrest, the accepted mechanism of death in cases of narcotic drug overdose. Nausea and vomiting are also associated with the use of mu receptor activation because opioids directly stimulate the chemoreceptor vomiting trigger zone in the medulla. Morphine provides effective and convenient pain relief, largely because there is no upper limit to the amount that can be given, provided enough time is allowed for tolerance to the respiratory effects to develop. Morphine, or compounds that bind the mu receptor, are also used to treat diarrhea and the cough associated with malignancy and tuberculosis.[7] Heroin, which is converted to morphine within the body, was originally marketed by Bayer as a cough suppressant.[8]

Activation of kappa receptors also produces analgesia, but it simultaneously induces nausea and dysphoria. Kappa receptors are located mainly on pain neurons located in the spinal cord and, to a lesser extent in the brain. They bind to an endogenously occurring ligand called dynorphin.

The exact function of dynorphin is unknown, but evidence suggests that it is produced to counter the pleasurable effects of produced by cocaine and is, to some degree, neuroprotective.[9] Some believe dynorphin may play an important role in determining an individual's risk for addiction. Blocking the actions of dynorphin helps to alleviate depression.[10]

Delta receptor activation also produces analgesia, but it can also cause seizures as well. Delta receptors normally bind to a class of endogenous ligands known as enkephalins, but unlike mu receptors, information about delta receptors is limited. Enkephalins are peptides that are produced by the pituitary gland. Several different enkephalins have been identified. β-Enkephalin resembles opiates because when it binds to a delta receptor, it relieves pain.[11]

4.10.1.2 Absorption

Morphine can be given orally, or by subcutaneous, intramuscular, or intravenous injection.[7] Increasingly, as the purity of street heroin has risen, heroin is also being inhaled ("chasing the dragon").[12] Heroin is also administered epidurally, either as an individual dose or continuous infusion.[13] Parenteral morphine is well absorbed, and in individuals with normal blood pressure, resultant plasma levels after subcutaneous, intramuscular, and intravenous injection are very similar.[14] The oral bioavailability of morphine is quite low due to extensive first pass hepatic metabolism. A 10-mg bolus given to healthy volunteers undergoing elective surgery produced peak blood of 200 to 400 ng/ml 5 min after injection.[15] After either intramuscular or subcutaneous injection, morphine plasma levels peak in 10 to 20 min. In healthy volunteers a dose of 10 mg/70 kg given intravenously produces a free morphine concentration of 80 ng/ml at 5 min, compared to a peak of 74 ng/ml at 15 min after the same dose was given as an intravenous bolus.[14] Oral administration is a mainstay in the management of patients with cancer. In stable patients receiving sufficient oral morphine to produce acceptable analgesia, the mean trough serum morphine concentration is on the order of 18 ng/ml with roughly equal concentrations of the active metabolite M6G.[16]

4.10.1.3 Distribution

The volume of distribution of morphine ranges from 2 to 5 L/kg in humans,[17] although values as high as 7 L/kg have been reported.[18] The wide variation could be explained by the health of the volunteers being studied. In patients with incompletely compensated heart failure and increased body water from any cause, higher values would be expected. Conversely, in patients with renal failure, where intravascular volume may be decreased, smaller values would be expected. Plasma protein binding of morphine in healthy humans ranges from 12 to 35% and appears to be independent of concentration over approximately a 1000-fold range, although a slight decrease (24 to 20% bound) was observed when the concentration was increased therapeutically by 60-fold.[19] Morphine is bound mainly to albumin with approximately 5% bound to γ-globulin and 5% to α-1-acid glycoprotein. In healthy humans, the blood/plasma concentration ratio for morphine averages 1.02.[17] This ratio was found to be consistent in the concentration range of 35 to 140 n*M*. The plasma half-life averaged 1.8 and 2.9 h in female and male surgical patients, respectively.[20]

Morphine is relatively hydrophilic and therefore distributes slowly into tissues, where it may be detected in fat, even after death.[21] Morphine crosses the blood–brain barrier, but not so freely as heroin and codeine, which possess an aromatic hydroxyl group at the C3 position. Morphine's passage across the blood–brain barrier is mediated by P-glycoprotein (P-gp) concentrated in brain capillary endothelium. Drugs that interfere with P-gp, such as doxyrubrin, can alter brain morphine uptake and disposition. Lopermide, which is widely used to treat diarrheal disease, avidly binds the mu receptor but, because it does not bind to P-gp, it never enters the brain and never causes any of the psychological changes produced by morphine.[22]

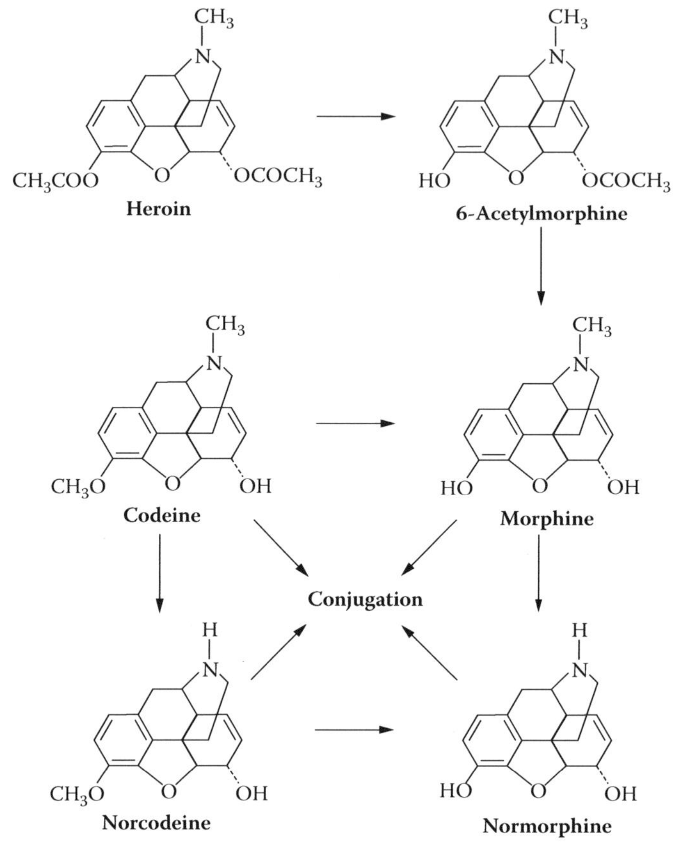

Figure 4.8 Metabolic pathway of heroin and morphine.

4.10.1.4 Metabolism and Excretion

The major pathway for morphine metabolism is conjugation with glucuronic acid (Figure 4.8). The free phenolic hydroxyl group undergoes glucuronidation to produce morphine-3-glucuronide (M3G), a highly water-soluble metabolite. Metabolism occurs primarily in the liver with 90% of a dose excreted in the urine and 10% in the feces. There is extensive enterohepatic circulation of both conjugated and unconjugated morphine. Approximately 87% of a dose of morphine is excreted in the 72-h urine, 75% as M3G, 10% as free morphine, and the remainder as morphine-6-glucuronide, morphine-3-sulfate, normorphine, and conjugates. The clearance of morphine was found to vary between 1.2 and 1.9 L/min/70 kg in several studies of humans.[19]

M3G is the predominant metabolite in young children. The total body morphine clearance is 80% of an adult at 6 months of age.[23] When the brains of experimental animals are directly injected with M3G, neuroexcitatory and anti-analgesic responses result, although this does not happen after system administration. Nonetheless, small amounts of M3G do cross the blood–brain barrier, and this may account for some reports of neuroexcitatory responses to morphine in humans. Attempts at correlating M3G plasma concentrations or M3G:morphine or M3G:M6G concentration ratios with the clinical activity of M3G have sometimes been successful, and sometimes not. To date, there are only two published studies describing the effects of injecting M3G directly into humans; both studies yielded equivocal results.[24]

M6G, on the other hand, is pharmacologically active and exerts important clinical opioid effects, especially when it is allowed to accumulate in the plasma of patients who have renal failure. However, after short-term morphine administration, the contribution of M6G to both analgesia and the occurrence of side effects is probably negligible.[25] M6G may have peripheral analgesic effects.[26] In a placebo-controlled, double blind, crossover study in ten healthy volunteers, M6G was given intravenously as a bolus followed by an infusion sufficient to maintain plasma concentrations of 500 ng/ml for 2 h. Analgesia was produced, but miotic effects were not, suggesting that the pain relief was a consequence of some peripheral effect exerted by M6G.

A small amount of morphine, on the order of 5%, is *N*-demethylated by hepatic CYP3A4, and to a lesser extent CYP2C8, to form normorphine.[27] This metabolite itself has pharmacological activity, but it is less potent than morphine and is present in lower concentrations.

4.10.2 Heroin

C.R. Wright first synthesized heroin, or 3,6-diacetylmorphine, from morphine in 1874. The Bayer Company of Germany advertised heroin as an antitussive in 1898. Under U.S. law (but not the laws of many other countries) heroin has no accepted medical use; it is classified as a Schedule I drug under the Controlled Substances Act of 1970.

Heroin is typically self-administered by intramuscular or intravenous injection and also by nasal insufflation ("snorting") or smoking. Peak heroin concentrations in blood are achieved within 1 to 5 min after intravenous and smoked administration[20] and within 5 min after intranasal and intramuscular administration.[28] In a study in which the method of smoked heroin delivery was optimized to reduce losses due to pyrolysis and sidestream smoke, Jenkins et al.[20] reported similar pharmacokinetic profiles for the smoked and intravenous routes. Mean elimination half-lives for two subjects across three doses of heroin were 3.3 and 3.6 min, after smoked and intravenous administration, respectively. The mean residence time of heroin was less than 10 min after all doses by both routes. Cone et al.[28] reported that the pharmacokinetic profile of intranasal heroin was equivalent to that for the intramuscular route. Mean elimination half-lives (hours plus or minus SD) were determined to be 0.09 ± 0.05, 0.07 ± 0.02, and 0.13 ± 0.07, following intranasal administration of 6 and 12 mg, and intramuscular administration of 6 mg of heroin, respectively. The relative potency of intranasal heroin was estimated to be approximately one half that of intramuscular administration.

Heroin may also be administered orally. In drug users this is an uncommon route since hydrolysis in the GI tract and loss due to first pass metabolism result in slow and inefficient delivery to the brain. Following low dose administration of 10 mg heroin hydrochloride, no heroin or 6-acetylmorphine was detected in blood.[29] Peak morphine concentrations ranging from 2 to 15 ng/ml (mean = 8 ng/ml, $n = 6$) were achieved 7.5 min to 4 h after drug administration. In another study, 400 mg of heroin was orally administered, followed 359 min later by a second dose of 400 mg.[30] In this study as well, heroin and 6-acetylmorphine were not detected in blood. Morphine and its conjugates were detected. Peak morphine concentrations were measured 1 to 2 h after the initial dose and were 0.73 and 1.34 mg/L in the two subjects. Girardin et al.[31] administered heroin by three different routes to eight heroin addicts. The intramuscular route demonstrated linear pharmacokinetics for heroin and the metabolites 6-acetylmorphine (6-AM) and morphine. The oral route resulted in low blood concentrations of heroin and 6-AM but linear kinetics for morphine and its glucuronides.

It is known from *in vitro* studies that heroin is rapidly deacetylated to an active metabolite, 6-AM, which is then hydrolyzed to morphine (Figure 4.8). Spontaneous hydrolysis to 6-AM may occur under various conditions. Heroin is susceptible to base-catalyzed hydrolysis but will also hydrolyze in the presence of protic compounds such as ethanol, methanol, and aqueous media.

The addition of two acetyl-ester groups to the morphine molecule produces a more lipophilic compound. Experimental evidence suggests that heroin and morphine may exert their effects via different receptor mechanisms.[32,33]

Following intravenous infusion of 70 mg of heroin to human volunteers, 45% of the dose was recovered in urine after 40 h. More than 38% was recovered as conjugated morphine, approximately 4% as free morphine, 1% as 6-acetylmorphine, and 0.1% as heroin.[14] Urinary elimination half-lives of 0.6, 4.4, and 7.9 h were reported for 6-AM, morphine, and conjugated morphine, respectively, after administration of 6 mg of heroin by the intramuscular route.[34]

4.10.3 Methadone

Methadone is a synthetic opioid, clinically available in the U.S. since 1947.[8] It exists in the dextro- and levo-rotatory forms with the levo-isoform possessing approximately 8 to 50 times more pharmacological activity.[27,34] Methadone acts on the CNS and cardiovascular system producing respiratory and circulatory depression. Methadone also produces miosis and increases the tone of smooth muscle in the lower gastrointestinal tract while decreasing the amplitude of contractions. It is used clinically for the treatment of severe pain and in maintenance programs for morphine and heroin addicts.[34]

Methadone is typically administered orally, with peak blood concentrations occurring after 4 h. Inturrisi and Verebely[35] reported a peak plasma concentration of 75 ng/ml at 4 h after a single 15-mg oral dose. Concentrations declined slowly, with a half-life of 15 h, reaching 30 ng/ml by 24 h. A single 10-mg intravenous dose of methadone resulted in initial plasma concentrations of 500 ng/ml declining to 50 ng/ml after 1 to 2 h.[29] Peak plasma concentrations (mean = 830 ng/ml) after 4 h were also observed with chronic oral administration of 100 to 200 mg/day.[28] Concentrations of methadone reach a maximum in brain tissue approximately 1 to 2 h after an oral dose.[27] Methadone is highly plasma protein bound (87%) with 70% bound to albumin.[28] Methadone distributes rapidly to tissues, especially the lungs, liver, kidneys, and spleen. The volume of distribution is 4 to 5 L/kg.[34]

Methadone is metabolized in the liver by *N*-demethylation to produce unstable metabolites, which undergo cyclization to form the metabolites 2-ethylidene-1,5-dimethyl-3,3-diphenylpyrrolidine (EDDP) and 2-ethyl-5-methyl-3,3-diphenylpyrroline (EMDP) (Figure 4.9). These metabolites and the parent drug undergo para-hydroxylation with subsequent conjugation with glucuronic acid. All three are excreted in the bile and are the major excretory products measured in the urine after methadone administration. Minor metabolites, methadol, and normethadol exhibit pharmacological activity similar to methadone but are produced in low concentrations. Metabolism to EDDP is achieved by multiple cytochrome P450 isoforms, namely, CYP2B6, 2C19, and 3A4.[30] Michaelis–Menten data demonstrated that the highest V_{max} and lowest K_m occurred with CYP2B6. CYP2B6 and 2C19 showed stereoselective

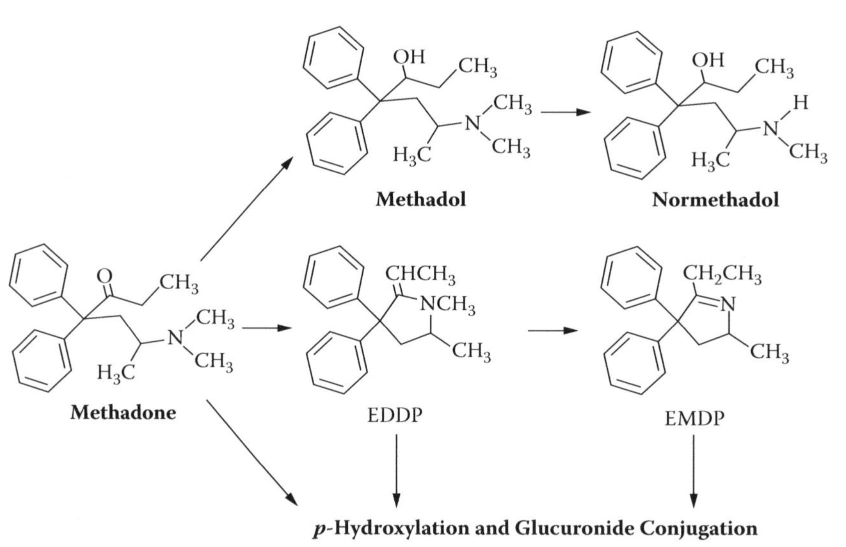

Figure 4.9 Metabolic pathway of methadone.

metabolism, with the former preferentially metabolizing *S*-methadone and the latter the R-enantiomer.[30] Shiran et al.[36] reported that methadone appears to inhibit CYP2D6 activity.

Large individual variations in the urine excretion of methadone are observed depending on urine volume and pH, the dose and rate of metabolism. Acidification of the urine may increase the urinary output of methadone from 5 to 22%.[37] Typically, following a 5-mg oral dose, methadone and EDDP account for 5% of the dose in the 24-h urine. In those individuals on maintenance therapy, methadone may account for 5 to 50% of the dose in the 24-h urine and EDDP may account for 3 to 25% of the dose. (S)- and (R)-methadone and EDDP have been reported in saliva[38] and methadone and (S)- and (R)-methadone in human breast milk.[39,40]

4.10.4 Oxycodone

Oxycodone is a semisynthetic opioid derived from thebaine and used for oral pain relief. It is commonly formulated as an immediate-release medication with acetaminophen or aspirin. A controlled-release oxycodone formulation is used for the treatment of moderate to severe pain; it provides controlled drug delivery over 12 h. The oral bioavailability of this formulation is 60 to 87%.[35] The results of clinical studies of patients with postoperative and cancer pain show that oxycodone has a potency 1.5 times that of morphine.

The absorption half-life of the immediate-release oral formulation is 0.4 h in healthy adults. In contrast the controlled-release form exhibits a biphasic absorption pattern with two apparent half-lives of 0.6 and 6.9 h.[41] Peak plasma concentrations are achieved in approximately 1.6 h with the immediate release compared with 2 to 3 h with the controlled-release formulation. After a 10-mg oral dose of the immediate release formulation, peak plasma concentrations ranged from 13 to 46 ng/ml (mean = 30 ng/ml, n = 12).[36] After the administration of 20 mg of the prolonged-release formulation the peak plasma concentration averaged 23 ng/ml in a group of 28 adults.[41] The plasma half-life has been reported to be 4 to 6 h with a volume of distribution of 1.8 to 3.7 L/kg.[42]

Oxycodone is metabolized in the liver by the cytochrome P450 isozymes and the elimination half-life is prolonged in individuals with liver disease, such as cirrhosis. Metabolism by *O*- and *N*-demethylation produces the metabolites oxymorphone and noroxycodone. The *O*-demethylated metabolite, oxymorphone, is a very powerful μ receptor agonist, providing ten times the relief of morphine in patients with cancer,[43] and at one time it was believed that most of oxycodone's ability to relieve pain was due to oxymorphone formation. However, recent studies have shown that so little oxymorphone is formed that it cannot account for the relief afforded by the parent compound.[44–46] Both the *O*- and *N*-demethylated forms are then conjugated with glucuronic acid. CYP2D6 metabolizes oxycodone and is encoded by a polymorphic gene with three mutations (*3, *4, and *5) with a combined 95% allelic frequency and approximately 10% prevalence.[47] Less than 65% of a single dose is excreted in the urine over a period of 24 h with 13 to 19% comprising free oxycodone.

4.10.5 Hydrocodone

Hydrocodone is a semisynthetic opioid derived from codeine.[8] It is utilized as an analgesic and antitussive available for oral administration, often in combination with acetaminophen or ibuprofen. As a rule, potent analgesics containing a methoxyl group at position 3 (e.g., hydrocodone, K_i = 19.8 nM) bind the mu receptor relatively weakly, but their *O*-demethylated metabolites (such as hydromorphone, K_i = 0.6 nM) bind more strangely. As with oxycodone, the possibility exists that some of their ability to relieve pain may actually derive from their active metabolites.[48]

Hydrocodone has multiple actions, mainly involving the CNS and smooth muscle. Peak serum concentrations after single therapeutic doses are typically less than 30 ng/ml and occur within 1.5 h after drug administration.[25] The plasma half-life has been reported to range from 3.4 to 8.8 h with a volume of distribution of 3.3 to 4.7 L/kg.[25] In humans, hydrocodone is metabolized by *O*-demethylation (by the action of CYP2D6) and *N*-demethylation (by the action of CYP3A4) and also reduction of the 6-keto groups. This produces multiple metabolites including hydromorphone, norhydrocodone, hydrocodol, and hydromorphol. The last two metabolites exist as stereoisomers (6-alpha-hydrocodol is also known as dihydrocodeine). Hydromorphone and hydromorphol are then conjugated to form glucuronides. The unconjugated metabolites are believed to exhibit pharmacological activity and, therefore, may contribute to the actions of the drug. Hydrocodone is principally excreted by the kidneys. Approximately 26% of the drug from a single dose is eliminated in the 72-h urine, with less than 15% as unchanged drug.

4.10.6 Fentanyl

Fentanyl is a fast-acting potent synthetic opioid introduced in the U.S. in the early 1960s for use as an anesthetic supplement. It interacts with the opioid mu receptors located in the brain, spinal cord, and smooth muscle. Fentanyl is highly lipophilic and, therefore, crosses the blood–brain barrier rapidly. Therapeutic use involves the CNS, producing pharmacological actions as pain relief and sedation. In addition to its use as an anesthetic agent, fentanyl is prescribed clinically to treat chronic pain. It is available in an oral transmucosal solid formulation and also as a transdermal delivery system (patches). In opioid nontolerant individuals effective analgesia occurs at blood concentrations of 1 to 2 ng/ml.[25] Surgical anesthesia occurs at concentrations of 10 to 20 ng/ml.

The transmucosal formulation of fentanyl is designed to be dissolved slowly in the mouth, permitting absorption through the buccal mucosa, and a more prolonged absorption, after swallowing, in the GI tract. Bioavailability is dependent on the fraction of the dose absorbed by both routes. Typically 25% of the dose is rapidly absorbed through the buccal mucosa and approximately 33% of the remaining dose, which is swallowed, becomes systemically available. The time to reach peak blood concentrations after this form of drug delivery is generally 20 to 40 min after drug administration.

The transdermal system provides continuous systemic delivery of fentanyl for 72 h. The amount of drug released from the system per hour is proportional to the surface area. Following application of the patch to the skin, a depot of fentanyl concentrates in the upper skin layers. This is then available to the systemic circulation. There is an initial rise in blood fentanyl concentration after application followed by a leveling off that occurs 12 to 24 h later. Peak blood concentrations occur between 24 and 72 h after application. The skin does not appear to metabolize fentanyl when delivered transdermally.

Fentanyl is highly lipophilic. It is rapidly distributed to tissues such as the brain, heart, kidneys, and lungs, followed by slower movement into muscle and fat.

Fentanyl is approximately 80% bound to plasma proteins, principally α-1-acid glycoprotein. The volume of distribution reportedly ranges from 3 to 8 L/kg. The plasma half-life is 3 to 12 h.[49] Fentanyl is metabolized in the liver and intestinal mucosa by cytochrome P450 3A4 isozyme by *N*-dealkylation to form the pharmacologically inactive metabolite norfentanyl.[35] Hydroxylated inactive metabolites include hydroxyfentanyl and hydroxynorfentanyl. Fentanyl is primarily excreted in the urine with up to 85% of a single dose eliminated in 3 to 4 days. Norfentanyl is the principal compound detected in urine comprising 26 to 55% of a single dose.[50]

4.10.7 Buprenorphine

Buprenorphine is derived from thebaine. It is a partial mu agonist with kappa antagonist activity. Buprenorphine has 25 to 50 times the potency of morphine. It is used to produce a longer-lasting analgesia than morphine. Effects of buprenorphine last longer because it is released more slowly from mu receptors than morphine. It is available as an injectable for intramuscular (IM) or intravenous administration in a 1-ml solution containing 0.3 mg buprenorphine (as buprenorphine HCl) for the relief of moderate to severe pain. It is also available to treat opioid dependence in the formulation of a tablet,[51] alone or in combination with naloxone, in 2- or 8-mg doses to be administered sublingually (SL).[25] The recommended sublingual daily dose is 12 to 16 mg/day.

Pharmacological effects occur within 15 min of IM administration, peaking at approximately 1 h and persisting for up to 6 h. After SL administration, peak pharmacological effects typically occur after 100 min. After an intravenous dose of 0.3 mg, plasma concentrations are typically less than 1 ng/ml. Sublingual maintenance therapy of 8 mg/day resulted in plasma buprenorphine concentrations of 1 to 8 ng/ml.[52]

The bioavailability of the buprenorphine/naloxone tablet appears to be greater than the buprenorphine-alone formulation, with the former similar to the drug in liquid form. Buprenorphine is approximately 96% plasma protein bound, primarily to α- and β-globulin. The plasma half-life is 2 to 4 h with a volume of distribution of 2.5 L/kg. The drug undergoes *N*-dealkylation by CYP3A4 isozyme to norbuprenorphine, a pharmacologically active metabolite. This metabolite and parent are subject to glucuronidation. Buprenorphine is eliminated primarily in the feces as free drug with low concentrations occurring in the urine.

4.10.8 Tramadol

Tramadol has about one tenth the pain-relieving ability of morphine.[53] There are two enantiomers, and both contribute to pain relief, but via different mechanisms. (+)-Tramadol and the metabolite (+)-*O*-desmethyl-tramadol, which is referred to as M1, are agonists of the mu opioid receptor. (+)-Tramadol inhibits serotonin reuptake and (–)-tramadol inhibits norepinephrine reuptake.[25] This latter action enhances the inhibitory effects on pain transmission in the spinal cord. Because the actions of the two enantiomers are complementary, they are usually supplied as a racemic mixture. However, because it is a serotonin-reuptake blocker, interaction with other medications can lead to the occurrence of serotonin syndrome.[54]

Tramadol is available as drops, capsules, and sustained-release formulations for oral use, suppositories for rectal use, and solution for intramuscular, intravenous, and subcutaneous injection. After oral administration, tramadol is rapidly and almost completely absorbed. Sustained-release tablets release the active ingredient over a period of 12 h, reach peak concentrations after 4.9 h, and have a bioavailability of 87 to 95% compared with capsules. One 100-mg dose given to healthy volunteers resulted in plasma levels of 375 ng/ml at 1.5 h.[55] Tramadol is 20% bound to plasma protein and it is rapidly distributed in the body; it is mainly metabolized by *O*- and *N*-demethylation forming glucuronides and sulfates that are excreted by the kidney.

The mean elimination half-life is about 6 h. The *O*-demethylation of tramadol to M1, the main analgesic effective metabolite, is catalyzed by cytochrome P450 (CYP) 2D6, whereas *N*-demethylation to M2 is catalyzed by CYP2B6 and CYP3A4. The wide variability in the pharmacokinetic properties of tramadol can partly be ascribed to CYP polymorphism. *O*- and *N*-demethylation of tramadol as well as renal elimination are stereoselective.[56]

Pharmacokinetic–pharmacodynamic characterization of tramadol is difficult because of differences between tramadol concentrations in plasma and at the site of action, and because of pharmacodynamic interactions between the two enantiomers of tramadol and its active metabolites.[53]

4.10.9 Hydromorphone

Sold as Dilaudid™ in the U.S., hydromorphone is a semisynthetic, differing from morphine only by presence of a 6-keto group, and the hydrogenation of the double bond at the 7–8 position of the molecule.[57] Like morphine, it acts primarily at the mu opioid receptors, and to a lesser degree at delta receptors.

As a hydrogenated ketone of morphine, it shares common pharmacologic properties with other opioid analgesics.[25] These include the expected changes in the CNS, including increased cerebrospinal fluid pressure, increased biliary pressure, and increased parasympathetic activity. It can also produce transient hyperglycemia. It is generally viewed as a second tier analgesic and is not that widely prescribed.

Hydromorphone is well absorbed from the small intestine and is extensively metabolized in the liver, mainly to 3-glucuronide, which, like morphine, is devoid of analgesic effect but can cause significant neuroexcitation. It undergoes extensive first pass metabolism (62%), accounting for its relatively low bioavailability. A single 8-mg dose of hydromorphone yields blood concentrations of approximately 2 ng/ml, while a 12-mg time-release formulation gives plasma concentrations half as high.[58,59]

Depending on the country where the drug is manufactured, a number of different time-release preparations are available. Palladone™, a controlled-release preparation consisting of hydromorphone HCl pellets, was withdrawn from the U.S. market in 2005. When taken with alcohol the pellets rapidly released their contents leading to dangerously elevated peak plasma concentrations.[60] Interaction with ethanol and "dose dumping" is not the only concern. Any CNS depressant may enhance the depressant effects of hydromorphone.

REFERENCES

1. Anon., The opium alkaloids, *Bull. Narcotics*, 19, 13–14, 1963.
2. Meine, T.J., M.T. Roe, A.Y. Chen, M.R. Patel, et al., Association of intravenous morphine use and outcomes in acute coronary syndromes: results from the CRUSADE Quality Improvement Initiative, *Am. Heart J.*, 149(6), 1043–1049, 2005.
3. Hoskin, P.J. and G.W. Hanks, Morphine: pharmacokinetics and clinical practice, *Br. J. Cancer,* 62(5), 705–707, 1990.
4. Hann, V. and P. Chazot, G-proteins, *Curr. Anaesth. Crit. Care*, 15(1), 79–81, 2004.
5. Bodnar, R.J. and G.E. Klein, Endogenous opiates and behavior: 2003, *Peptides,* 25(12), 2205–2256, 2004.
6. Evans, C.J., Secrets of the opium poppy revealed, *Neuropharmacology,* 47(Suppl. 1), 293–299, 2004.
7. Skaer, T.L., Practice guidelines for transdermal opioids in malignant pain, *Drugs*, 64(23), 2629–38, 2004.
8. Karch, S.B., *Karch's Pathology of Drug Abuse,* 3rd ed., CRC Press, Boca Raton, FL, 2002.
9. Hauser, K.F., J.V. Aldrich, K.J. Anderson, G. Bakalkin, et al., Pathobiology of dynorphins in trauma and disease, *Front. Biosci.*, 10, 216–235, 2005.
10. Morley, J.E., Anorexia of aging: physiologic and pathologic, *Am. J. Clin. Nutr.*, 66(4), 760–773, 1997.
11. Bodnar, R.J. and G.E. Klein, Endogenous opiates and behavior: 2004, *Peptides*, 26(12), 2629–2711, 2005.
12. Klous, M.G., A.D. Huitema, E.J. Rook, M.J. Hillebrand, et al., Pharmacokinetic comparison of two methods of heroin smoking: "chasing the dragon" versus the use of a heating device, *Eur. Neuropsychopharmacol.*, 15(3), 263–269, 2005.
13. Robertson, S.A. and P.M. Taylor, Pain management in cats — past, present and future. Part 2. Treatment of pain — clinical pharmacology, *J. Feline Med. Surg.,* 6(5), 321–333, 2003.
14. Stuart-Harris, R., S.P. Joel, P. McDonald, D. Currow, et al., The pharmacokinetics of morphine and morphine glucuronide metabolites after subcutaneous bolus injection and subcutaneous infusion of morphine, *Br. J. Clin. Pharmacol.*, 49(3), 207–214, 2000.
15. Berkowitz, B.A., S.H. Ngai, J.C. Yang, J. Hempstead, et al., The disposition of morphine in surgical patients, *Clin. Pharmacol. Ther.*, 17(6), 629–635, 1975.
16. Klepstad, P., S. Kaasa, and P.C. Borchgrevink, Start of oral morphine to cancer patients: effective serum morphine concentrations and contribution from morphine-6-glucuronide to the analgesia produced by morphine, *Eur. J. Clin. Pharmacol.*, 55(10), 713–719, 2000.
17. Milne, R.W., R.L. Nation, and A.A. Somogyi, The disposition of morphine and its 3- and 6-glucuronide metabolites in humans and animals, and the importance of the metabolites to the pharmacological effects of morphine, *Drug Metab. Rev.*, 28(3), 345–472, 1996.
18. Lotsch, J., A. Stockmann, G. Kobal, K. Brune, et al., Pharmacokinetics of morphine and its glucuronides after intravenous infusion of morphine and morphine-6-glucuronide in healthy volunteers, *Clin. Pharmacol. Ther.*, 60(3), 316–325, 1996.

19. Mazoit, J.X., P. Sandouk, P. Zetlaoui, and J.M. Scherrmann, Pharmacokinetics of unchanged morphine in normal and cirrhotic subjects, *Anesth. Analg.*, 66(4), 293–298, 1987.
20. Jenkins, A.J., R.M. Keenan, J.E. Henningfield, and E.J. Cone, Pharmacokinetics and pharmacodynamics of smoked heroin, *J. Anal. Toxicol.*, 18(6), 317–330, 1994.
21. Levisky, J.A., D.L. Bowerman, W.W. Jenkins, D.G. Johnson, et al., Drugs in postmortem adipose tissues: evidence of antemortem deposition, *Forensic Sci. Int.*, 121(3), 157–160, 2001.
22. Daugherty, L.M., Loperamide hydrochloride, *Am. Pharm.*, NS30(12), 45–48, 1990.
23. Bouwmeester, N.J., B.J. Anderson, D. Tibboel, and N.H. Holford, Developmental pharmacokinetics of morphine and its metabolites in neonates, infants and young children, *Br. J. Anaesth.*, 92(2), 208–217, 2004.
24. Skarke, C., G. Geisslinger, and J. Lotsch, Is morphine-3-glucuronide of therapeutic relevance? *Pain*, 116(3), 177–180, 2005.
25. Lotsch, J., Opioid metabolites, *J. Pain Symptom Manage.*, 29(5 Suppl.), S10–24, 2005.
26. Tegeder, I., S. Meier, M. Burian, H. Schmidt, et al., Peripheral opioid analgesia in experimental human pain models, *Brain*, 126(Pt. 5), 1092–1102, 2003.
27. Projean, D., P.E. Morin, T.M. Tu, and J. Ducharme, Identification of CYP3A4 and CYP2C8 as the major cytochrome P450s responsible for morphine *N*-demethylation in human liver microsomes, *Xenobiotica*, 33(8), 841–854, 2003.
28. Cone, E.J., B.A. Holicky, T.M. Grant, W.D. Darwin, et al., Pharmacokinetics and pharmacodynamics of intranasal "snorted" heroin, *J. Anal. Toxicol.*, 17(6), 327–337, 1993.
29. Jenkins, A.J., B.A. Holicky, T.M. Grant, W.D. Darwin, et al., Blood concentrations and pharmacological effects after oral heroin administration, paper presented at Society of Forensic Toxicologists/The International Association of Forensic Toxicologists, Joint Conference (October 1994), abstr. 127, 1994.
30. Gyr, E., R. Brenneisen, D. Bourquin, T. Lehmann, et al., Pharmacodynamics and pharmacokinetics of intravenously, orally and rectally administered diacetylmorphine in opioid dependents, a two-patient pilot study within a heroin-assisted treatment program, *Int. J. Clin. Pharmacol. Ther.*, 38(10), 486–491, 2000.
31. Girardin, F., K.M. Rentsch, M.A. Schwab, M. Maggiorini, et al., Pharmacokinetics of high doses of intramuscular and oral heroin in narcotic addicts, *Clin. Pharmacol. Ther.*, 74(4), 341–352, 2003.
32. Rady, J.J., A.E. Takemori, P.S. Portoghese, and J.M. Fujimoto, Supraspinal delta receptor subtype activity of heroin and 6-monoacetylmorphine in Swiss Webster mice, *Life Sci.*, 55(8), 603–609, 1994.
33. Gilbert, A.K., S. Hosztafi, L. Mahurter, and G.W. Pasternak, Pharmacological characterization of dihydromorphine, 6-acetyldihydromorphine and dihydroheroin analgesia and their differentiation from morphine, *Eur. J. Pharmacol.*, 492(2–3), 123–130, 2004.
34. Cone, E.J., P. Welch, J.M. Mitchell, and B.P. Paul, Forensic drug testing for opiates: I, *J. Anal. Toxicol.*, 15, 1–7, 1991.
35. Inturrisi, C.E. and K. Verebely, Disposition of methadone in man after a single oral dose, *Clin. Pharmacol. Ther.*, 13(6), 923–930, 1972.
36. Shiran, M.R., J. Chowdry, A. Rostami-Hodjegan, S.W. Ellis, et al., A discordance between cytochrome P450 2D6 genotype and phenotype in patients undergoing methadone maintenance treatment, *Br. J. Clin. Pharmacol.*, 56(2), 220–224, 2003.
37. Chamberlain, N., Patterns of drug use in dependent opioid users in methadone treatment, *N.Z. Med. J.*, 110(1047), 258–259, 1997.
38. Rosas, M.E., K.L. Preston, D.H. Epstein, E.T. Moolchan, et al., Quantitative determination of the enantiomers of methadone and its metabolite (EDDP) in human saliva by enantioselective liquid chromatography with mass spectrometric detection, *J. Chromatogr. B Anal. Technol. Biomed. Life Sci.*, 796(2), 355–370, 2003.
39. Begg, E.J., T.J. Malpas, L.P. Hackett, and K.F. Ilett, Distribution of R- and S-methadone into human milk during multiple, medium to high oral dosing, *Br. J. Clin. Pharmacol.*, 52(6), 681–685, 2001.
40. McCarthy, J.J. and B.L. Posey, Methadone levels in human milk, *J. Hum. Lact.*, 16(2), 115–120, 2000.
41. Kalso, E., Oxycodone, *J. Pain Symptom Manage.*, 29(5 Suppl.), S47–56, 2005.
42. Davis, M.P., J. Varga, D. Dickerson, D. Walsh, et al., Normal-release and controlled-release oxycodone: pharmacokinetics, pharmacodynamics, and controversy, *Support. Care Cancer*, 11(2), 84–92, 2003.

43. Beaver, W.T., S.L. Wallenstein, R.W. Houde, and A. Rogers, Comparisons of the analgesic effects of oral and intramuscular oxymorphone and of intramuscular oxymorphone and morphine in patients with cancer, *J. Clin. Pharmacol.*, 17(4), 186–198, 1977.
44. Kaiko, R.F., Pharmacokinetics and pharmacodynamics of controlled-release opioids, *Acta Anaesthesiol. Scand.*, 41(1 Pt. 2), 166–174, 1997.
45. Heiskanen, T., K.T. Olkkola, and E. Kalso, Effects of blocking CYP2D6 on the pharmacokinetics and pharmacodynamics of oxycodone, *Clin. Pharmacol. Ther.*, 64(6), 603–611, 1998.
46. Poyhia, R., T. Seppala, K.T. Olkkola, and E. Kalso, The pharmacokinetics and metabolism of oxycodone after intramuscular and oral administration to healthy subjects, *Br. J. Clin. Pharmacol.*, 33(6), 617–621, 1992.
47. Wong, S.H., M.A. Wagner, J.M. Jentzen, C. Schur, et al., Pharmacogenomics as an aspect of molecular autopsy for forensic pathology/toxicology: does genotyping CYP 2D6 serve as an adjunct for certifying methadone toxicity? *J. Forensic Sci.*, 48(6), 1406–1415, 2003.
48. Chen, Z.R., R.J. Irvine, A.A. Somogyi, and F. Bochner, Mu receptor binding of some commonly used opioids and their metabolites, *Life Sci.*, 48(22), 2165–2171, 1991.
49. Poklis, A., Fentanyl: a review for clinical and analytical toxicologists, *J. Toxicol. Clin. Toxicol.*, 33(5), 439–447, 1995.
50. Poklis, A. and R. Backer, Urine concentrations of fentanyl and norfentanyl during application of Duragesic transdermal patches, *J. Anal. Toxicol.*, 28(6), 422–425, 2004.
51. Stock, C. and J.H. Shum, Bupreorphine: a new pharmacotherapy for opioid addictions treatment, *J. Pain Palliat. Care Pharmacother.*, 18(3), 35–54, 2004.
52. Perez de los Cobos, J., S. Martin, A. Etcheberrigaray, J. Trujols, et al., A controlled trial of daily versus thrice-weekly buprenorphine administration for the treatment of opioid dependence, *Drug Alcohol Depend.*, 59(3), 223–233, 2000.
53. Grond, S. and A. Sablotzki, Clinical pharmacology of tramadol, *Clin. Pharmacokinet.*, 43(13), 879–923, 2004.
54. Jones, D. and D.A. Story, Serotonin syndrome and the anaesthetist, *Anaesth. Intensive Care*, 33(2), 181–187, 2005.
55. Gambaro, V., C. Benvenuti, L. De Ferrari, L. Dell'Acqua, et al., Validation of a GC/MS method for the determination of tramadol in human plasma after intravenous bolus, *Farmaco*, 58(9), 947–950, 2003.
56. Pedersen, R.S., P. Damkier, and K. Brosen, Tramadol as a new probe for cytochrome P450 2D6 phenotyping: a population study, *Clin. Pharmacol. Ther.*, 77(6), 458–467, 2005.
57. Babul, N., A.C. Darke, and N. Hagen, Hydromorphone metabolite accumulation in renal failure, *J. Pain Symptom Manage.*, 10(3), 184–186, 1995.
58. Vashi, V., S. Harris, A. El-Tahtawy, D. Wu, et al., Clinical pharmacology and pharmacokinetics of once-daily hydromorphone hydrochloride extended-release capsules, *J. Clin. Pharmacol.*, 45(5), 547–554, 2005.
59. Murray, A. and N. Hagen, Hydromorphone, *J. Pain Symptom Manage.*, 29(5, Suppl. 1), 57–66, 2005.
60. Murray, S. and E. Wooltorton, Alcohol-associated rapid release of a long-acting opioid, *CMAJ*, 173(7), 756, 2005.

4.11 PHENCYCLIDINE

Phencyclidine, PCP, or 1-(1-phenylcyclohexyl) piperidine, is an arylcyclohexamine with structural similarities to ketamine. It is a lipophilic weak base with a pKa of 8.5. Phencyclidine was originally synthesized and marketed under the trade name Sernyl® by Parke-Davis for use as an intravenously administered anesthetic agent in humans. Distribution began in 1963 but was discontinued in 1965 due to a high incidence (10 to 20%) of post-operative delirium and psychoses. However, its use continued as a veterinary tranquilizer for large animals until 1978, when all manufacture was prohibited and PCP was placed in Schedule II of the federal Controlled Substances Act (1970).

Illicit use of PCP as a hallucinogenic agent was first reported in San Francisco in 1967.[1] It was first abused in oral form but then gained popularity in the smoked form as this mode of drug delivery allowed better control over dose. Because illicit synthesis is relatively easy and inexpensive, abuse became widespread in the 1970s and early 1980s. Today, use of PCP tends to be highly regionalized and located in certain areas of the U.S., notably the Washington D.C./Baltimore corridor, New York City, and Los Angeles.[2]

4.11.1 Pharmacology

Phencyclidine binds with high affinity to sites located in the cortex and limbic structures of the brain. Binding results in blockade of *N*-methyl-D-aspartic acid (NMDA)-type glutamate receptors. The actions of glutamate and aspartate at the NMDA receptor allow movement of cations across the cell membrane. PCP exerts its action by binding to the glutamate receptor, thus preventing the flux of cations.[3] PCP is also known to exert effects on catecholamines, serotonin, gamma-hydroxy butyric acid, and acetylcholine neurotransmitter release, but its role is incompletely defined. Due to its action on several systems, the physiological and behavioral effects of PCP are varied and depend on not only the dose, but also the route of administration and user's previous experience.

4.11.2 Absorption

Phencyclidine is typically self-administered by the oral, intravenous, or smoked routes. After oral administration to healthy human volunteers, the bioavailability was found to vary between 50 and 90%.[4] In this study, peak plasma concentrations were achieved after 1.5 h and appeared to correlate with the time to reach maximum pharmacological effects. However, because there have been no comprehensive clinical controlled studies of phencyclidine, a correlation between PCP blood concentrations and pharmacological effects has not been definitively documented. Maximum serum PCP concentrations ranged between 2.7 and 2.9 ng/ml after 1 mg PCP administered orally.[4]

PCP is commonly self-administered by the smoked route. Liquid PCP is soaked in parsley flakes and rolled as a cigarette; powdered PCP is sprinkled over a marijuana joint, or the end of a tobacco cigarette is dipped in liquid PCP and then smoked. Cook et al.[5] studied the pharmacokinetic properties of PCP deposited on parsley cigarettes. Upon smoking, PCP is partially volatilized to 1-phenylcyclohexene (PC). These investigators found that 69 ± 5% of the PCP available in the cigarette was inhaled, 39% as PCP and 30% as PC.[5] The pharmacological and toxicological properties of PC have not been established. Peak plasma concentrations of PCP were reached within 5 to 20 min. In 80% of the subjects, a second peak was observed in plasma PCP concentrations, occurring 1 to 3 h after the end of smoking. This may have been due to trapping of PCP in the mouth, where it could be released and absorbed by the GI tract or, alternatively, it could be due to absorption by the lung and bronchial tissue with slower release into the systemic circulation.[6] Long-term users of PCP report feeling the effects of the drug within 2 to 5 min of smoking, with a peak effect after 15 to 30 min and residual effects for 4 to 6 h.[7]

4.11.3 Distribution

Plasma protein binding of PCP in healthy individuals remains relatively constant between 60 and 70% over the concentration range of 0.007 to 5000 ng/ml.[5] PCP binding to serum albumin accounts for only 24% of the binding,[6] which suggests binding to another protein may occur to a significant extent. When studied *in vitro*, α_1-acid glycoprotein was also found to bind phencyclidine.[6] The volume of distribution has been shown to be large, between 5.3 and 7.5 L/kg,[8] providing evidence of extensive distribution to extravascular tissues.

Wall et al.[9] administered 1.3 μg/kg of 3H-PCP intravenously to human volunteers and collected blood samples for 72 h. Data from this study suggested a two-compartment pharmacokinetic model with a plasma half-life for PCP of 7 to 16 h. Domino et al.[10] further analyzed the data from Wall et al. and developed a more complex three-compartment PK model. The reported half-lives for each compartment were 5.5 min, 4.6 h, and 22 h. The specific tissues and organs represented by the multicompartment model were not identified. Half-lives of greater than 3 days have been reported in cases of PCP overdose.[11]

4.11.4 Metabolism and Excretion

PCP is metabolized by the liver through oxidative hydroxylation. Unchanged PCP, two monohydroxylated and one dihydroxylated metabolite, have been identified in urine after oral and intravenous administration.[12] The monohydroxlyated metabolites have been identified as 4-phenyl-4-(1-piperidinyl)-cyclohexanol (PPC) and 1-(1-phenylcyclohexyl)-4-hydroxypiperidine (PCHP). These metabolites are pharmacologically inactive in humans and PPC is present in both *cis*- and *trans*-isomeric forms. The *cis/trans* ratio was found to be 1:1.4 in human urine.[5] The dihydroxylated metabolite was identified as 4-(4-hydroxypiperidino)-4-phenylcyclohexanol (HPPC). These metabolites are present in urine as glucuronide conjugates in addition to their unconjugated forms.[8]

Approximately 30 to 50% of a labeled intravenous dose is excreted over a 72-h period in urine as unchanged drug (19.4%) and 80.6% as polar metabolites, mainly 4-phenyl-4-(1-piperidinyl) cyclohexanol.[5] Only 2% of a dose is excreted in feces.[10] After 10 days, an average of 77% of an intravenous dose is found in the feces and urine.[9] Green et al.[12] reported urine PCP concentrations between 40 and 3400 ng/ml in ambulatory users.

Urine pH is an important determinant of renal elimination of PCP. In a study in which urine pH was uncontrolled (6.0 to 7.5), the average total clearance of PCP was 22.8 ± 4.8 L/h after intravenous administration.[4] In the same study, renal clearance was 1.98 ± 0.48 L/h. When the urine was made alkaline, the renal clearance of PCP was found to decrease to 0.3 ± 0.18 L/h. If the urine was acidified (pH 6.1) in the same subjects, renal clearance increased to 2.4 ± 0.78 L/h.[13] Aronow et al.[14] determined that if the urine pH was decreased to <5.0, renal clearance increased significantly to 8.04 ± 1.56 L/h. There is disagreement about the utility of urine acidification in the treatment of PCP overdose, even though excretion may be increased by as much as 100-fold.[15] It should be noted that acidification may increase the risk of metabolic complications.[16]

REFERENCES

1. Nicholl, A.M., The non therapeutic use of psychoactive drugs, *N. Engl. J. Med.,* 308, 925–933, 1983.
2. Epidemiologic trends in drug abuse, data from the Drug Abuse Early Warning Network, Vol. 11, Department of Health and Human Services, National Institute on Drug Abuse, Rockville, MD, June 1994.
3. Stone, J.A., Phencyclidine. In-Service Training and Continuing Education AACC/TDM, American Association for Clinical Chemistry, Inc., Washington, D.C., 17(8), 199–202, 1996.
4. Cook, C.E., Brine, D.R., Jeffcoat, A.R., Hill, J.M., and Wall, M.E., Phencyclidine disposition after intravenous and oral doses, *Clin. Pharmacol. Ther.,* 31, 625–634, 1982.
5. Cook, C.E., Brine, D.R., Quin, G.D., Perez-Reyes, M., and DiGuiseppi, S.R., Phencyclidine and phenylcyclohexene disposition after smoking phencyclidine, *Clin. Pharmacol. Ther.,* 31, 635–641, 1982.
6. Busto, U., Bendayan, R., and Sellers, E.M., Clinical pharmacokinetics of non-opiate abused drugs, *Clin. Pharmacokinet.,* 16, 1–26, 1989.
7. Perry, D.C., PCP revisited, *Clin. Toxicol.,* 9, 339–348, 1976.
8. Baselt, R.C. and Cravey, R.H., *Disposition of Toxic Drugs and Chemicals in Man,* 4th ed., Chemical Toxicology Institute, Foster City, CA, 1995.
9. Wall, M.E., Brine, D.R., Jeffcoat, R.A., and Cook, C.E., Phencyclidine metabolism and disposition in man following a 100 μg intravenous dose, *Res. Commun. Substance Abuse,* 2, 161–172, 1981.
10. Domino, S.E., Domino, L.E., and Domino, E.F., Comparison of two and three compartment models of phencyclidine in man, *Subst. Alcohol Actions Misuse,* 2, 205–211, 1982.

11. Done, A.K., Aronow, R., and Miceli, J.N., The pharmacokinetics of phencyclidine in overdosage and its treatment, National Institute on Drug Abuse, Rockville, MD, Res. Monograph 21, 210–217, 1978.
12. Green, D.E., Chao, F.C., Loeffler, K.O., and Lemon, R., Phencyclidine blood levels by probability based matching GC/MS, *Proc. West. Pharm. Soc.,* 19, 355–361, 1976.
13. Perez-Reyes, M., DiGuiseppi, S., Brine, D.R., Smith, H., and Cook, C.E., Urine pH and phencyclidine excretion, *Clin. Pharmacol. Ther.,* 32, 635–641, 1982.
14. Aronow, R., Miceli, J.N., and Done, A.K., Clinical observations during phencyclidine intoxication and treatment based on ion-trapping, National Institute on Drug Abuse, Rockville, MD, Res. Monograph Ser. 21, 218–228, 1978.
15. Milhorn, H.T., Diagnosis and management of phencyclidine intoxication, *Am. Fam. Physician,* 43, 1293–1301, 1991.
16. Ellenhorn, M.J. and Barceloux, D.G., *Medical Toxicology, Diagnosis and Treatment of Human Poisoning,* Elsevier, New York, 1988, 764–777.

4.12 KETAMINE

Ketamine, a weakly basic compound structurally and pharmacologically similar to phencyclidine, is utilized in the U.S. to induce anesthesia.[1] It is available in solution for intravenous or intramuscular injection. Since the drug is pharmacologically similar to PCP it has the potential of producing hallucinogenic effects and, therefore, in recent years has become a drug of abuse.

After intravenous administration of 175 mg/70 kg to five individuals, the average peak serum concentration was 1.0 mg/L achieved at 12 min.[2] The concentration declined by 50% within 30 min. The plasma half-life is reported to be 3 to 4 h with a volume of distribution of 3 to 5 L/kg.[1] Continuous infusion of 41 μg/kg/min after a 2-mg/kg bolus produced an average (n = 31) steady-state plasma concentration of 2.2 mg/L.[3]

Two metabolites are formed that achieve serum concentrations similar to ketamine and may also exhibit the depressant effects of the parent compound. Norketamine is produced by *N*-demethylation.[4] Norketamine is then dehydrogenated to form dehydronorketamine. Parent drug and metabolites are then subject to hydroxylation and conjugation. Approximately 2% of a single dose of ketamine is excreted in the 72-h urine as unchanged drug. In a recent study urine ketamine concentrations ranged from 6 to 7744 ng/ml (mean = 1083 ng/ml) in 33 subjects following illegal consumption.[5]

REFERENCES

1. Baselt, R.C. and Cravey, R.H., *Disposition of Toxic Drugs and Chemicals in Man,* 4th ed., Chemical Toxicology Institute, Foster City, CA, 1995.
2. Wieber, J., Gugler, R., Hengstmann, J.H., and Dengler, H.J., Pharmacokinetics of ketamine in man, *Anaesthesia,* 24, 260–263, 1975.
3. Idvall, J., Ahlgren, I., Aronsen, K.F., and Stenberg, P., Ketamine infusions: pharmacokinetics and clinical effects, *Br. J. Anaesth.*, 51, 1167–1173, 1979.
4. Jenkins, A.J., Hallucinogens. In *Principles of Forensic Toxicology*, 2nd ed., B.S. Levine, Ed., AACC Press, Washington, D.C., 2003.
5. Moore, K.A., Sklerov, J., Levine, B., and Jacobs, A.J., Urine concentrations of ketamine and norketamine following illegal consumption, *J. Anal. Toxicol.*, 25, 583–588, 2001.

CHAPTER 5

Pharmacodynamics: Effects of Abused Drugs on Human Performance: Laboratory Assessment

Stephen J. Heishman, Ph.D.* **and Carol S. Myers, Ph.D.**
Clinical Pharmacology and Therapeutics Branch, National Institute on Drug Abuse, National Institutes of Health, Department of Health and Human Services, Baltimore, Maryland

CONTENTS

* Dr. Heishman contributed to this chapter in his personal capacity. The views expressed are his and do not necessarily represent the views of the National Institutes of Health or the U.S. government.

5.1 INTRODUCTION

The experimental investigation of the effects of psychoactive drugs on human performance has enjoyed a long history. Some of the earliest university laboratories in departments of psychology and physiology were dedicated to the study of caffeine, nicotine, and other drugs.[1,2] Advances in technology and methodology have resulted in a comprehensive body of research, and for most drugs of abuse, we have a general idea of their effects on performance. For example, it is well known that psychomotor stimulants, such as D-amphetamine, increase one's ability to sustain attention over prolonged periods of time when performing monotonous tasks.[3,4] However, numerous inconsistencies exist in the literature concerning the effects of certain drugs on various aspects of human performance, and few studies take into account nonpharmacological variables that, in addition to the drug dose, ultimately determine behavioral effects of psychoactive drugs.[5,6]

The purpose of this chapter is to provide an overview of the effects of abused drugs on human performance as assessed in the laboratory. This is not an exhaustive review of the literature. Rather, we take as our starting point several general overviews[7–9] and drug-specific reviews[3,4,6,10–18] and update these findings with recent studies. The classes of drugs included in this review are (1) psychomotor stimulants, including D-amphetamine, cocaine, and 3,4-methylenedioxymethamphetamine (MDMA, ecstasy); (2) nicotine and tobacco; (3) sedative-hypnotics, focusing on benzodiazepines as the prototypical sedative-hypnotic in use today (effects of ethanol are discussed elsewhere in this volume); (4) opioid analgesics and anesthetics; and (5) marijuana. Within each drug category, results will be organized into sensory, motor, attentional, and cognitive abilities. Such a classification scheme allows a focus on behavior compared with, for example, a classification based on specific performance tests.

5.2 PSYCHOMOTOR STIMULANTS

5.2.1 Cocaine and D-Amphetamine

The psychomotor stimulants, cocaine and D-amphetamine, are considered together because they share a similar psychopharmacological profile.[19,20] Low to moderate doses of both drugs given acutely to nontolerant, nonanxious subjects produce increases in positive mood (euphoria), energy, and alertness. Experienced cocaine users were unable to distinguish between intravenous (IV) cocaine and D-amphetamine,[21] and cross-tolerance between cocaine and D-amphetamine with respect to their anorectic effect has been demonstrated.[22] Additionally, the toxic psychosis observed after days or weeks of continued use of both psychostimulants is very similar. The fully developed toxic syndrome, characterized by vivid auditory and visual hallucinations, paranoid delusions, and disordered thinking, is often indistinguishable from paranoid schizophrenia.[20] Derlet et al.[23] reported that the most prominent presenting symptoms seen in 127 cases of amphetamine toxicity were agitation, suicidal ideation, hallucinations, delusions, confusion, and chest pain. Once drug use ceases, symptoms usually resolve within 1 week.

Research studies on human performance have typically involved the administration of cocaine and D-amphetamine in single doses that do not produce toxic psychosis. In the studies reviewed, D-amphetamine was administered orally (PO). Given that the performance effects of D-amphetamine have been studied for more than 60 years and its widespread use during World War II,[24] it is not surprising that much is known about the effects of D-amphetamine on vigilance and attention. However, the effect of psychostimulants on higher-order cognitive processes has not been widely studied.

5.2.1.1 Sensory Abilities

A frequently used measure of central nervous system (CNS) functioning is critical flicker frequency (CFF) threshold. The task requires subjects to view a light stimulus and to note the point (frequency) at which the steady light begins to flicker (or vice versa) as the experimenter changes the frequency of the light. An increase in CFF threshold indicates increased cortical and behavioral arousal, whereas a decrease suggests lowered CNS arousal.[25] D-Amphetamine reliably increases CFF threshold.[8,25] In the only study, to our knowledge, intranasal cocaine (100 mg) had no effect on CFF threshold.[26]

5.2.1.2 Motor Abilities

Finger tapping is considered to be a measure of relatively pure motor activity. One study found that D-amphetamine (10 mg) produced a 5% increase in tapping rate,[27] whereas three other studies reported no effect.[28–30] The circular lights test is a measure of gross motor coordination in which subjects extinguish lights by pressing buttons that are arranged in a 72-cm-diameter circle on a wall-mounted panel. The test is typically performed for 1 min. D-Amphetamine (25 mg) increased response rate on the circular lights test in one study,[31] but another study reported no effect of 20 mg D-amphetamine.[32] The effect of cocaine on finger tapping and circular lights performance has not been examined.

5.2.1.3 Attentional Abilities

Attention is a broad psychological category encompassing behaviors such as searching, scanning, and detecting visual and auditory stimuli for brief or long periods of time.[33,34] In nearly all performance tests assessing attention, responding is measured in some temporal form, such as reaction or response time, time off target, or response rate. If appropriate, response accuracy is also reported. Because of differential drug effects, it can be helpful to distinguish among focused, selective, divided, and sustained attention.[6]

Focused attention involves attending to one task for a brief period of time, usually about 5 min or less. In this regard, D-amphetamine[7] and cocaine[26] have been shown to improve performance in auditory and visual reaction time tests, although other studies have reported no effect of D-amphetamine. A brief, frequently used test of psychomotor skills and attention is the digit symbol substitution test (DSST), which originated as a paper and pencil subtest of the Wechsler Adult Intelligence Scale and now exists in a computerized version.[35] The DSST requires subjects to draw the symbol or type the pattern associated with each numeral 1 to 9. The number of attempted and correct symbols or patterns during the 90-s test is recorded. In general, D-amphetamine[7,36] and cocaine[37–39] enhanced performance on the DSST, although Foltin et al.[40] reported that cocaine decreased number of attempted trials, and others have reported no effect of smoked cocaine[41] or D-amphetamine.[42,43]

A few recent studies have looked at behavioral inhibition using reaction time tasks that require the participant to make quick responses to "go" signals and inhibit responding to "stop" signals. An impairment in the ability to inhibit responses is used as a measure of impulsivity. Cocaine administered orally to cocaine users dose-dependently impaired the ability to inhibit responses.[44] However, in another study in which cocaine was smoked, there was no effect on reaction time.[41] In contrast, D-amphetamine administered orally to healthy volunteers improved inhibition, but only in those people who had slow baseline stop responses.[45]

Examining selective attention, two studies reported that D-amphetamine improved accuracy,[46,47] and either increased[46] or decreased[47] reaction time. The effect of D-amphetamine and cocaine on divided attention has not been widely investigated; two studies reported small increases in accuracy on a divided attention test after administration of D-amphetamine.[48,49] Several studies have shown that D-amphetamine reliably enhanced performance in tests of visual and auditory vigilance.[7,50] The time of effect in these studies was 1 to 4 h after drug administration, suggesting that D-amphetamine improved performance by preventing the vigilance decrement that typically occurs in tests of sustained attention.

5.2.1.4 Cognitive Abilities

Psychostimulants have produced inconsistent effects on tests of cognition. Several studies have investigated the effect of cocaine on a test of repeated acquisition and performance of response sequences. In the acquisition component, subjects attempt to learn by trial and error a predetermined sequence of 10 numbers within 20 trials. Subjects learn a new sequence each time they perform the test. In the performance component, the response sequence remains constant throughout the experiment, and thus subjects repeat an already learned sequence. Two studies have reported no effect of either intranasal (IN) or IV cocaine on the test.[37,40] However, Higgins et al.[51] reported that cocaine (96 mg, IN) decreased response rate during the acquisition phase and increased response accuracy during the performance component. In a similar serial acquisition procedure, cocaine has been shown to have no effect.[52,53]

Cocaine[26] and D-amphetamine[7] had no effect on simple arithmetic skills. With respect to memory, most studies have also indicated no effect of D-amphetamine on immediate recall of lists of numbers.[7] However, Soetens et al.[54] reported that D-amphetamine (10 mg) administered PO before learning and intramuscularly (IM) after learning enhanced recall of a word list for up to 3 days. D-Amphetamine also enhanced performance on a working memory task, but only in subjects with a low baseline working memory capacity. In contrast, amphetamine diminished performance in high-baseline subjects.[55]

5.2.1.5 Summary

The performance effects of D-amphetamine have been studied to a greater extent than those of cocaine; however, because of their similar pharmacology, both drugs generally produce comparable effects. Psychostimulants in low to moderate doses typically produce behavioral and cortical arousal, and thus D-amphetamine reliably increases CFF threshold and has been shown in some studies to increase finger tapping rate and gross motor coordination. A relatively large body of literature indicates that D-amphetamine and cocaine enhance attentional abilities, including brief tests requiring focused attention and vigilance tasks requiring sustained attention. The majority of studies have shown that cocaine and D-amphetamine have no effect on learning, memory, and other cognitive processes, such as solving arithmetic problems.

5.2.2 3,4-Methylenedioxymethamphetamine (MDMA; Ecstasy)

Since the late 1980s, MDMA (ecstasy) has become an increasingly popular recreational drug among teenagers and young adults. MDMA has structural similarities to hallucinogens and psychomotor stimulants and acts to release presynaptic monoamines, primarily serotonin. Cardiovascular effects are similar to other stimulants and include increases in heart rate and blood pressure due to peripheral norepinephrine release. Users report a sense of well-being, heightened responsiveness to emotions, and feelings of intimacy toward other people. These effects are sometimes accompanied by mild hallucinations and perceptual disturbances, thought to be due to the drug's interaction with postsynaptic 5-HT2 receptors.[56] There have been reports of MDMA-generated psychotic syndrome, anxiety-related disorders, and other psychiatric symptoms.

MDMA is most often taken orally in a typical dose range per tablet of 50 to 100 mg.[57,58] Neurotoxicity of MDMA to serotonergic systems has been demonstrated in animal studies; therefore for ethical reasons most research has been accomplished using light to heavy MDMA users. Methodological confounds associated with this include the sometimes extensive previous or concurrent use of other drugs, the existence of premorbid psychiatric syndromes often not explored or reported, and variability in the components of street drugs sold as "ecstasy."

5.2.2.1 Sensorimotor Abilities

Prepulse inhibition (PPI) of acoustic startle is the reduction of a startle response to a stimulus when that stimulus is preceded by a weaker stimulus. PPI has been used as an operational measure to study sensorimotor gating in a variety of populations. In a double-blind, placebo-controlled study, MDMA (1.7 mg) was administered orally to healthy, non-MDMA-using volunteers to determine the effect on PPI. MDMA produced a slight but significant increase in startle reactivity.[59] Using a trail-making test to assess psychomotor speed, there were no differences in performance between current and former MDMA users, polydrug users, and drug naïve participants.[60] Similarly, users of MDMA were asked to perform a simple reaction time task after administration of 75 and 125 mg of MDMA and neither dose affected task performance.[61]

5.2.2.2 Attentional Abilities

There are several reports of decrements in attentional processes among MDMA users. Focused attention, as assessed by the DSST, was significantly worse among MDMA users who were administered 125 mg MDMA.[61] In another study employing a similar task, MDMA users who were abstinent for 3 weeks prior to testing were significantly less accurate than non-MDMA users at baseline.[62] On a divided attention task requiring attention to simultaneously presented visual and auditory cues, participants who were regular users of both cannabis and MDMA performed more poorly than cannabis users only and than participants who used neither drug. These MDMA/cannabis users also performed more poorly than either comparison group on a selective attention task requiring visual memory, target selection, and response inhibition.[63] Adolescent MDMA users performed significantly worse as compared to drug-naïve adolescents on both selective and divided attention tasks.[64] However, another group reported no impairment in divided attention in either current or former MDMA users.[60]

Reports of sustained attention performance are mixed. In studies that used the Continuous Performance Task (CPT), no differences were observed between MDMA users and drug-naïve controls.[64,65] Using a visual search scan, regular (>10 times) and novice ($\leq$10 times) users of MDMA were compared to MDMA-naïve participants. Subjects were tested off-drug, when the user groups were actively self-administering MDMA, and at three times (up to 7 days) after the last drug use. Visual scanning was impaired only when the user groups were on MDMA.[66] This was confirmed in a second study in which these groups were tested only while they were drug-free, and there were no differences in sustained attention performance between the three groups.[67] In contrast is a report of MDMA users who were abstinent for 3 weeks prior to testing, yet still had performance decrements on a sustained attention task that required arithmetic calculations.[62]

5.2.2.3 Cognitive Abilities

Many studies that have assessed cognitive processes have demonstrated impairment in both active and abstinent users of MDMA, particularly on memory performance. Memory decrements have been reported long after users had ceased taking the drug. For example, immediate[67] and delayed recall was significantly worse in novice[66] and regular MDMA users,[66–68] compared to MDMA-naïve participants, whether they were on or off drug.[66,67] Memory scores remained poor in the regular MDMA users up to 7 days after drug use.[66] Other studies have confirmed that memory difficulties can persist after drug use has ended. MDMA users who were abstinent 1 week,[69] 3 weeks,[62] 2 months,[70] 6 months,[68,71] and at least 1 year[70] showed impaired performances on short-term memory,[62,69–71] delayed recall,[68,70] working memory,[62,71] and logical reasoning[62] compared to MDMA-naïve control groups. However, another study found no decrements in working memory in MDMA users,[60] and Parrott[18] mentioned several unpublished reports in which unimpaired learning or memory task performance was observed in users.

One problem, as noted earlier, is that cognitive deficits reported in these studies might be confounded by concurrent use of other drugs. For example, one investigator[72] reported that it was impossible to recruit MDMA users who did not also use cannabis. Exploring the relationship of these two drugs, one group reported that cannabis-only users and drug-naïve participants performed significantly better on tests of working memory, immediate recall, selective and divided attention, and logical thinking compared to users of MDMA + cannabis.[63] In that group, the use of cannabis was related to more pronounced cognitive deficits. In contrast, other investigators have reported that both drug-using groups each performed significantly worse than non-users on several measures of memory and other cognitive processes,[72,73] suggesting that coincident cannabis use might account for the cognitive impairment in MDMA users. However, in one of those studies[72] the MDMA + cannabis group did perform worse on two delayed recall tasks and others also have reported similar findings on various cognitive tasks.[17,18,57,58]

5.2.2.4 Summary

Simple cognitive processes such as reaction time seem to be normal among MDMA users, with the exception of one report of altered sensorimotor gating. More complex cognitive processes, such as attentional processes, appear to be more susceptible to disruption by MDMA. Although the literature is mixed, the use of MDMA has been reported to disrupt focused, divided, selective, and sustained attention. There is a growing body of evidence that even light recreational use of MDMA can have long-lasting effects on memory, including verbal and visual recall and working memory. The degree of memory impairment is associated with the extent and intensity of drug use and might be enhanced by concurrent cannabis use, and memory deficits can be long lasting.

5.3 NICOTINE AND TOBACCO

The vast majority of people who use nicotine (either cigarettes or smokeless tobacco products) use the drug on a daily basis and are considered to be addicted to or dependent on nicotine. In contrast, a minority of people who use the other psychoactive drugs considered in this chapter for nonmedical purposes develop a drug dependence. Daily smokers accumulate plasma levels of nicotine that increase during the day, decline overnight, but never reach zero. This poses a unique problem when conducting behavioral studies with smokers. When improvements in performance are observed after nicotine is given to smokers who have been tobacco-deprived overnight (a common design strategy), it is impossible to determine whether such improvements represent a true enhancement of performance or the alleviation of withdrawal-induced performance deficits. The latter explanation would simply represent a reversal to the person's normal smoking behavioral baseline, not a true enhancement above baseline performance. Unlike other drugs of abuse that are typically tested in nondependent, nontolerant subjects, this issue must always be considered when interpreting the effects of nicotine on smokers' performance.

Two papers have thoroughly reviewed the literature on the effects of nicotine and cigarette smoking on human performance.[6,15] In general, both reviews concluded that nicotine does not universally enhance performance and cognition and that any nicotine-induced performance improvements are small in magnitude. Heishman et al.[6] suggested that the limited performance-enhancing effects of nicotine are not likely to be an important factor in the initiation of cigarette smoking by adolescents (the modal age for starting tobacco use is between 11 and 15; beginning after high school is rare[74]). However, once an individual is dependent on nicotine, data suggest that nicotine deprivation maintains smoking, at least in part, because nicotine can reverse withdrawal-induced performance decrements.[6]

Because the majority of studies in this area are methodologically deficient, only studies that used placebo-control conditions and single- or double-blind drug administration procedures are included in this section. Additionally, because of the problem of interpreting nicotine-induced changes in smokers' performance as discussed above, a distinction will be made between studies that administered nicotine to subjects under conditions of nicotine deprivation and no deprivation. Studies involving no nicotine deprivation include nondeprived smokers and nonsmokers.

5.3.1 Sensory Abilities

Sherwood et al.[75] administered nicotine polacrilex gum (0 and 2 mg) three times at 1-h intervals to smokers who were overnight deprived and measured CFF after each administration. CFF threshold was increased over predose baseline after the first 2-mg dose, but no further increase after the second and third doses was observed. Thus, the initial dose appeared to reverse a deprivation-induced deficit, and subsequent doses maintained normal functioning. Baseline CFF was not measured before subjects were tobacco abstinent. No effect of nicotine on CFF was reported following administration of nicotine polacrilex or subcutaneous (SC) nicotine injections to 24-h abstinent smokers, nonabstinent smokers, and nonsmokers.[76–79] The lack of effect of nicotine in the absence of nicotine deprivation is consistent with the data of Sherwood et al.,[75] further suggesting that nicotine reverses withdrawal-induced deficits, but does not produce true enhancement of CFF threshold.

5.3.2 Motor Abilities

Perkins et al.[80] administered placebo and nicotine nasal spray (15 μg/kg) to smokers who were tobacco deprived for at least 12 h. Nicotine reliably increased finger tapping rate in all subjects, and produced a nonsignificant trend toward improved hand steadiness. In a subsequent study, Perkins et al.[81] reported that nicotine (5, 10, and 20 μg/kg) increased finger tapping rate, but impaired hand steadiness and hand tremor in nonsmokers and overnight tobacco abstinent smokers. Finger tapping rate was also increased by nicotine in nonsmokers who were administered nicotine nasal solution or spray[80,82] or SC nicotine injections.[77] In contrast, Foulds et al.[79] found that nicotine injections (0.3 and 0.6 mg, SC) had no effect on finger tapping rate in nonsmokers, and only 0.3 mg nicotine produced a slight tapping rate increase in 24-h abstinent smokers. Heishman and Henningfield[83] administered nicotine polacrilex gum (0, 2, 4, 8 mg) to nonsmokers each day for 8 days and found that the 8-mg dose impaired gross motor performance on the circular lights test.

5.3.3 Attentional Abilities

Numerous studies investigating focused attention have used reaction time tests. Nicotine polacrilex gum (2 mg) produced faster motor reaction time, but did not affect recognition reaction time in overnight deprived smokers,[75] nonabstinent smokers,[76] and a group of nonabstinent smokers and nonsmokers.[78] Le Houezec et al.[84] found that SC nicotine (0.8 mg) increased the number of fast reaction times, but did not affect task accuracy. Griesar et al.[85] reported faster reaction time following administration of transdermal nicotine patch compared to placebo patch in nonsmokers. However, Hindmarch et al.[76] reported no effect of 2-mg polacrilex on reaction time in nonsmokers.

Selective attention can be defined as the ability to attend to a target stimulus while simultaneously ignoring irrelevant or distracting stimuli. In 12-h tobacco-deprived smokers, nicotine polacrilex (2 and 4 mg) reversed deprivation-induced impairments in letter searching to predeprivation baseline[86] and had no effect on Stroop and letter cancellation tests.[87] The Stroop test compares the time required for subjects to name the ink color of color words that are incongruent (e.g., the word red printed in blue ink) vs. the ink color of neutral stimuli, such as non-color words or colored squares. Typically, the incongruent task takes more time than the neutral stimulus task because the tendency to read the color word interferes with naming its ink color; the difference in time between the two tasks is considered a measure of selective attention or distractibility.[88] In two studies comparing abstinent smokers and nonsmokers on the Stroop test, nicotine nasal spray (5, 10, and 20 μg/kg) improved response time, but impaired accuracy with regard to the Stroop conflict,[81] whereas nicotine injections (0.3 and 0.6 mg, SC) had no effect.[79] Using the Stroop test with nonsmokers, Wesnes and Revell[89] found no effect of 1.5-mg nicotine tablets, whereas Provost and Woodward[90] reported faster response time after 2-mg nicotine polacrilex. In two studies with nonsmokers, nicotine polacrilex (2 and 4 mg) had no effect on letter searching response time or accuracy,[91] whereas 8-mg polacrilex impaired letter searching accuracy.[83]

Using a divided attention test that required subjects to perform simultaneously a central tracking task and respond to peripheral visual stimuli, Sherwood et al.[75] found that 2-mg polacrilex decreased tracking errors, but had no effect on reaction time to the peripheral lights in overnight deprived smokers. There were fewer tracking errors after the third nicotine dose compared to the first dose, and placebo responding was unchanged, suggesting a true enhancement of performance. In the same divided attention test, nicotine decreased errors on the tracking task in nonabstinent smokers[76,78] but had no effect in nonsmokers.[76]

The rapid visual information processing (RVIP) test has been used in numerous studies investigating the effects of smoking and nicotine on sustained attention. This test requires subjects to press a button when they detect three consecutive even or odd digits in a series of single digits presented on a video monitor at 600-ms intervals. In tobacco-deprived smokers, RVIP accuracy was improved after subjects smoked cigarettes,[92] were administered nicotine polacrilex,[87,93] or received SC injections of nicotine.[79] However, there was no effect on RVIP performance in smokers who were abstinent for 2 h and given polacrilex (4 mg)[94] and in nondeprived smokers allowed to smoke one cigarette.[95] Wesnes et al.[96] reported that the decline in signal detection during an 80-min vigilance test was less after active nicotine tablets compared with placebo in 12-h deprived smokers. Testing nonsmokers, three studies reported that nicotine had no effect on the RVIP test compared to placebo conditions,[77,97,98] whereas Foulds et al.[79] reported faster reaction time after nicotine injections (0.3 and 0.6 mg, SC). Levin et al.[99] found that transdermal nicotine decreased errors of omission on a continuous performance test in nonsmokers. Nonsmokers were also administered nicotine tablets in the Wesnes et al.[96] study, and no difference between abstinent smokers and nonsmokers was observed, suggesting that nicotine functioned to reverse deprivation-induced deficits in the 12-h abstinent smokers.

5.3.4 Cognitive Abilities

Testing a verbal rote learning paradigm in overnight-deprived smokers, Andersson and Post[100] reported that after the first cigarette, anticipatory responding was improved in the placebo compared to the nicotine condition, but after the second cigarette, there was no difference between conditions. Another study reported that, after learning a word-pair list, smoking a cigarette reduced errors when subjects were tested 1 week later.[101]

The effects of nicotine and smoking on memory have been widely investigated. In two studies conducted with 10-h abstinent smokers,[102,103] most subjects recalled a greater number of words after nicotine tablets or cigarettes; however, some subjects' recall improved after placebo tablets or denicotinized cigarettes, and some showed no difference between conditions. More recent studies with 12- to 24-h abstinent smokers found that nicotine nasal spray[81] and SC nicotine injections[79] improved recognition memory. In a study with minimally tobacco deprived (1 h) smokers, three experiments found no effect of smoking after word list presentation on delayed intentional word recall.[104] In contrast, three experiments found improved free recall when subjects either smoked[104,105] or received 2-mg polacrilex gum[106] before list presentation. Krebs et al.[107] reported that subjects' recall of prose passages was better after smoking a 0.7-mg nicotine cigarette compared to 0.1- or 1.5-mg nicotine cigarettes, suggesting that optimal arousal was produced by the medium, compared with the high, nicotine-containing cigarette. Reaction time on the Sternberg memory test, which measures scanning and retrieval from short-term memory, was faster after smoking[75,108] and administration of nicotine polacrilex[109] compared to placebo conditions; however, Foulds et al.[79] reported no effect of SC nicotine on the Sternberg memory test in 24-h abstinent smokers and nonsmokers.

In contrast to these positive effects of nicotine on memory, three studies[86,93,110] reported no effect of nicotine on tests of immediate and delayed recall in nicotine-deprived smokers, and Houston et al.[111] reported that immediate and delayed recall was impaired after smoking a nicotine cigarette compared to a nicotine-free cigarette. In studies of nondeprived smokers or nonsmokers, two reported that nicotine improved some aspects of memory in patients with Alzheimer's disease,[77,112] two found enhanced reaction time on the Sternberg memory test,[78,109] four reported no effect of nicotine on tests of immediate and delayed recall,[76,77,91,113] and two found that nicotine polacrilex impaired immediate and/or delayed recall accuracy.[83,114] Foulds et al.[79] reported that SC nicotine enhanced response time but decreased accuracy in a digit recall test in nonsmokers.

Several studies have examined the effect of nicotine on other cognitive abilities. Snyder and Henningfield[86] reported that polacrilex (2 and 4 mg) enhanced response time but had no effect on accuracy in an arithmetic test and had no effect on either speed or accuracy in a test of logical reasoning in 12-h abstinent smokers. However, Foulds et al.[79] reported that nicotine injections (0.3 and 0.6 mg, SC) improved response time on the logical reasoning test in 24-h deprived smokers. Five studies conducted with nonsmokers reported no effect of nicotine on several cognitive tests, including the ability to generate correct answers to word and number problems[114] and logical reasoning and mental arithmetic.[79,83,91,113]

5.3.5 Summary

As discussed previously, results of studies conducted with nicotine-deprived smokers are difficult to interpret. Without pre-deprivation baseline data, which few studies report, it is difficult to conclude whether nicotine reversed deprivation-induced deficits or enhanced performance beyond that observed in the nondeprived state. In general, however, nicotine and smoking at least reversed deprivation-induced deficits in certain abilities in abstinent smokers, but such beneficial effects have not been observed consistently across a range of performance measures. For example, about half of the studies that measured sustained attention and memory reported a positive effect of nicotine; however, the effects were limited to some subjects or one aspect of test performance.

The strongest conclusions concerning the effects of nicotine and smoking on human performance can be drawn from studies conducted with nondeprived smokers and nonsmokers. These studies indicated that nicotine enhanced finger tapping rate and motor responding in tests of focused and divided attention. Additionally, nicotine produced faster motor responses in the Sternberg memory test, enhanced recognition memory, and reversed the vigilance decrement in a sustained attention test. However, no studies reported true enhancement of sensory abilities, selective attention, learning, and other cognitive abilities.

5.4 SEDATIVE-HYPNOTICS: BENZODIAZEPINES

Since their advent in the 1960s, benzodiazepines have been prescribed widely as anxiolytic and sedative-hypnotic medications, essentially replacing barbiturates because of their greater safety margin. Compared with barbiturates, an acute benzodiazepine overdose is much less likely to produce fatal respiratory depression.[20] There are currently more than a dozen benzodiazepines available for medical use; all produce sedation with varying potency. Benzodiazepines with longer duration of action, such as diazepam and lorazepam, are typically prescribed for the treatment of anxiety disorders, whereas those with shorter duration of action, such as triazolam, are used as hypnotics for insomnia. A concern with benzodiazepines being used at night to induce sleep has been the potential for sedation and impaired performance the next day. A review of 52 studies[115] indicated that all benzodiazepine hypnotics, at high enough doses, produced next-day performance impairment. The degree of impairment was dose related, suggesting that the lowest effective hypnotic dose should be prescribed.

As with all drugs that produce changes in mood, benzodiazepines have the potential to be abused,[116,117] and methodologies have been developed to test the abuse liability of benzodiazepines and related drugs in the laboratory.[118] The pattern of benzodiazepine abuse varies from occasional episodes of intoxication to daily, compulsive use of large doses. Tolerance and physical dependence develop with continued use, such that individuals taking therapeutic doses of benzodiazepines for several months typically experience withdrawal symptoms even if the dose is gradually tapered.[20] The benzodiazepine withdrawal syndrome includes insomnia, restlessness, dizziness, nausea, headache, inability to concentrate, and fatigue. Although unpleasant, benzodiazepine withdrawal is not life-threatening, unlike withdrawal from barbiturates.

The effects of benzodiazepines have been studied extensively with respect to human performance and cognition. Because of their sedative effects, not surprisingly, benzodiazepines generally impair all aspects of performance.[7,119] However, some decrements, such as the well-studied anterograde amnesia, have been shown to be independent of general sedation.[12] Benzodiazepines will be considered as the prototypic sedative-hypnotic drug, recognizing that other CNS depressant drugs, such as barbiturates and ethanol, produce somewhat distinct performance impairment profiles. In the studies reviewed, benzodiazepines were administered PO.

5.4.1 Sensory Abilities

Consistent with their depressant and sedative effects, benzodiazepines administered acutely typically decrease CFF threshold.[119,120] Specifically, significant decreases have been reported for 1 mg alprazolam, 10 mg diazepam, and 15 mg quazepam;[121] 4 to 11 mg midazolam;[122] 7.5 to 50 mg oxazepam;[123] 1 and 2 mg lorazepam;[124] and 0.5 mg triazolam and 1 mg flunitrazepam.[120] As is evident, this effect on CFF threshold was observed at therapeutic doses of each drug, and when multiple doses were tested, the effect was dose-related. However, there are reports of acute, therapeutic doses of diazepam (5 mg)[125] and lorazepam (1 and 2 mg)[125,126] having no effect on CFF threshold. One study investigating numerous benzodiazepines[120] reported next-day impairment after acute doses of triazolam (0.5 mg) and lormetazepam (1 to 2 mg). No studies were found that examined the effect of chronic benzodiazepine administration on CFF threshold.

Blom et al.[121] recorded horizontal saccadic eye movements as subjects viewed the successive illumination of red light stimuli. They reported that alprazolam, diazepam, and quazepam reduced peak saccadic velocity; alprazolam produced the greatest degree of impairment. Maximal reductions occurred 1 to 4 h after dosing, and effects had not returned to placebo levels at 8 h. Rettig et al.[127] reported that 1 mg lormetazepam and 15 mg midazolam given the night before increased imbalance of the ocular muscles as measured by the Maddox Wing test. This muscular imbalance produces strabismus, which is the inability of both eyes to converge directly on a visual stimulus. Such ocular impairment could be the basis of a wide range of benzodiazepine-induced performance deficits.

5.4.2 Motor Abilities

Numerous studies have reported that various benzodiazepines decrease finger tapping rate.[119,122,124,128] Kunsman et al.[119] noted that finger tapping rate was generally less sensitive to the effects of benzodiazepines than more complex tasks, such as reaction time and tracking. However, the studies reporting decreases in tapping rate used doses that were in the therapeutic range; thus simple motor skills can be impaired at clinically relevant doses.

A large number of studies have shown that benzodiazepines impair gross motor coordination, as measured by the ability to balance on one leg and the circular lights test. Alprazolam (0.5 to 2 mg),[129] lorazepam (1 and 4 mg),[130,131] and triazolam (0.25 to 0.75)[132–135] impaired balance or circular lights performance in a dose-related manner. In a population of sedative abusers, acute administration of 40 or 80 mg diazepam and 1 or 2 mg triazolam impaired circular lights performance, and diazepam, but not triazolam, impaired performance the next day.[136] Stoops and Rush[137] reported that tolerance to impaired performance on the circular lights task developed over several sessions of triazolam (0.375 mg) administration. Bond et al.[128] reported that 1 mg alprazolam increased body sway as measured in an automated ataxiameter.

In contrast to these reports of benzodiazepine-induced motor impairment, Kumar et al.[138] found that chronic administration of 1 mg lorazepam and 0.5 mg alprazolam for 5 days had no effect on fine motor coordination as assessed using a standard pegboard test. Additionally, Tobler et al.[139] reported that performance on a typing test was not impaired the day after an acute dose of 7.5 mg midazolam.

5.4.3 Attentional Abilities

The effects of benzodiazepines on reaction time tests and the DSST have been investigated in many studies, the majority of which reported impairment of attentional abilities necessary to perform such tests successfully. Because these tests typically are of short duration (less than 5 min), focused attention is primarily required, although other abilities are also involved. Numerous studies have reported that simple or choice reaction time to visual stimuli was increased (slowed) by acute, therapeutic doses of various benzodiazepines, including adinazolam,[140] alprazolam,[129] diazepam and flunitrazepam,[141] lorazepam,[130,142] oxazepam,[123] temazepam,[119] and triazolam.[132] Linnoila et al.[143,144] reported that diazepam, alprazolam, and adinazolam impaired reaction time and accuracy in a word recognition test. Flurazepam (30 mg, but not 15 mg) produced next-day impairment of simple and choice visual reaction time, whereas 15 mg midazolam had no residual effect.[145] In contrast, diazepam (5 mg) and lorazepam (1 mg) had no effect on an auditory reaction time test.[125] It is possible that, compared with visual tests, auditory reaction time tests are less sensitive to the impairing effects of benzodiazepines. To investigate this, Pompeia et al.[146] compared the effects of equipotent doses of lorazepam and flunitrazepam on visual and auditory event-related potentials. Both benzodiazepines produced performance decrements on auditory delayed recall; however, flunitrazepam increased P3 latencies in both visual and auditory modalities, whereas lorazepam increased visual latencies only.

Like reaction time tests, nearly all studies have reported that acute administration of benzodiazepines impair performance on the DSST. Lorazepam (1 to 9 mg),[125,130,142,147–149] triazolam (0.25 to 0.75 mg),[132,134,135,148,150–153] alprazolam (0.5 to 4 mg),[129,147] temazepam (15 to 60 mg),[119,150] diazepam (5 to 10 mg),[147,154] clonazepam,[155] and estazolam (1 to 4 mg)[152] have been shown to impair response speed and/or accuracy on the DSST in a dose-related manner. However, Kelly et al.[156] reported that diazepam (5 or 10 mg) had no effect on DSST performance. It is unlikely that low doses of diazepam accounted for the lack of effect, as suggested by Kelly et al.,[156] because numerous studies have reported DSST impairment after 10 mg diazepam.[7] In a test similar to the DSST symbol copying, Saano et al.[125] reported no effect of diazepam (5 mg) and lorazepam (1 mg). Acute triazolam (0.375 mg) administration decreased the number of trials completed on the DSST task, but tolerance to this decrement developed with each of three subsequent doses.[137]

Another test requiring focused attention is digit or letter cancellation, in which subjects mark through a certain numeral in a page of random numbers or a certain letter in a page of text or random letters. The typical duration of cancellation tests is 1 to 2 min. Two studies reported that diazepam (10 or 15 mg)[157] and lorazepam (1 and 2 mg)[124] impaired digit cancellation performance. Interestingly, Brown et al.[157] found that impaired focused attention was not correlated with the ability to encode associative information. These studies confirm numerous previous studies that reported benzodiazepine-induced decrements in cancellation tests.[7]

Brief tests of tracking abilities can also be considered tests of focused attention. In such tests, subjects attempt to maintain a moving target within a certain area of the video monitor or a cursor within a moving target. Tracking performance is uniformly impaired by benzodiazepines at doses similar to those reported above for reaction time and DSST impairment.[119,143,144] One study investigating the effects of multiple doses of three benzodiazepines reported that lorazepam produced the greatest degree of tracking impairment, followed by alprazolam and then diazepam.[147] Because the manipulandum used to control the moving target in some studies was a steering wheel, tracking tests have occasionally been considered laboratory tests of driving ability. In studies of on-road driving, Volkerts et al.[158] reported that driving was impaired the morning after dosing with oxazepam (50 mg) and slightly impaired after lormetazepam (1 mg). Brookhuis et al.[159] found that next-day driving was significantly impaired after flurazepam (30 mg) and less impaired after lormetazepam (2 mg). Diazepam (15 mg) impaired performance on a clinical test for drunkenness, which comprised 13 tests assessing motor, vestibular, mental, and behavioral functioning.[160]

Compared with focused attention, fewer studies have examined the effects of benzodiazepines on selective attention. Two studies have shown that performance on the Stroop test was impaired by lorazepam.[119,131] Acute administration of triazolam and lorazepam produced dose-dependent decrements in response rate and accuracy in a simultaneous matching-to-sample task, which required subjects to determine which of two comparison visual stimuli was identical to the sample stimulus.[148,161] The drug effects differed as a function of task difficulty, such that the benzodiazepine-induced impairment was reduced when discriminability of the non-matching stimulus was increased.

Benzodiazepines have been shown to impair divided attention.[119] Two groups of investigators reported that oxazepam (7.5 to 50 mg)[123] and alprazolam (0.5 mg)[162] impaired performance on a test that required subjects to divide their attention between a central tracking task and responding to stimuli in the peripheral visual field. Using a similar test of divided attention, Moskowitz et al.[145] found that 30 mg flurazepam and 15 mg midazolam impaired performance the day after drug administration.

Consistent with the other types of attention, benzodiazepines impair performance in tests of sustained attention or vigilance.[14,143,145] There is no evidence that benzodiazepines exacerbate the vigilance decrement normally observed during prolonged, tedious tests. The impairment caused by benzodiazepines in tests of sustained attention is not secondary to sedation, but rather a direct effect on perceptual sensitivity, resulting in decreased hits and increased response time in detecting stimulus targets.

5.4.4 Cognitive Abilities

The most widely studied aspect of cognition with respect to benzodiazepines is memory.[12,163] One of the most reliable effects of benzodiazepines is to impair recall of information presented after drug administration (anterograde amnesia). In contrast, information presented before administration of benzodiazepines is not affected. The memory decrement produced by benzodiazepines is a function of task difficulty, such that little or no impairment is observed for immediate recall of a few items, whereas more complex or delayed memory tests reveal profound impairment.[12] The benzodiazepine antagonist flumazenil has been used to block the sedative effects of benzodiazepines, but the amnestic effect was not affected, suggesting that benzodiazepine-induced amnesia is independent of sedation.[122,164] It has also been demonstrated that some benzodiazepines selectively impaired explicit memory (e.g., recall of a word list), but left other aspects of memory intact.[163] In this way, benzodiazepines have been used as pharmacological tools to identify distinct memory processes.

Roy-Byrne et al.[165] reported that diazepam (10 mg) impaired attentional processes during auditory presentation of a word list and immediate recognition of words that had been presented twice; however, naming examples of a category, such as vegetables (semantic memory), and self-evaluation of memory performance (meta-cognition) were not affected. Triazolam (0.25 to 0.5 mg) impaired free recall of a word list, but had no effect on implicit (memory without awareness of the source of information) or semantic memory.[166,167] Linnoila et al.[143] reported that adinazolam (15 or 30 mg) impaired attention during list presentation, but had no effect on delayed (1 min) free recall of words. Using a battery of tests that assessed numerous memory functions, Bishop et al.[124] reported that lorazepam (1 and 2 mg) impaired explicit (free recall), semantic, and implicit memory, but had no effect on working memory (manipulation of information for less than 30 s) and procedural memory (knowledge required for skills reflected as improved performance with practice). Similarly, a higher dose of lorazepam (2.5 mg) disrupted several memory processes (delayed recall, implicit and semantic memory), but did not affect short-term memory.[168] Such selective drug effects on memory and similarly selective clinical amnestic syndromes resulting from brain injury or disease[163] have allowed a greater understanding of cognitive functioning and the processes subserving learning and memory.

A large number of studies have investigated the effect of acute benzodiazepine administration on either immediate or delayed recall or recognition of word lists, numbers, or pictures in healthy volunteers. Impaired memory has been reported for adinazolam (20 to 30 mg),[140] alprazolam (0.5 to 2 mg),[129,144,169] diazepam (5 to 15 mg),[157,170] estazolam (1 to 4 mg),[152] lorazepam (1 to 4 mg),[130,171] temazepam (15 to 60 mg),[150] and triazolam (0.25 to 0.75 mg).[132–135,150,152,172] Acute administration of triazolam[135] and lorazepam[131] has been observed to significantly impair working memory. In addition, Buchanan et al.[173] reported that triazolam (0.25 mg) interfered with the facilitating effect that emotional stimuli have on long-term memory (both delayed recall and recognition). Diazepam (15 mg) also was reported to produce impairments in facial emotional recognition.[174] Testing subjects with histories of sedative abuse, Roache and Griffiths[136,142] reported that immediate and delayed recall and recognition of digits and symbols were impaired by diazepam (40 or 80 mg), lorazepam (1.5 to 9 mg), and triazolam (1 or 2 mg). After 5 days of dosing healthy subjects with either alprazolam (0.5 mg) or lorazepam (1 mg), anterograde amnesia was observed for word lists.[138] Hindmarch et al.[120] examined the effects of several benzodiazepines on the Sternberg memory test, which measures scanning and retrieval from short-term memory. They reported that acute administration of flunitrazepam (1 mg), lormetazepam (1 to 2 mg), and triazolam (0.5 mg) significantly slowed response time on the test and that performance remained impaired the next day with lormetazepam and triazolam. However, Kelly et al.[156] reported no effect of diazepam (5 and 10 mg) on the Sternberg test.

The effect of a number of benzodiazepines has been investigated on the repeated acquisition and performance of response sequences task, which comprises separate acquisition (learning) and performance components.[175] This task thus allows independent assessment of drug effects on acquisition of new information and performance of already learned information. In general, doses of benzodiazepines that increased errors in the acquisition component did not impair the performance component, although high doses decreased response rate and increased errors in both components. Impairment of acquisition of the response sequence has been reported following acute administration of alprazolam (1 to 3 mg),[175] diazepam (5 to 30 mg),[11,175,176] estazolam (1 to 4 mg),[152] lorazepam (2.8 to 5.6 mg),[149] temazepam (15 to 60 mg),[150] and triazolam (0.375 to 0.75 mg).[150–152,175,176] In these studies, only the highest doses impaired the performance component of the task. In one of the few studies to examine the chronic effects of benzodiazepines on cognitive processes, Bickel et al.[177] administered diazepam (80 mg daily) for 3 days to sedative abusers and found increased errors and decreased response rate in the acquisition component on day 1 that decreased on days 2 and 3, suggesting the development of tolerance. In the performance component, response rate was decreased on day 1; the magnitude of effect decreased over days. Performance error rate was relatively unaffected.

Few studies have examined the effects of benzodiazepines on other cognitive abilities. Rusted et al.[170] reported that 5 and 10 mg diazepam impaired performance on a logical reasoning test, but had no effect on a mental rotation task. Judd et al.[178] found that 30 mg flurazepam, but not 15 mg midazolam, impaired arithmetic (addition) abilities the day after drug administration. In contrast, flurazepam had no effect on reading comprehension.

5.4.5 Summary

When administered acutely to nontolerant, healthy volunteers, therapeutic doses of benzodiazepines produce sedation, which typically impairs most aspects of performance in a dose-dependent manner. In patients taking benzodiazepines medically and in individuals who abuse benzodiazepines recreationally, both of whom have developed tolerance, it is necessary to increase the dose of benzodiazepine to observe impaired performance. Benzodiazepines have been shown to decrease CFF threshold, a direct indication of CNS depression, and to impair ocular performance. Motor abilities are impaired by benzodiazepines, including fine (finger tapping) and gross (balance, circular lights, and body sway) motor coordination. Numerous studies have documented that benzodiazepines impair tests requiring focused, selective, divided, and sustained attention. One of the best-studied cognitive effects of benzodiazepines is their ability to produce anterograde amnesia, memory loss for information presented after drug administration. It has been demonstrated that these memory deficits are not secondary to benzodiazepine-induced sedation and that explicit memory (free recall of presented stimuli) functions are typically impaired, whereas other memory processes can remain unaffected. Benzodiazepines have also been shown to impair the acquisition (learning) of new information.

5.5 OPIOID ANALGESICS AND ANESTHETICS

The class of drugs referred to as opioids consists of a wide range of naturally occurring derivatives from the opium poppy, *Papaver somniferum*, such as morphine and codeine; semisynthetic derivatives from opium, such as heroin and hydromorphone; and completely synthetic opioids, such as meperidine and fentanyl. The primary pharmacological effect of all opioids is analgesia; a common side effect is sedation. At high doses, respiratory depression occurs, which is the usual cause of death from acute opioid overdose. The full range of clinical pain can be effectively treated with various opioids, and fentanyl and related synthetic congeners (sufentanil, alfentanil) are generally used clinically as anesthetics, but are also used for postoperative analgesia.

Opioids can be classified according to their pharmacological actions into those that function like morphine, producing their agonist effects primarily through the mu opioid receptor, and those that produce mixed effects, such as agonist-antagonists or partial agonists.[179] Mixed agonist-antagonists function as agonists at one type of opioid receptor (e.g., delta or kappa) and as an antagonist at other (e.g., mu) receptors. Partial agonists produce only limited effects at a given receptor. Morphine-like opioids are used clinically for moderate to severe pain, whereas agonist-antagonists and partial agonists produce less analgesia and are thus useful in the treatment of mild pain.

Previous reviews have concluded that opioids produce minimal impairment of human performance even at high doses.[179,180] However, more recent reviews[16,181] challenge this benign notion. In healthy, nontolerant research subjects, opioids impair psychomotor performance to a greater extent than cognitive abilities. Typically, opioids slow responses in tests requiring speed, but do not impair test accuracy. In contrast, individuals who have developed tolerance to opioids, such as patients suffering chronic pain[181] or persons maintained on methadone,[180] generally show little or no behavioral impairment after administration of their maintenance dose. The time required for tolerance to develop to any performance-impairing effects of methadone has been estimated at 3 to 4 weeks in methadone-maintained patients.[180] The studies reviewed here report the performance effects of opioids in nontolerant research volunteers, unless otherwise indicated.

5.5.1 Sensory Abilities

Studies investigating the effects of morphine, meperidine, buprenorphine, and nalbuphine on CFF threshold have, in general, found impaired functioning, consistent with the CNS depressant effect of opioids.[16] Veselis et al.[182] targeted fentanyl plasma concentrations of 1.0, 1.5, and 2.5 ng/ml using continuous IV infusion and found that CFF threshold was decreased at 1.5 ng/ml, whereas other performance measures were affected only at concentrations greater than 2.5 ng/ml. Morphine (10 mg, PO) was also found to decrease CFF threshold.[183] In contrast, pentazocine (30 mg) had no effect on CFF threshold;[184] however, other studies using higher doses of pentazocine have reported decreased CFF threshold.[16]

Zacny and colleagues have examined the effects of several opioids on the Maddox Wing test, a measure of ocular muscle imbalance indicating divergence of the eyes. Administration of morphine (2.5 to 10 mg, IV),[185] butorphanol (0.5 to 2.0 mg, IV),[186] dezocine (2.5 to 10 mg, IV),[187] pentazocine (30 mg, IM),[184] hydromorphone (1.3 mg, IV),[188] nalbuphine (2.5 to 10 mg, IV),[189] and an anesthetic combination of propofol and alfentanil[190] impaired performance on the Maddox Wing test in a dose-related manner. In contrast, fentanyl (25 to 100 μg, IV)[191] and meperidine (0.25 to 1.0 mg, IV)[192] were found to have no effect on Maddox Wing performance. Additionally, fentanyl (50 μg, IV)[193] and an IV combination of fentanyl (50 μg) plus propofol (35 mg),[194] an IV anesthetic, had no effect on the Maddox Wing test. Thus, many opioids have been shown to decrease CFF threshold, a measure of overall CNS arousal, whereas some, but not all, opioids impaired ocular muscle balance.

5.5.2 Motor Abilities

Compared with other measures of performance, few studies have investigated the effects of opioids on pure motor abilities, such as finger tapping and coordination.[16] Kerr et al.[195] used individually tailored steady-state infusions to target several plasma concentrations of morphine (20, 40, and 80 ng/ml). They found that only the high dose of morphine impaired finger tapping and the ability to maintain low constant levels of isometric force, which required precise motor control. Finger tapping rate was decreased in a group of patients with cancer who had received an increase of greater than 30% in their dose of opioid (morphine, hydromorphone, oxycodone, or codeine) compared to a group of patients who did not receive a dosage increase.[196] Finger tapping rate was also decreased following a short-term anesthetic regimen of propofol and alfentanil.[190] In contrast, pentazocine (30 mg) had no effect on finger tapping.[184] Butorphanol (0.5 to 2 mg, IV) and nalbuphine (2.5 to 10 mg, IV) were shown to impair a measure of eye–hand coordination.[189] Slightly over half the studies investigating the effect of opioids on body sway, a measure of gross motor coordination, reported impairment.[16]

5.5.3 Attentional Abilities

A relatively large number of studies have investigated the effects of opioids on tests requiring focused attention. Morphine (2.5 to 10 mg, IV)[185] and propofol (70 mg, IV)[193] impaired an auditory simple reaction time test, and fentanyl (1 to 2.5 ng/ml, IV)[182] impaired a visual choice reaction time test. Jenkins et al.[197] reported that IV (3 to 20 mg) and smoked (2.6 to 10.5 mg) heroin impaired performance on a simple visual reaction time task. However, other studies reported no effect of butorphanol (0.5 to 2.0 mg, IV),[186] fentanyl (25 to 100 μg, IV),[191] meperidine (0.25 to 1.0 mg, IV),[192] and nalbuphine (2.5 to 10 mg, IV)[189] on an auditory simple reaction time test. It may be that visual reaction time tests are more sensitive than auditory tests to the effects of opioids, which would be consistent with opioid-induced impairment on the Maddox Wing test, discussed in the preceding section.

Numerous studies have reported that performance on the DSST was impaired by various opioids, including morphine (2.5 to 10 mg),[185,198] fentanyl (1 to 2.5 ng/ml),[182] pentazocine (30 mg),[184] butorphanol (0.5 to 2 mg),[186] dezocine (2.5 to 10 mg),[187] propofol (22 to 70 mg),[193,199] nalbuphine (2.5 to 10 mg, IV),[189] and the combination of fentanyl (50 μg) plus propofol (35 mg).[194] In contrast, meperidine was found to have no effect on the DSST.[192] Because the DSST is a timed test, it would appear that opioids slow speeded responses in a fairly consistent manner in opioid-naïve subjects. However, in opioid abusers or opioid-dependent persons, Preston and colleagues have reported no effect on DSST performance of several opioids, including morphine (7.5 to 30 mg, IM),[200] hydromorphone (0.125 to 3 mg, IM),[201] buprenorphine (0.5 to 8 mg, IM),[202] pentazocine (7.5 to 120 mg, IM),[203] butorphanol (0.375 to 1.5 mg, IV),[204] and nalbuphine (3 to 24 mg, IM).[205]

Many of these same studies have also reported opioid-induced impairment of a 1-min tracking test in which subjects tracked a randomly moving target on a video monitor with a mouse-controlled cursor. This task measures visual-motor coordination and focused attentional abilities and was impaired by fentanyl (25 to 100 μg, IV),[191,193] meperidine (0.25 to 1.0 mg, IV),[192] butorphanol (0.5 to 2 mg, IV),[186] dezocine (2.5 to 10 mg, IV),[187] and propofol (0.08 to 0.32 mg/kg, IV) alone[199] and in combination with fentanyl (50 μg, IV).[194] Morphine (2.5 to 10 mg, IV) had no effect on the same tracking task.[185] In one of the few studies to investigate the effects of opioids on divided attention, pentazocine (30 mg, IM) was shown to impair the choice reaction time component, but had no effect on the tracking component of a divided attention test.[184] Fentanyl (100 μg, IV) slowed reaction time and movement time in a driving simulator.[206] However, patients suffering noncancer pain receiving transdermal fentanyl for at least 2 weeks showed no impairment on a battery of computerized tests designed to assess driving ability.[207] Further, Galski et al.[208] showed that patients on chronic opioid treatment were not impaired in off-road tests and in a driving simulator. Some studies with morphine have documented impaired sustained attention; however, the few studies that have been conducted with other opioids found no effect on a variety of vigilance tasks.[16,183]

5.5.4 Cognitive Abilities

A relatively large number of studies have examined the effects of opioids on memory and other cognitive functions; a minority of these studies have reported impairment.[16] Kerr et al.[195] found that steady-state levels of morphine (20 to 80 ng/ml, IV) slowed reading time of prose passages. When asked questions about the passage immediately after reading, subjects' recall was not impaired, but delayed questioning revealed impaired comprehension. In methadone-maintained patients, a single methadone dose equal to 100% of their daily stabilization dose impaired delayed recall of a prose passage, whereas 50% of their daily dose slightly improved recall.[209] Fentanyl (1 to 2.5 ng/ml, IV) was shown to impair a range of memorial abilities, including auditory-verbal recall of common words, picture recall, and digit recall.[182] In a group of patients with cancer whose opioid (morphine, hydromorphone, oxycodone, or codeine) dose was increased by at least 30%, decreases were observed in an arithmetic test, backward digit span, and a test of visual memory.[196] Propofol (0.08 to 0.32 mg/kg, IV) impaired delayed, but not immediate recall of a word list only at the highest dose level.[199] In another study, propofol (70 mg, IV), but not fentanyl (50 μg, IV), impaired immediate free recall of words.[193] Walker et al.[189] reported that butorphanol (0.5 to 2 mg, IV), but neither nalbuphine nor pentazocine, slowed responding on a test of logical reasoning.

5.5.5 Summary

Administration of acute, therapeutic doses of opioids to nontolerant research subjects produces effects typical of CNS depressant drugs, including decreased CFF threshold. Many, but not all, opioids produce ocular muscle imbalance as assessed in the Maddox Wing test. Finger tapping and gross motor coordination were found to be impaired in some, but not all, studies. A relatively large number of studies have reported that opioids produce decrements in brief tests requiring focused attention and fine motor coordination, such as visual reaction time, DSST, and visual-motor tracking. Very few studies have examined the effects of opioids on selective, divided, and sustained attention. The effects of opioids on cognitive functioning are mixed, with the majority of studies indicating no impairment, but some well-designed studies showing decrements in memory. When administered to opioid-tolerant individuals, such as opioid abusers or patients with chronic pain, opioids typically produce little or no performance impairment, including impairment of skills related to driving.

5.6 MARIJUANA

Marijuana consists of the dried and crushed leaves and stems of the plant *Cannabis sativa*, which grows worldwide. In the U.S., marijuana is typically rolled in cigarettes (joints) or cigar wrappers (blunts) and smoked. In various parts of the world, other preparations of the cannabis plant are eaten or fumes from the ignited plant material are inhaled. The acute effects of smoked marijuana and Δ^9-tetrahydrocannabinol (THC), the primary psychoactive constituent of marijuana, have been investigated in numerous studies over the past several decades.[10,11] One of the most reliable behavioral effects of acute marijuana is impairment of memory processes; less consistent impairment has been reported for motor and attentional tests. Documenting the effects of chronic marijuana use has been somewhat elusive, with early studies reporting no impairment of cognitive functioning;[210] however, more recent studies have shown chronic marijuana users to be impaired in perceptual-motor abilities,[211] attention,[212,213] mathematical and verbal skills,[214] and learning and memory.[213,215]

Unless otherwise noted, the studies reviewed here examined the acute effects of marijuana and were conducted with experienced marijuana users who smoked standard marijuana cigarettes provided by the National Institute on Drug Abuse (NIDA). These marijuana cigarettes resemble in size an unfiltered tobacco cigarette, weigh 700 to 900 mg, and are assayed by NIDA to determine the percentage of THC by weight. Doses are typically manipulated by using cigarettes that differ in THC content or by varying the number of puffs administered to subjects (five to eight puffs are equivalent to one cigarette). Placebo cigarettes have had active THC removed chemically from the plant material, but when burned, smell identical to an active marijuana cigarette.

Over the years, an intriguing research question with important practical implications has been whether marijuana impairs performance beyond the period of acute intoxication, which typically lasts 2 to 6 h after smoking one or two cigarettes. Studies have documented performance decrements 12 to 24 h after smoking marijuana.[216] One series of studies reported that 24 h after smoking a single marijuana cigarette (2.2% THC), experienced aircraft pilots were impaired attempting to land a plane in a flight simulator;[217,218] however, a third study failed to replicate this next-day effect.[219] In another series of studies, a comprehensive battery of tests revealed that only time estimation[220] and memory[221] were impaired 9 to 17 h after smoking two marijuana cigarettes (2.1 to 2.9% THC), leading the authors to conclude that evidence for next-day performance effects of marijuana was weak. Yet another series of studies found next-day impairment on tests of memory and mental arithmetic after smoking two or four marijuana cigarettes (2.6% THC) over a 4-h period,[222] but not after smoking one marijuana cigarette.[222,223] Thus, residual impairment after acute marijuana dosing appears to be a dose-related phenomenon, with effects more likely to be observed at higher marijuana doses.

Recently, two studies have examined the residual effects of long-term marijuana use.[224,225] In both studies, marijuana smokers were abstinent for 28 days during which time a battery of neuropsychological tests was repeatedly administered. Daily, chronic smokers were compared to less frequent smokers. Bolla et al.[224] reported that daily smokers were impaired on tests of memory, executive functioning, and psychomotor skills after 28 days of marijuana abstinence. In contrast,

Pope et al.[225] found neuropsychological impairment during the first week of abstinence, but by day 28, there were no differences between daily smokers and control subjects. Both studies found that daily smokers evidenced greater impairment than less frequent smokers, which is consistent with the dose-related effect noted above for acute marijuana studies.

Another controversial issue has been the amotivational syndrome supposedly caused by heavy, chronic marijuana use. This syndrome has been characterized by feelings of lethargy and apathy and an absence of goal-directed behavior.[226,227] However, studies conducted in countries where segments of the population use marijuana heavily[228–230] and laboratory-based studies in the U.S.[231,232] have not found empirical support for an amotivational syndrome.

5.6.1 Sensory Abilities

Few studies have investigated the effects of marijuana on CFF threshold. Block et al.[233] reported that one marijuana cigarette (2.6% THC) decreased CFF threshold compared to placebo. However, Liguori et al.[234] found no effect of marijuana (1.8 and 4.0% THC) on CFF threshold. Although more a perceptual process than a sensory ability, a commonly reported effect of marijuana is to increase the subjective passage of time relative to clock time. This typically results in subjects either overestimating an experimenter-generated time interval[220] or underproducing a subject-generated interval.[235] However, Heishman et al.[236] reported that marijuana (3.6% THC; 4, 8, or 16 puffs) had no effect on either time estimation or production.

5.6.2 Motor Abilities

In their review, Chait and Pierri[11] indicated that marijuana produced moderate impairment of balance (increased body sway) and hand steadiness. Consistent with this motor impairment, one marijuana cigarette decreased postural balance as subjects attempted to maintain balance while standing on a platform that moved at random intervals,[237] impaired equilibrium in a computerized test of body sway,[234] and impaired balance in subjects attempting to stand on one leg.[238] Cone et al.[239] found that two marijuana cigarettes (2.8% THC) impaired performance on the circular lights task; however, Heishman et al.[240] reported no effect of marijuana (1.3 and 2.7% THC, two cigarettes) on circular lights performance. Marijuana impaired performance in a test of perceptual motor speed and accuracy.[241] In contrast, several studies have shown that marijuana did not influence finger tapping rate.[11]

5.6.3 Attentional Abilities

A relatively large number of studies have investigated the effects of marijuana on focused attention, including reaction time tests and the DSST. Marijuana (1.8 and 3.6% THC) was shown to slow responding on a simple, visual reaction time task;[242] however, others have not found marijuana to impair simple reaction time performance.[11,40,236] Similarly, some studies have shown that marijuana impairs complex or choice reaction time tasks,[11,233] whereas others have shown no effect.[234] O'Leary et al.[243] found no effect of a 20-mg marijuana cigarette on reaction time in a dichotic listening task.

In general, marijuana also impaired performance on the DSST. In concentrations ranging from 1.8 to 3.6% THC, marijuana has been shown to decrease number of attempted responses (speed) and/or decrease number of correct responses (accuracy) on the DSST.[235,236,238,240,242,244–246] Oral THC (10 and 20 mg) also impaired DSST performance.[247] However, other studies have reported no effect of marijuana (1.3 to 3.6% THC) on the DSST.[40,220,248] The reasons for a lack of effect in these latter studies is unclear given that doses of marijuana were comparable and, in one study,[248] task presentation was identical to those studies reporting impairment. Marijuana (1.2% THC) also impaired selective attention as evidenced by slower responding and greater interference scores in the Stroop color naming test.[249]

Divided attention has generally been shown to be impaired by marijuana. Many divided attention tests consist of a central or primary task and a secondary or peripheral task. Several studies have shown that marijuana impaired detection accuracy and/or stimulus reaction time in one or both test components.[235,245,250] Hart et al.[251] reported that oral THC (20 mg, q.i.d.) and smoked marijuana (3.1% THC, q.i.d.) decreased tracking speed in a divided attention task. Kelly et al.[252] used a complex, 5-min divided attention test, in which an arithmetic task (addition and subtraction of three-digit numbers) was presented in the center of the video monitor and three other stimulus detection tasks were presented in the corners of the monitor. Performance was impaired in a dose-related manner after smoking one marijuana cigarette (2.0 or 3.5% THC). This finding illustrates that marijuana readily disrupts performance in complex tasks requiring continuous monitoring and the ability to shift attention rapidly between various stimuli.

These same attentional abilities are required when operating a motor vehicle. Not surprisingly, laboratory tests that model various components of driving[241] and standardized tests used by law enforcement officials to determine whether a person can safely drive[253,254] have been shown to be impaired by marijuana. Liguori et al.[234] reported that smoked marijuana (1.8 and 4.0% THC) increased braking latency in a driving simulator. Finally, tests of on-road driving found that marijuana moderately increased lateral movement of the vehicle within the driving lane on a highway.[255,256]

Marijuana also impairs sustained attention. In a 30-min vigilance task, hashish users exhibited more false alarms than non-using control subjects.[257] This finding is consistent with the observation that the impairing effects of marijuana on sustained attention are most evident in tests that last 30 to 60 min; tests with durations of 10 min are not adversely affected by marijuana.[11]

5.6.4 Cognitive Abilities

Marijuana has been shown to impair learning in the repeated acquisition and performance of response sequences tasks. Increased errors in the acquisition phase were reported after smoked marijuana (2.0 and 3.5% THC)[244] and oral THC (10 and 20 mg).[247] However, other studies[40,52] have found no effect of smoked marijuana on this test, and one study[251] reported that oral THC (20 mg, q.i.d.) increased the number of completed trials. Block et al.[233] reported that one marijuana cigarette (2.6% THC) impaired paired-associative learning.

As stated previously, one of the most reliable effects of marijuana is the impairment of memory processes. Numerous studies have found that smoked marijuana decreased the number of words or digits recalled and/or increased the number of intrusion errors in either immediate or delayed tests of free recall after presentation of information to be remembered.[220,222,233,236,245,246,249,252] Curran et al.[258] reported that oral THC (15 mg) impaired explicit memory and a selective reminding task, but had no effect on implicit and working memory. Using an extensive battery of cognitive tests, Block et al.[233] reported that marijuana (2.6% THC) slowed response time for producing word associations, slowed reading of prose, and impaired tests of reading comprehension, verbal expression, and mathematics. Heishman et al.[222] also found that simple addition and subtraction skills were impaired by smoking one, two, or four marijuana cigarettes (2.6% THC). Finally, Kelly et al.[252] reported that marijuana (2.0 and 3.5% THC) slowed response time in a spatial orientation test requiring subjects to determine whether numbers and letters were displayed normally or as a mirror image when they were rotated between 90° and 270°. In contrast to these findings, Hart et al.[259] reported that although smoked marijuana (1.8 and 3.9% THC) slowed responding on several measures, it had no effect on accurate performance of tasks measuring cognitive flexibility, arithmetic skills, and reasoning ability.

5.6.5 Summary

Laboratory studies in which subjects smoked marijuana have documented that marijuana impaired sensory-perceptual abilities by reducing CFF threshold and by increasing the subjective passage of time relative to clock time. Marijuana impaired gross motor coordination as measured by body sway and postural balance. However, inconsistent findings have been reported for fine motor control; hand steadiness was impaired, whereas several studies have shown no effect of marijuana on finger tapping. Marijuana has been shown to impair complex, but not simple, reaction time tests. A majority of studies have found that marijuana disrupted performance on the DSST. Complex divided attention tests, including driving a vehicle, were readily impaired by marijuana, as were tests requiring sustained attention for more than 30 min. Numerous studies have documented that smoked marijuana and oral THC impaired learning, memory, and other cognitive processes.

5.7 CONCLUSION

It is evident that a large body of literature exists concerning the effects of psychomotor stimulants, nicotine and tobacco, benzodiazepines, opioids, and marijuana on human performance. As a result, we know much in general about the effects of these psychoactive drugs on sensory, motor, attentional, and cognitive abilities. However, there are some gaps in this literature that need to be filled with data from well-designed, well-controlled studies. For example, few studies have investigated the effects of D-amphetamine or cocaine on cognitive abilities, and, for all drugs, sensory and perceptual processes have received little research attention compared with other aspects of behavior. It is also important to continue investigating specific mechanisms underlying general effects of drugs on behavior. For example, we are beginning to understand the differential effects of benzodiazepines on various components of memory;[124,163] similar studies should be conducted examining the effects of marijuana on memory or the effects of nicotine on cognitive processes. Not only will we learn more about the potentially deleterious effects of drugs on human performance, but drugs can be used as tools to further our understanding of basic processes of performance and cognition.

Two other approaches for future research include the measurement of plasma drug concentrations concomitant with performance and a greater number of drug interaction studies. Very few of the studies reviewed in this chapter provided data on the amount of drug actually delivered to subjects. This is especially critical in studies with tobacco and marijuana because the large variability in smoking behaviors (e.g., length of puffs and depth of inhalations)[246,260] and the low bioavailability of smoked drugs[6,261] result in highly variable delivered drug doses.[262] Virtually none of the tobacco studies and only a few of the marijuana studies reviewed reported plasma drug concentrations. Such data are necessary to relate performance impairment with a known drug concentration. Relatively few studies have investigated the interactive effects of drugs on human behavior.[40,144,151,235] Such basic information is critically needed because the simultaneous use of drugs with different pharmacological effects (e.g., ethanol and marijuana; nicotine and all drugs) is common practice today. It is likely that the combined effect of two or more drugs is very different from that of each drug alone.

Last, laboratory research emphasizing applications of performance effects of psychoactive drugs to the workplace remains relatively uncharted (see Kelly et al., Chapter 6 of this book). Performance assessment batteries need to be tested in the laboratory to determine their validity, reliability, and generalizability to the workplace. Although few performance measures have undergone such rigorous laboratory testing, the methodology exists for assessing the validity, reliability, and sensitivity of a performance task.[263–265] Because much of the drug-induced impairment observed in the workplace will be subtle in nature, laboratory studies should pay greater attention to long-lasting (next day) drug effects and drug withdrawal effects. Additionally, controlled laboratory studies can provide important information concerning a drug's time course of action and its interaction with other drugs.

ACKNOWLEDGMENT

Drs. Heishman and Myers were supported by the NIH Intramural Research Program, NIDA.

REFERENCES

1. Hollingworth, H.L., The influence of caffeine on mental and motor efficiency, *Arch. Psychol.*, 22, 1, 1912.
2. Bates, R.L., The effects of cigarettes and cigarette smoking on certain psychological and physical functions, *J. Comp. Psychol.*, 2, 371, 1922.
3. Weiss, B. and Laties, V.G., Enhancement of human performance by caffeine and the amphetamines, *Pharmacol. Rev.*, 14, 1, 1962.
4. Koelega, H.S., Stimulant drugs and vigilance performance: a review, *Psychopharmacology*, 111, 1, 1993.
5. McNair, D.M., Antianxiety drugs and human performance, *Arch. Gen. Psychiatry*, 29, 611, 1973.
6. Heishman, S.J., Taylor, R.C., and Henningfield, J.E., Nicotine and smoking: a review of effects on human performance, *Exp. Clin. Psychopharmacol.*, 2, 345, 1994.
7. Foltin, R.W. and Evans, S.M., Performance effects of drugs of abuse: a methodological survey, *Hum. Psychopharmacol. Clin. Exp.*, 8, 9, 1993.
8. Hindmarch, I., Psychomotor function and psychoactive drugs, *Br. J. Clin. Pharmacol.*, 10, 189, 1980.
9. Nicholson, A.N. and Ward, J., Eds., Psychotropic drugs and performance, *Br. J. Clin. Pharmacol.*, 18, 1S, 1984.
10. Beardsley, P.M. and Kelly, T.H., Acute effects of cannabis on human behavior and central nervous system function, in *The Health Effects of Cannabis*, Kalant, H., Corrigall, W., Hall, W., and Smart, R., Eds., Addiction Research Foundation, Toronto, 1999, 127.
11. Chait, L.D. and Pierri, J., Effects of smoked marijuana on human performance: a critical review, in *Marijuana/Cannabinoids: Neurobiology and Neurophysiology*, Murphy, L. and Bartke, A., Eds., CRC Press, Boca Raton, FL, 1992, 387.
12. Curran, H.V., Benzodiazepines, memory and mood: a review, *Psychopharmacology*, 105, 1, 1991.
13. Ghoneim, M.M. and Mewaldt, S.P., Benzodiazepines and human memory: a review, *Anesthesiology*, 72, 926, 1990.
14. Koelega, H.S., Benzodiazepines and vigilance performance: a review, *Psychopharmacology*, 98, 145, 1989.
15. Sherwood, N., Effects of nicotine on human psychomotor performance, *Hum. Psychopharmacol. Clin. Exp.*, 8, 155, 1993.
16. Zacny, J.P., A review of the effects of opioids on psychomotor and cognitive functioning in humans, *Exp. Clin. Psychopharmacol.*, 3, 432, 1995.
17. Montoya, A.G. et al., Long-term neuropsychiatric consequences of "ecstasy" (MDMA): a review, *Harvard Rev. Psychiatry*, 10, 212, 2002.
18. Parrott, A.C., Human psychopharmacology of ecstasy (MDMA): a review of 15 years of empirical research, *Hum. Psychopharmacol. Clin. Exp*, 16, 557, 2001.
19. Gavin, F.H. and Ellinwood, E.H., Cocaine and other stimulants: actions, abuse, and treatment, *N. Engl. J. Med.*, 318, 1173, 1988.
20. Jaffe, J.H., Drug addiction and drug abuse, in *The Pharmacological Basis of Therapeutics*, Gilman, A.G., Rall, T.W., Nies, A.S., and Taylor, P., Eds., Pergamon Press, New York, 1990, 522.
21. Fischman, M.W. and Schuster, C.R., Cocaine self-administration in humans, *Fed. Proc.*, 41, 241, 1982.
22. Woolverton, W.L., Kandel, D., and Schuster, C.R., Tolerance and cross-tolerance to cocaine and D-amphetamine, *J. Pharmacol. Exp. Ther.*, 205, 525, 1978.
23. Derlet, R.W. et al., Amphetamine toxicity: experience with 127 cases, *J. Emerg. Med.*, 7, 157, 1989.
24. Myerson, A., Effect of benzedrine sulphate on mood and fatigue in normal and in neurotic persons, *Arch. Neurol. Psychiatry*, 36, 816, 1936.
25. Smith, J.M. and Misiak, H., Critical Flicker Frequency (CFF) and psychotropic drugs in normal human subjects — a review, *Psychopharmacology*, 47, 175, 1976.
26. Farre, M. et al., Alcohol and cocaine interactions in humans, *J. Pharmacol. Exp. Ther.*, 266, 1364, 1993.

27. Peck, A.W. et al., A comparison of bupropion hydrochloride with dexamphetamine and amitriptyline in healthy subjects, *Br. J. Clin. Pharmacol.*, 7, 469, 1979.
28. Bye, C. et al., A comparison of the effects of 1-benzylpiperazine and dexamphetamine on human performance tests, *Eur. J. Clin. Pharmacol.*, 6, 163, 1973.
29. Evans, M.A. et al., Effects of marihuana-dextroamphetamine combination, *Clin. Pharmacol. Ther.*, 20, 350, 1976.
30. Hamilton, M.J., Smith, P.R., and Peck, A.W., Effects of bupropion, nomifensine and dexamphetamine on performance, subjective feelings, autonomic variables and electroencephalogram in healthy volunteers, *Br. J. Clin. Pharmacol.*, 15, 367, 1983.
31. Higgins, S.T. and Stitzer, M.L., Monologue speech: effects of D-amphetamine, secobarbital and diazepam, *Pharmacol. Biochem. Behav.*, 34, 609, 1989.
32. Heishman, S.J. and Stitzer, M.L., Effects of D-amphetamine, secobarbital, and marijuana on choice behavior: social versus nonsocial options, *Psychopharmacology*, 99, 156, 1989.
33. Kinchla, R.A., Attention, *Annu. Rev. Psychol.*, 43, 711, 1992.
34. Warm, J.S., Ed., *Sustained Attention in Human Performance*, Wiley, New York, 1984.
35. McLeod, D.R. et al., An automated version of the digit symbol substitution task (DSST), *Behav. Res. Meth. Instr.*, 14, 463, 1982.
36. Holdstock, L. and de Wit, H., Individual difference in responses to ethanol and D-amphetamine: a within-subject study, *Alcohol. Clin. Exp. Res.*, 25, 540, 2001.
37. Higgins, S.T. et al., Effects of intranasal cocaine on human learning, performance and physiology, *Psychopharmacology*, 102, 451, 1990.
38. Higgins, S.T. et al., Acute behavioral and cardiac effects of cocaine and alcohol combinations in humans, *Psychopharmacology*, 111, 285, 1993.
39. Rush, C.R. and Baker, R.W., Behavioral pharmacological similarities between methylphenidate and cocaine in cocaine abusers, *Exp. Clin. Psychopharmacol.*, 9, 59, 2001.
40. Foltin, R.W. et al., Behavioral effects of cocaine alone and in combination with ethanol or marijuana in humans, *Drug Alcohol Depend.*, 32, 93, 1993.
41. Jenkins, A.J. et al., Correlation between pharmacological effects and plasma cocaine concentrations after smoked administration, *J. Anal. Toxicol.*, 26, 382, 2002.
42. Rush, C.R. et al., Reinforcing and subject-rated effects of methylphenidate and D-amphetamine in non-drug-abusing humans, *J. Clin. Psychopharmacol.*, 21, 273, 2001.
43. Cousins, M.S., Stamat, H.M., and de Wit, H., Acute doses of D-amphetamine and buproprion increase cigarette smoking, *Psychopharmacology*, 157, 243, 2001.
44. Fillmore, M.T., Rush, C.R., and Hays, L., Acute effects of oral cocaine on inhibitory control of behavior in humans, *Drug Alcohol Depend.*, 67, 157, 2002.
45. de Wit, H., Crean, J., and Richards, J.B., Effects of D-amphetamine and ethanol on a measure of behavioral inhibition in humans, *Behav. Neurosci.*, 114, 830, 2000.
46. McKetin, R. et al., Changes in auditory selective attention and event-related potentials following oral administration of D-amphetamine in humans, *Neuropsychopharmacology*, 21, 380, 1999.
47. Servan-Schreiber, D. et al., Dopamine and the mechanisms of cognition: Part II. D-amphetamine effects in human subjects performing a selective attention task, *Biol. Psychiatry*, 43, 723, 1998.
48. Perez-Reyes, M. et al., Interaction between ethanol and dextroamphetamine: effects on psychomotor performance, *Alcohol. Clin. Exp. Res.*, 16, 75, 1992.
49. Mills, K.C. et al., The influence of stimulants, sedatives, and fatigue on tunnel vision: risk factors for driving and piloting, *Hum. Factors*, 43, 310, 2001.
50. Kelly, T.H., Foltin, R.W., and Fischman, M.W., The effects of repeated amphetamine exposure on multiple measures of human behavior, *Pharmacol. Biochem. Behav.*, 38, 417, 1991.
51. Higgins, S.T. et al., Effects of cocaine and alcohol, alone and in combination, on human learning and performance, *J. Exp. Anal. Behav.*, 58, 87, 1992.
52. Foltin, R.W. and Fischman, M.W., The effects of combinations of intranasal cocaine, smoked marijuana, and task performance on heart rate and blood pressure, *Pharmacol. Biochem. Behav.*, 36, 311, 1990.
53. Foltin, R.W. et al., Effects of cocaine, alone and in combination with task performance, on heart rate and blood pressure, *Pharmacol. Biochem. Behav.*, 31, 387, 1988.

54. Soetens, E., D'Hooge, R., and Hueting, J.E., Amphetamine enhances human-memory consolidation, *Neurosci. Lett.*, 161, 9, 1993.
55. Mattay, V.S. et al., Effects of dextroamphetamine on cognitive performance and cortical activation, *NeuroImage*, 12, 268, 2000.
56. Glennon, R.A., Titeler, M., and McKenney, J.D., Evidence for 5-HT2 involvement in the mechanism of action of hallucinogenic agents, *Life Sci.*, 35, 2505, 1984.
57. McGuire, P., Long term psychiatric and cognitive effects of MDMA use, *Toxicol. Lett.*, 112–113, 153, 2000.
58. Kalant, H., The pharmacology and toxicology of "ecstasy" (MDMA) and related drugs, *Can. Med. Assoc. J.*, 165, 917, 2001.
59. Vollenweider, F.X. et al., Opposite effects of 3,4-methylenedioxymethamphetamine (MDMA) on sensorimotor gating in rats versus healthy humans, *Psychopharmacology*, 143, 365, 1999.
60. Thomasius, R. et al., Mood, cognition and serotonin transporter availability in current and former ecstasy (MDMA) users, *Psychopharmacology*, 167, 85, 2003.
61. Cami, J. et al., Human pharmacology of 3,4-methylenedioxymethamphetamine ("ecstasy"): psychomotor performance and subjective effects, *J. Clin. Psychopharmacol.*, 20, 455, 2000.
62. McCann, U.D. et al., Cognitive performance in (±) 3,4-methylenedioxymethamphetamine (MDMA, "ecstasy") users: a controlled study, *Psychopharmacology*, 143, 417, 1999.
63. Gouzoulis-Mayfrank, E. et al., Impaired cognitive performance in drug free users of recreational ecstasy (MDMA), *J. Neurol. Neurosurg. Psychiatry*, 68, 719, 2000.
64. Jacobsen, L.K. et al., Preliminary evidence of hippocampal dysfunction in adolescent MDMA ("ecstasy") users: possible relationship to neurotoxic effects, *Psychopharmacology*, 2003 Nov 28 [Epub ahead of print].
65. Gamma, A. et al., No difference in brain activation during cognitive performance between ecstasy (3,4-methylenedioxymethamphetamine) users and control subjects: a [H215O]-positron emission tomography study, *J. Clin. Psychopharmacol.*, 21, 66, 2001.
66. Parrott, A.C. and Lasky, J., Ecstasy (MDMA) effects upon mood and cognition: before, during and after a Saturday night dance, *Psychopharmacology*, 139, 261, 1998.
67. Parrott, A.C. et al., Cognitive performance in recreational users of MDMA or "ecstasy": evidence for memory deficits, *J. Psychopharmacol.*, 12, 79, 1998.
68. Morgan, M.J. et al., Ecstasy (MDMA): are the psychological problems associated with its use reversed by prolonged abstinence? *Psychopharmacology*, 159, 294, 2002.
69. Verkes, R.J. et al., Cognitive performance and serotonergic function in users of ecstasy, *Psychopharmacology*, 153, 196, 2001.
70. Reneman, L. et al., Cortical serotonin transporter density and verbal memory in individuals who stopped using 3,4-methylenedioxymethamphetamine (MDMA or "ecstasy"), *Arch. Gen. Psychiatry*, 58, 901, 2001.
71. Wareing, M., Fisk, J.E., and Murphy, P.N., Working memory deficits in current and previous users of MDMA ("ecstasy"), *Br. J. Psychol.*, 91, 181, 2000.
72. Rodgers, J., Cognitive performance amongst recreational users of "ecstasy," *Psychopharmacology*, 151, 19, 2000.
73. Croft, R.J. et al., The relative contributions of ecstasy and cannabis to cognitive impairment, *Psychopharmacology*, 153, 373, 2001.
74. Johnston, L.D., O'Malley, P.M., and Bachman, J.G., National survey results on drug use from the Monitoring the Future Study, 1975–1994 (NIH Publication No. 95-4026). U.S. Government Printing Office, Washington, D.C., 1995.
75. Sherwood, N., Kerr, J.S., and Hindmarch, I., Psychomotor performance in smokers following single and repeated doses of nicotine gum, *Psychopharmacology*, 108, 432, 1992.
76. Hindmarch, I., Kerr, J.S., and Sherwood, N., Effects of nicotine gum on psychomotor performance in smokers and non-smokers, *Psychopharmacology*, 100, 535, 1990.
77. Jones, G.M.M. et al., Effects of acute subcutaneous nicotine on attention, information processing and short-term memory in Alzheimer's disease, *Psychopharmacology*, 108, 485, 1992.
78. Kerr, J.S., Sherwood, N., and Hindmarch, I., Separate and combined effects of the social drugs on psychomotor performance, *Psychopharmacology*, 104, 113, 1991.

79. Foulds, J. et al., Cognitive performance effects of subcutaneous nicotine in smokers and never-smokers, *Psychopharmacology*, 127, 31, 1996.
80. Perkins, K.A. et al., Behavioral performance effects of nicotine in smokers and nonsmokers, *Pharmacol. Biochem. Behav.*, 37, 11, 1990.
81. Perkins, K.A. et al., Chronic and acute tolerance to subjective, behavioral and cardiovascular effects of nicotine in humans, *J. Pharmacol. Exp. Ther.*, 270, 628, 1994.
82. West, R.J. and Jarvis, M.J., Effects of nicotine on finger tapping rate in non-smokers, *Pharmacol. Biochem. Behav.*, 25, 727, 1986.
83. Heishman, S.J. and Henningfield, J.E., Tolerance to repeated nicotine administration on performance, subjective, and physiological responses in nonsmokers, *Psychopharmacology*, 152, 321, 2000.
84. Le Houezec, J. et al., A low dose of subcutaneous nicotine improves information processing in nonsmokers, *Psychopharmacology*, 114, 628, 1994.
85. Griesar, W.S., Zajdel, D.P., and Oken, B.S., Nicotine effects on alertness and spatial attention in nonsmokers, *Nicotine Tob. Res.*, 4, 185, 2002.
86. Snyder, F.R. and Henningfield, J.E., Effects of nicotine administration following 12 h of tobacco deprivation: assessment on computerized performance tasks, *Psychopharmacology*, 97, 17, 1989.
87. Parrott, A.C. and Craig, D., Cigarette smoking and nicotine gum (0, 2 and 4 mg): effects upon four visual attention tasks, *Neuropsychobiology*, 25, 34, 1992.
88. Stroop, J.R., Studies of interference in serial verbal reactions, *J. Exp. Psychol.*, 18, 643, 1935.
89. Wesnes, K. and Revell, A., The separate and combined effects of scopolamine and nicotine on human information processing, *Psychopharmacology*, 84, 5, 1984.
90. Provost, S.C. and Woodward, R., Effects of nicotine gum on repeated administration of the Stroop test, *Psychopharmacology*, 104, 536, 1991.
91. Heishman, S.J., Snyder, F.R., and Henningfield, J.E., Performance, subjective, and physiological effects of nicotine in nonsmokers, *Drug Alcohol Depend.*, 34, 11, 1993.
92. Wesnes, K. and Warburton, D.M., Effects of smoking on rapid information processing performance, *Neuropsychobiology*, 9, 223, 1983.
93. Parrott, A.C. and Winder, G., Nicotine chewing gum (2 mg, 4 mg) and cigarette smoking: comparative effects upon vigilance and heart rate, *Psychopharmacology*, 97, 257, 1989.
94. Michel, C. et al., Cardiovascular, electrocortical, and behavioral effects of nicotine chewing gum, *Klin. Wochenschr.*, 66 (Suppl. 11), 72, 1988.
95. Herbert, M., Foulds, J., and Fife-Schaw, C., No effect of cigarette smoking on attention or mood in non-deprived smokers, *Addiction*, 96, 1349, 2001.
96. Wesnes, K., Warburton, D.M., and Matz, B., Effects of nicotine on stimulus sensitivity and response bias in a visual vigilance task, *Neuropsychobiology*, 9, 41, 1983.
97. Wesnes, K. and Revell, A., The separate and combined effects of scopolamine and nicotine on human information processing, *Psychopharmacology*, 84, 5, 1984.
98. Wesnes, K. and Warburton, D.M., Effects of scopolamine and nicotine on human rapid information processing performance, *Psychopharmacology*, 82, 147, 1984.
99. Levin, E.D. et al., Transdermal nicotine effects on attention, *Psychopharmacology*, 140, 135, 1998.
100. Andersson, K. and Post, B., Effects of cigarette smoking on verbal rote learning and physiological arousal, *Scand. J. Psychol.*, 15, 263, 1974.
101. Colrain, I.M. et al., Effects of post-learning smoking on memory consolidation, *Psychopharmacology*, 108, 448, 1992.
102. Warburton, D.M., Rusted, J.M., and Fowler, J., A comparison of the attentional and consolidation hypotheses for the facilitation of memory by nicotine, *Psychopharmacology*, 108, 443, 1992.
103. Warburton, D.M., Rusted, J.M., and Muller, C., Patterns of facilitation of memory by nicotine, *Behav. Pharmacol.*, 3, 375, 1992.
104. Rusted, J., Graupner, L., and Warburton, D., Effects of post-trial administration of nicotine on human memory: evaluating the conditions for improving memory, *Psychopharmacology*, 119, 405, 1995.
105. Rusted, J.M. et al., Effortful processing is a requirement for nicotine-induced improvements in memory, *Psychopharmacology*, 138, 362, 1998.
106. Phillips, S. and Fox, P., An investigation into the effects of nicotine gum on short-term memory, *Psychopharmacology*, 140, 429, 1998.

107. Krebs, S.J., Petros, T.V., and Beckwith, B.E., Effects of smoking on memory for prose passages, *Physiol. Behav.*, 56, 723, 1994.
108. Houlihan, M.E., Pritchard, W.S., and Robinson, J.H., Effects of smoking/nicotine on performance and event-related potentials during a short-term memory scanning task, *Psychopharmacology*, 156, 388, 2001.
109. West, R. and Hack, S., Effect of cigarettes on memory search and subjective ratings. *Pharmacol. Biochem. Behav.*, 38, 281, 1991.
110. Rusted, J. and Eaton-Williams, P., Distinguishing between attentional and amnestic effects in information processing: the separate and combined effects of scopolamine and nicotine on verbal free recall, *Psychopharmacology*, 104, 363, 1991.
111. Houston, J.P., Schneider, N.G., and Jarvik, M.E., Effects of smoking on free recall and organization, *Am. J. Psychiatry*, 135, 220, 1978.
112. Newhouse, P.A. et al., Intravenous nicotine in Alzheimer's disease: a pilot study, *Psychopharmacology*, 95, 171, 1988.
113. Sakurai, Y. and Kanazawa, I., Acute effects of cigarettes in non-deprived smokers on memory, calculation and executive functions, *Hum. Psychopharmacol. Clin. Exp.*, 17, 369, 2002.
114. Dunne, M.P., MacDonald, D., and Hartley, L.R., The effects of nicotine upon memory and problem solving performance, *Physiol. Behav.*, 37, 849, 1986.
115. Johnson, L. and Chernik, D.A., Sedative-hypnotics and human performance, *Psychopharmacology*, 76, 101, 1982.
116. Griffiths, R.R. and Wolf, B., Relative abuse liability of different benzodiazepines in drug abusers, *J. Clin. Psychopharmacol.*, 10, 237, 1990.
117. Woods, J.H., Katz, J.L., and Winger, G., Abuse liability of benzodiazepines, *Pharmacol. Rev.*, 39, 251, 1987.
118. de Wit, H. and Griffiths, R.R., Testing the abuse liability of anxiolytic and hypnotic drugs in humans, *Drug Alcohol Depend.*, 28, 83, 1991.
119. Kunsman, G.W. et al., The use of microcomputer-based psychomotor tests for the evaluation of benzodiazepine effects on human performance: a review with emphasis on temazepam, *Br. J. Clin. Pharmacol.*, 34, 289, 1992.
120. Hindmarch, I., Sherwood, N., and Kerr, J.S., Amnestic effects of triazolam and other hypnotics, *Prog. Neuropsychopharmacol. Biol. Psychiatry*, 17, 407, 1993.
121. Blom, M.W. et al., The effects of alprazolam, quazepam and diazepam on saccadic eye movements, parameters of psychomotor function and the EEG, *Fund. Clin. Pharmacol.*, 4, 653, 1990.
122. Curran, H.V. and Birch, B., Differentiating the sedative, psychomotor and amnesic effects of benzodiazepines: a study with midazolam and the benzodiazepine antagonist, flumazenil, *Psychopharmacology*, 103, 519, 1991.
123. Kerr, J.S., Hindmarch, I., and Sherwood, N., Correlation between doses of oxazepam and their effects on performance of a standardised test battery, *Eur. J. Clin. Pharmacol.*, 42, 507, 1992.
124. Bishop, K.I., Curran, H.V., and Lader, M., Do scopolamine and lorazepam have dissociable effects on human memory systems? A dose-response study with normal volunteers, *Exp. Clin. Psychopharmacol.*, 4, 292, 1996.
125. Saano, V., Hansen, P.P., and Paronen, P., Interactions and comparative effects of zoplicone, diazepam and lorazepam on psychomotor performance and on elimination pharmacokinetics in healthy volunteers, *Pharmacol. Toxicol.*, 70, 135, 1992.
126. Curran, H.V., Schifano, F., and Lader, M., Models of memory dysfunction? A comparison of the effects of scopolamine and lorazepam on memory, psychomotor performance and mood, *Psychopharmacology*, 103, 83, 1991.
127. Rettig, H.C. et al., Effects of hypnotics on sleep and psychomotor performance: a double-blind randomized study of lormetazepam, midazolam and zopiclone, *Anaesthesia*, 45, 1079, 1990.
128. Bond, A., Silveira, J.C., and Lader, M., Effects of single doses of alprazolam and alcohol alone and in combination on physiological performance, *Hum. Psychopharmacol. Clin. Exp.*, 6, 219, 1991.
129. Evans, S.M., Troisi, J.R., and Griffiths, R.R., Tandospirone and alprazolam: comparison of behavioral effects and abuse liability in humans, *J. Pharmacol. Exp. Ther.*, 271, 683, 1994.
130. Preston, K.L. et al., Subjective and behavioral effects of diphenhydramine, lorazepam and methocarbamol: evaluation of abuse liability, *J. Pharmacol. Exp. Ther.*, 262, 707, 1992.

131. Mintzer, M.Z. and Griffiths, R.R., Lorazepam and scopolamine: a single-dose comparison of effects on human memory and attentional processes, *Exp. Clin. Psychopharmacol.*, 11, 56, 2003.
132. Evans, S.M., Funderburk, F.R., and Griffiths, R.R., Zolpidem and triazolam in humans: behavioral and subjective effects and abuse liability, *J. Pharmacol. Exp. Ther.*, 255, 1246, 1990.
133. Kirk, T., Roache, J.D., and Griffiths, R.R., Dose-response evaluation of the amnestic effects of triazolam and pentobarbital in normal subjects, *J. Clin. Psychopharmacol.*, 10, 160, 1990.
134. Roache, J.D. et al., Differential effects of triazolam and ethanol on awareness, memory, and psychomotor performance, *J. Clin. Psychopharmacol.*, 13, 3, 1993.
135. Mintzer, M.Z. and Griffiths, R.R., Triazolam-amphetamine interaction: dissociation of effects on memory versus arousal, *J. Psychopharmacol.*, 17, 17, 2003.
136. Roache, J.D. and Griffiths, R.R., Diazepam and triazolam self-administration in sedative abusers: concordance of subject ratings, performance and drug self-administration, *Psychopharmacology*, 99, 309, 1989.
137. Stoops, W.W. and Rush, C.R., Differential effects in humans after repeated administrations of zolpidem and triazolam, *Am. J. Drug Alcohol Abuse*, 29, 281, 2003.
138. Kumar, R. et al., Anxiolytics and memory: a comparison of lorazepam and alprazolam, *J. Clin. Psychiatry*, 48, 158, 1987.
139. Tobler, I. et al., Effects of night-time motor activity and performance in the morning after midazolam intake during the night, *Arzniemittelforschung*, 41, 581, 1991.
140. Fleishaker, J.C. et al., Psychomotor and memory effects of two adinazolam formulations assessed by a computerized neuropsychological test battery, *J. Clin. Pharmacol.*, 33, 463, 1993.
141. Ingum, J. et al., Relationship between drug plasma concentrations and psychomotor performance after single doses of ethanol and benzodiaepines, *Psychopharmacology*, 107, 11, 1992.
142. Roache, J.D. and Griffiths, R.R., Lorazepam and meprobamate dose effects in humans: behavioral effects and abuse liability, *J. Pharmacol. Exp. Ther.*, 243, 978, 1987.
143. Linnoila, M. et al., Effects of adinazolam and diazepam, alone and in combination with ethanol, on psychomotor and cognitive performance and on autonomic nervous system reactivity in healthy volunteers, *Eur. J. Clin. Pharmacol.*, 38, 371, 1990.
144. Linnoila, M. et al., Effects of single doses of alprazolam and diazepam, alone and in combination with ethanol, on psychomotor and cognitive performance and on autonomic nervous system reactivity in healthy volunteers, *Eur. J. Clin. Pharmacol.*, 39, 21, 1990.
145. Moskowitz, H., Linnoila, M., and Roehrs, T., Psychomotor performance in chronic insomniacs during 14-day use of flurazepam and midazolam, *J. Clin. Psychopharmacol.*, 10, 44S, 1990.
146. Pompeia, S. et al., Lorazepam induces an atypical dissociation of visual and auditory event-related potentials, *J. Psychopharmacol.,* 17, 31, 2003.
147. Ellinwood, E.H. et al., Comparative pharmacokinetics and pharmacodynamics of lorazepam, alprazolam and diazepam, *Psychopharmacology*, 86, 392, 1985.
148. Roache, J.D. et al., Benzodiazepine-induced impairment of matching-to-sample performance in humans, *Pharmacol. Biochem. Behav.*, 36, 945, 1990.
149. Rush, C.R. et al., Acute behavioral effects of lorazepam and caffeine, alone and in combination, in humans, *Behav. Pharmacol.*, 5, 245, 1994.
150. Rush, C.R. et al., A comparison of the acute behavioral effects of triazolam and temazepam in normal volunteers, *Psychopharmacology*, 112, 407, 1993.
151. Rush, C.R. et al., Acute behavioral effects of triazolam and caffeine, alone and in combination, in humans, *Exp. Clin. Psychopharmacol.*, 2, 211, 1994.
152. Rush, C.R., Madakasira, S., and Goldman, N.H., Acute behavioral effects of estazolam and triazolam in non-drug-abusing volunteers, *Exp. Clin. Psychopharmacol.*, 4, 300, 1996.
153. Rush, C.R. and Baker, R.W., Behavioral pharmacological similarities between methylphenidate and cocaine in cocaine abusers, *Exp. Clin. Psychopharmacol.*, 9, 59, 2001.
154. Freidman, H. et al., Pharmacokinetics and pharmacodynamics of oral diazepam: effect of dose, plasma concentration, and time, *Clin. Pharmacol. Ther.*, 52, 139, 1992.
155. Dowd, S.M. et al., The behavioral and cognitive effects of two benzodiazepines associated with drug-facilitated sexual assault, *J. Forensic Sci.,* 47, 1101, 2002.
156. Kelly, T.H. et al., Behavioral response to diazepam in a residential laboratory, *Biol. Psychiatry*, 31, 808, 1992.

157. Brown, G.G., Rich, J.B., and Simkins-Bullock, J., Correlated changes in focused attention and associative encoding following diazepam ingestion, *Exp. Clin. Psychopharmacol.*, 4, 114, 1996.
158. Volkerts, E.R. et al., A comparative study of on-the-road and simulated driving performance after nocturnal treatment with lormetazepam 1 mg and oxazepam 50 mg, *Hum. Psychopharmacol. Clin. Exp.*, 7, 297, 1992.
159. Brookhuis, K.A., Volkerts, E.R., and O'Hanlon, J.F., Repeated dose effects of lormetazepam and flurazepam upon driving performance, *Eur. J. Clin. Pharmacol.*, 39, 83, 1990.
160. Kuitunen, T., Drug and ethanol effects on the clinical test for drunkenness: single doses of ethanol, hypnotic drugs and antidepressant drugs, *Pharmacol. Toxicol.*, 75, 91, 1994.
161. Roache, J.D., Spiga, R., and Burt, D.B., Triazolam and ethanol effects on human matching-to-sample performance vary as a function of pattern size and discriminability, *Drug Alcohol Depend.*, 32, 219, 1993.
162. Mills, K.C. et al., The influence of stimulants, sedatives, and fatigue on tunnel vision: risk factors for driving and piloting, *Hum. Factors,* 43, 310, 2001.
163. Danion, J.N. et al., Pharmacology of human memory and cognition: illustrations from the effects of benzodiazepines and cholinergic drugs, *J. Psychopharmacol.*, 7, 371, 1993.
164. Hommer, D., Weingartner, H., and Breier, A., Dissociation of benzodiazepine-induced amnesia from sedation by flumazenil pretreatment, *Psychopharmacology*, 112, 455, 1993.
165. Roy-Byrne, P.P. et al., Effects of diazepam on cognitive processes in normal subjects, *Psychopharmacology*, 91, 30, 1987.
166. Weingartner, H.J. et al., Selective effects of triazolam on memory, *Psychopharmacology*, 106, 341, 1992.
167. Weingartner, H.J. et al., Specific memory and sedative effects of the benzodiazepine triazolam, *J. Psychopharmacol.*, 7, 305, 1993.
168. Matthews, A., Kirkby, K.C., and Martin, F., The effects of single-dose lorazepam on memory and behavioural learning, *J. Psychopharmacol.*, 16, 345, 2002.
169. Barbee, J.G., Black, F.W., and Todorov, A.A., Differential effects of alprazolam and buspirone upon acquisition, retention, and retrieval processes in memory, *J. Neuropsychiatry Clin. Neurosci.*, 4, 308, 1992.
170. Rusted, J.M., Eaton-Williams, P., and Warburton, D.M., A comparison of the effects of scopolamine and diazepam on working memory, *Psychopharmacology*, 105, 442, 1991.
171. Schifano, F. and Curran, H.V., Pharmacological models of memory dysfunction? A comparison of the effects of scopolamine and lorazepam on word valence ratings, priming and recall, *Psychopharmacology*, 115, 430, 1994.
172. Bixler, E.O. et al., Next-day memory impairment with triazolam use, *Lancet*, 337, 827, 1991.
173. Buchanan, T.W., Karafin, M.S., and Adolphs, R., Selective effects of triazolam on memory for emotional, relative to neutral, stimuli: differential effects on gist versus detail, *Behav. Neurosci.*, 117, 517, 2003.
174. Coupland, N.J. et al., Effects of diazepam on facial emotion recognition, *J. Psychiatry Neurosci.*, 28, 452, 2003.
175. Bickel, W.K., Hughes, J.R., and Higgins, S.T., Human behavioral pharmacology of benzodiazepines: effects on repeated acquisition and performance of response chains, *Drug Dev. Res.*, 20, 53, 1990.
176. Bickel, W.K., Higggins, S.T., and Hughes, J.R., The effects of diazepam and triazolam on repeated acquisition and performance of response sequences with an observing response, *J. Exp. Anal. Behav.*, 56, 217, 1991.
177. Bickel, W.K., Higgins, S.T., and Griffiths, R.R., Repeated diazepam administration: effects on the acquisition and performance of response chains in humans, *J. Exp. Anal. Behav.*, 52, 47, 1989.
178. Judd, L.L., Ellinwood, E., and McAdams, L.A., Cognitive performance and mood in patients with chronic insomnia during 14-day use of flurazepam and midazolam, *J. Clin. Psychopharmacol.*, 10, 56S, 1990.
179. Jaffe, J.H. and Martin, W.R., Opioid analgesics and antagonists, in *The Pharmacological Basis of Therapeutics*, Gilman, A.G., Rall, T.W., Nies, A. S., and Taylor, P., Eds., Pergamon Press, New York, 1990, 485.
180. Chesher, G.B., Understanding the opioid analgesics and their effects on skills performance, *Alcohol Drugs Driving*, 5, 111, 1989.

181. Chapman, S.L., Byas-Smith, M.G., and Reed, B.A., Effects of intermediate- and long-term use of opioids on cognition in patients with chronic pain, *Clin. J. Pain*, 18, S83, 2002.
182. Veselis, R.A. et al., Impaired memory and behavioral performance with fentanyl at low plasma concentrations, *Anesth. Analg.*, 79, 952, 1994.
183. O'Neill, W.M. et al., The cognitive and psychomotor effects of morphine in healthy subjects: a randomized controlled trial of repeated (four) oral doses of dextropropoxyphene, morphine, lorazepam and placebo, *Pain*, 85, 209, 2000.
184. Saarialho-Kere, U., Mattila, M.J., and Seppala, T., Parenteral pentazocine: effects on psychomotor skills and respiration, and interactions with amitriptyline, *Eur. J. Clin. Pharmacol.*, 35, 483, 1988.
185. Zacny, J.P. et al., A dose–response analysis of the subjective, psychomotor and physiological effects of intravenous morphine in healthy volunteers, *J. Pharmacol. Exp. Ther.*, 268, 1, 1994.
186. Zacny, J.P. et al., Comparing the subjective, psychomotor and physiological effects of intravenous butorphanol and morphine in healthy volunteers, *J. Pharmacol. Exp. Ther.*, 270, 579, 1994.
187. Zacny, J.P., Lichtor, J.L., and de Wit, H., Subjective, behavioral, and physiologic responses to intravenous dezocine in healthy volunteers, *Anesth. Analg.*, 74, 523, 1992.
188. Hill, J.L. and Zacny, J.P., Comparing the subjective, psychomotor, and physiological effects of intravenous hydromorphone and morphine in healthy volunteers, *Psychopharmacology*, 152, 31, 2000.
189. Walker, D.J. et al., Subjective, psychomotor, and physiological effects of cumulative doses of mixed-action opioids in healthy volunteers, *Psychopharmacology*, 155, 362, 2001.
190. Haavisto, E. and Kauranen, K., Psychomotor performance after short-term anaesthesia, *Eur. Acad. Anaesthesiol.*, 19, 436, 2002.
191. Zacny, J.P. et al., Subjective and behavioral responses to intravenous fentanyl in healthy volunteers, *Psychopharmacology*, 107, 319, 1992.
192. Zacny, J.P. et al., Subjective, behavioral and physiologic responses to meperidine in healthy volunteers, *Psychopharmacology*, 111, 306, 1993.
193. Thapar, P. et al., Using alcohol as a standard to assess the degree of impairment induced by sedative and analgesic drugs in ambulatory surgery, *Anesthesiology*, 82, 53, 1995.
194. Thapar, P. et al., Objective and subjective impairment from often-used sedative/analgesic combinations in ambulatory surgery, using alcohol as a benchmark, *Ambul. Anesth.*, 80, 1092, 1995.
195. Kerr, B. et al., Concentration-related effects of morphine on cognitive and motor control in human subjects, *Neuropsychopharmacology*, 5, 157, 1991.
196. Bruera, E. et al., The cognitive effects of the administration of narcotic analgesics in patients with cancer pain, *Pain*, 39, 13, 1989.
197. Jenkins, A.J. et al., Pharmacokinetics and pharmacodynamics of smoked heroin, *J. Anal. Toxicol.*, 18, 317, 1994.
198. Marsch, L.A. et al., Effects of infusion rate of intravenously administered morphine on physiological, psychomotor, and self-reported measures in humans, *J. Pharmacol. Exp. Ther.*, 299, 1056, 2001.
199. Zacny, J.P. et al., Subjective and psychomotor effects of subanesthetic doses of propofol in healthy volunteers, *Anesthesiology*, 76, 696, 1992.
200. Preston, K.L., Bigelow, G.E., and Liebson, I.A., Comparative evaluation of morphine, pentazocine and ciramadol in postaddicts, *J. Pharmacol. Exp. Ther.*, 240, 900, 1987.
201. Preston, K.L., Liebson, I.A., and Bigelow, G.E., Discrimination of agonist-antagonist opioids in humans trained on a two-choice saline-hydromorphone discrimination, *J. Pharmacol. Exp. Ther.*, 261, 62, 1992.
202. Strain, E.C. et al., Acute effects of buprenorphine, hydromorphone and naloxone in methadone-maintained volunteers, *J. Pharmacol. Exp. Ther.*, 261, 985, 1992.
203. Strain, E.C. et al., Precipitated withdrawal by pentazocine in methadone-maintained volunteers, *J. Pharmacol. Exp. Ther.*, 267, 624, 1993.
204. Preston, K.L., Bigelow, G.E., and Liebson, I.A., Discrimination of butorphanol and nalbuphine in opioid-dependent humans, *Pharmacol. Biochem. Behav.*, 37, 511, 1990.
205. Preston, K.L., Bigelow, G.E., and Liebson, I.A., Antagonist effects of nalbuphine in opioid-dependent human volunteers, *J. Pharmacol. Exp. Ther.*, 248, 929, 1989.
206. Stevenson, G.W. et al., Driving ability after fentanyl or diazepam: a controlled double-blind study, *Invest. Radiol.*, 21, 717, 1986.

207. Sabatowski, R., Driving ability under long-term treatment with transdermal fentanyl, *J. Pain Symptom Manage.*, 25, 38, 2003.
208. Galski, T., Williams, J.B., and Ehle, H.T., Effects of opioids on driving ability, *J. Pain Symptom Manage.*, 19, 200, 2000.
209. Curran, H.V. et al., Effects of methadone on cognition, mood and craving in detoxifying opiate addicts: a dose–response study, *Psychopharmacology*, 154, 153, 2001.
210. Schaeffer, J., Andrysiak, T., and Ungerleider, J.T., Cognition and long-term use of ganja (cannabis), *Science*, 213, 465, 1981.
211. Varma, V.K. et al., Cannabis and cognitive functions: a prospective study, *Drug Alcohol Depend.*, 21, 147, 1988.
212. Huestegge, L. et al., Visual search in long-term cannabis users with early age of onset, in *Progress in Brain Research*, Hyona, J., Munoz, D.P., Heide, W., and Radach, R., Eds., Elsevier, New York, 2002, 377.
213. Solowij, N. et al., Cognitive functioning of long-term heavy cannabis users seeking treatment, *J. Am. Med. Assoc.*, 287, 1123, 2002.
214. Block, R.I. and Ghoneim, M.M., Effects of chronic marijuana use on human cognition, *Psychopharmacology*, 110, 219, 1993.
215. Pope, H.G. and Yurgelun-Todd, D., The residual cognitive effects of heavy marijuana use in college students, *J. Am. Med. Assoc.*, 275, 521, 1996.
216. Pope, H.G., Gruber, A.J., and Yurgelun-Todd, D., The residual neuropsychological effects of cannabis: the current status of research, *Drug Alcohol Depend.*, 38, 25, 1995.
217. Leirer, V.O., Yesavage, J.A., and Morrow, D.G., Marijuana carry-over effects on aircraft pilot performance, *Aviat. Space Environ. Med.*, 62, 221, 1991.
218. Yesavage, J.A. et al., Carry-over effects of marijuana intoxication on aircraft pilot performance: a preliminary report, *Am. J. Psychiatry*, 142, 1325, 1985.
219. Leirer, V.O., Yesavage, J.A., and Morrow, D.G., Marijuana, aging, and task difficulty effects on pilot performance, *Aviat. Space Environ. Med.*, 60, 1145, 1989.
220. Chait, L.D., Fischman, M.W., and Schuster, C.R., "Hangover" effects the morning after marijuana smoking, *Drug Alcohol Depend.*, 15, 229, 1985.
221. Chait, L.D., Subjective and behavioral effects of marijuana the morning after smoking, *Psychopharmacology*, 100, 328, 1990.
222. Heishman, S.J. et al., Acute and residual effects of marijuana: profiles of plasma THC levels, physiological, subjective, and performance measures, *Pharmacol. Biochem. Behav.*, 37, 561, 1990.
223. Fant, R.V. et al., Acute and residual effects of marijuana in humans, *Pharmacol. Biochem. Behav.*, 60, 777, 1998.
224. Bolla, K.I. et al., Dose-related neurocognitive effects of marijuana use, *Neurology*, 59, 1337, 2002.
225. Pope, H.G. et al., Neuropsychological performance in long-term cannabis users, *Arch. Gen. Psychiatry*, 58, 909, 2001.
226. McGlothin, W.H. and West, L.J., The marihuana problem: an overview, *Am. J. Psychiatry*, 125, 370, 1968.
227. Kupfer, D.J. et al., A comment on the "amotivational syndrome" in marijuana smokers, *Am. J. Psychiatry*, 130, 1319, 1973.
228. Comitas, L., *Cannabis* and work in Jamaica: a refutation of the amotivational syndrome, *Ann. N.Y. Acad. Sci.*, 282, 24, 1976.
229. Stefanis, C., Dornbush, R., and Fink, M., *Hashish: Studies of Long-Term Use*, Raven Press, New York, 1977.
230. Page, J.B., The amotivational syndrome hypothesis and the Costa Rica study: relationship between methods and results, *J. Psychoactive Drugs*, 15, 261, 1983.
231. Mendelson, J.H. et al., Operant acquisition of marihuana in man, *J. Pharmacol. Exp. Ther.*, 198, 42, 1976.
232. Kelly, T.H. et al., Multidimensional behavioral effects of marijuana, *Prog. Neuropsychopharmacol. Biol. Psychiatry*, 14, 885, 1990.
233. Block, R.I., Farinpour, R., and Braverman, K., Acute effects of marijuana on cognition: relationships to chronic effects and smoking techniques, *Pharmacol. Biochem. Behav.*, 43, 907, 1992.
234. Liguori, A., Gatto, C.P., and Robinson, J.H., Effects of marijuana on equilibrium, psychomotor performance, and simulated driving, *Behav. Pharmacol.*, 9, 599, 1998.

235. Chait, L.D. and Perry, J.L., Acute and residual effects of alcohol and marijuana, alone and in combination, on mood and performance, *Psychopharmacology*, 115, 340, 1994.
236. Heishman, S.J., Arasteh, K., and Stitzer, M.L., Comparative effects of alcohol and marijuana on mood, memory, and performance, *Pharmacol. Biochem. Behav.*, 58, 93, 1997.
237. Greenberg, H.S. et al., Short-term effects of smoking marijuana on balance in patients with multiple sclerosis and normal volunteers, *Clin. Pharmacol. Ther.*, 55, 324, 1994.
238. Greenwald, M.K. and Stitzer, M.L., Antinociceptive, subjective and behavioral effects of smoked marijuana in humans, *Drug Alcohol Depend.*, 59, 261, 2000.
239. Cone, E.J. et al., Acute effects of smoking marijuana on hormones, subjective effects and performance in male human subjects, *Pharmacol. Biochem. Behav.*, 24, 1749, 1986.
240. Heishman, S.J., Stitzer, M.L., and Bigelow, G.E., Alcohol and marijuana: comparative dose effect profiles in humans, *Pharmacol Biochem. Behav.*, 31, 649, 1988.
241. Kurzthaler, I. et al., Effect of cannabis use on cognitive functions and driving ability, *J. Clin. Psychiatry*, 60, 395, 1999.
242. Wilson, W.H. et al., Effects of marijuana on performance of a computerized cognitive-neuromotor test battery, *Psychiatry Res.*, 51, 115, 1994.
243. O'Leary, D.S. et al., Effects of smoking marijuana on brain perfusion and cognition, *Neuropsychopharmacology*, 26, 802, 2002.
244. Kelly, T.H., Foltin, R.W., and Fischman, M.W., Effects of smoked marijuana on heart rate, drug ratings and task performance by humans, *Behav. Pharmacol.*, 4, 167, 1993.
245. Azorlosa, J.L. et al., Marijuana smoking: effect of varying Δ^9-tetrahydrocannabinol content and number of puffs, *J. Pharmacol. Exp. Ther.*, 261, 114, 1992.
246. Heishman, S.J., Stitzer, M.L., and Yingling, J.E., Effects of tetrahydrocannabinol content on marijuana smoking behavior, subjective reports, and performance, *Pharmacol. Biochem. Behav.*, 34, 173, 1989.
247. Kamien, J.B. et al., The effects of Δ^9-tetrahydrocannabinol on repeated acquisition and performance of response sequences and on self-reports in humans, *Behav. Pharmacol.*, 5, 71, 1994.
248. Azorlosa, J.L., Greenwald, M.K., and Stitzer, M.L., Marijuana smoking: effects of varying puff volume and breathhold duration, *J. Pharmacol. Exp. Ther.*, 272, 560, 1995.
249. Hooker, W.D. and Jones, R.T., Increased susceptibility to memory intrusions and the Stroop interference effect during acute marijuana intoxication, *Psychopharmacology*, 91, 20, 1987.
250. Marks, D.F. and MacAvoy, M.G., Divided attention performance in cannabis users and non-users following alcohol and cannabis separately and in combination, *Psychopharmacology*, 99, 397, 1989.
251. Hart, C.L. et al., Comparison of smoked marijuana and oral Δ^9-tetrahydrocannabinol in humans, *Psychopharmacology*, 164, 407, 2002.
252. Kelly, T.H. et al., Performance-based testing for drugs of abuse: dose and time profiles of marijuana, amphetamine, alcohol, and diazepam, *J. Anal. Toxicol.*, 17, 264, 1993.
253. Heishman, S.J., Singleton, E.G., and Crouch, D.J., Laboratory validation study of Drug Evaluation and Classification program: ethanol, cocaine, and marijuana, *J. Anal. Toxicol.*, 20, 468, 1996.
254. Heishman, S.J., Singleton, E.G., and Crouch, D.J., Laboratory validation study of Drug Evaluation and Classification program: alprazolam, D-amphetamine, codeine, and marijuana, *J. Anal. Toxicol.*, 22, 503, 1998.
255. Robbe, H.W.J., *Influence of Marijuana on Driving*, University of Limburg Press, Maastricht, 1994.
256. Ramaekers, J.G., Robbe, H.W.J., and O'Hanlon, J.F., Marijuana, alcohol and actual driving performance, *Hum. Psychopharmacol. Clin. Exp.*, 15, 551, 2000.
257. Bahri, T. and Amir, T., Effect of hashish on vigilance performance, *Percept. Mot. Skills*, 78, 11, 1994.
258. Curran, H.V. et al., Cognitive and subjective dose–response effects of acute oral Δ^9-tetrahydrocannabinol (THC) in infrequent cannabis users, *Psychopharmacology*, 164, 61, 2002.
259. Hart, C.L. et al., Effects of acute smoked marijuana on complex cognitive performance, *Neuropsychopharmacology*, 25, 757, 2001.
260. Herning, R.I., Jones, R.T., Bachman, J., and Mines, A.H., Puff volume increases when low-nicotine cigarettes are smoked, *Br. Med. J.*, 283, 1, 1981.
261. Ohlsson, A. et al., Plasma delta-9-tetrahydrocannabinol concentrations and clinical effects after oral and intravenous administration and smoking, *Clin. Pharmacol. Ther.*, 28, 409, 1980.

262. Huestis, M.A., Henningfield, J.E., and Cone, E.J., Blood cannabinoids. I. Absorption of THC and formation of 11-OH-THC and THCCOOH during and after smoking marijuana, *J. Anal. Toxicol.*, 16, 276, 1992.
263. Parrott, A.C., Performance tests in human psychopharmacology (1): test reliability and standardization, *Hum. Psychopharmacol. Clin. Exp.*, 6, 1, 1991.
264. Parrott, A.C., Performance tests in human psychopharmacology (2): content validity, criterion validity, and face validity, *Hum. Psychopharmacol. Clin. Exp.*, 6, 91, 1991.
265. Parrott, A.C., Performance tests in human psychopharmacology (3): construct validity and test interpretation, *Hum. Psychopharmacol. Clin. Exp.*, 6, 197, 1991.

CHAPTER 6

Performance-Based Assessment of Behavioral Impairment in Occupational Settings

Thomas H. Kelly, Ph.D.,[1] Richard C. Taylor, M.A.,[2] Stephen J. Heishman, Ph.D.,[2] and Jonathan Howland, Ph.D.[3]

[1] Department of Behavioral Science, University of Kentucky College of Medicine, Lexington, Kentucky

[2] Clinical Pharmacology and Therapeutics Branch, National Institute on Drug Abuse, National Institutes of Health, Department of Health and Human Services, Baltimore, Maryland

[3] Social and Behavioral Sciences Department, Boston University School of Public Health, Boston, Massachusetts

CONTENTS

6.1 INTRODUCTION

A number of technologies for the assessment of performance impairment have emerged in recent years.[1] These technologies, which include biological sample testing, neuropsychological assessment, personality assessment, and performance testing, are designed to identify risks to safety and/or productivity (e.g., poor health, sleep deprivation, use of behaviorally active drugs/medications), to alter behaviors associated with the development of these risks (e.g., health promotion, reducing drug-taking behavior), and to support the development and evaluation of interventions designed to enhance safety and productivity.[2] Each of these technologies has strengths and limitations.

Biological sample testing is highly specific for the assessment of risk factors associated with the presence of drugs and/or neurotoxins. The primary advantage of biological sample testing is the reliability and validity with which the presence of these risk factors can be detected (e.g., published standards for the development and implementation of drug-testing programs are available).[3] If the integrity of testing procedures is maintained, these technologies can provide accurate information regarding prior exposure to a wide variety of agents. There are a number of disadvantages associated with these technologies, however. The costs associated with development and maintenance of testing programs can be substantial. The collection of biological samples can be invasive. The time required to produce a result following collection of a biological sample can be impractical in applications in which immediate results are necessary. Perhaps the most complicated disadvantage associated with biological sample testing technologies available at the current time is that they provide uncertain information regarding performance effects. Drugs (and their metabolites) remain in biological samples for many hours/days after exposure, well beyond the period of time that is associated with performance-impairing effects. The detection of metabolites in biological samples, therefore, does not always provide sufficient information to determine whether or not a drug is producing effects on human performance.

Neuropsychological testing technologies attempt to measure neurological and behavioral function. These technologies generally involve one-time measurements of physiological and behavioral responses to tests, and clinical interpretations of the results of the tests are based, in part, on comparisons with scores (i.e., norms) collected from populations of individuals with similar characteristics (e.g., age, gender, race).[4] The reliability and validity of neuropsychological testing technologies are regularly and repeatedly tested, and these procedures can be used to assess the acute and long-term effects of environmental perturbations, such as injuries, disease states, and drug exposure, on human capabilities. An appropriately trained professional should conduct neuropsychological test battery administration and interpretation, and as such, the efficiency and expense of this technology may limit its use in applied settings. On the other hand, while designed for acute clinical assessment, many components of neuropsychological test batteries can be administered in a reliable manner on a repeated basis as part of an automated performance testing system. Additional research is needed to determine the validity of the use of components of neuropsychological test batteries in this manner.

Personality testing technologies attempt to identify and measure personality dimensions that differentiate individuals who have increased safety and/or productivity risks (e.g., drug users) from those who do not. Examples of such screening tools include integrity tests, attitude tests, and the measurement of risk factor profiles. Personality testing technologies have been evaluated most critically when used for pre-employment screening; their use in repeated assessments of workers has received less attention. A major concern with regard to this technology is the high rate of false positives (i.e., identification of an individual as being at risk when the individual is, in fact, not at any risk) that has been associated with its use.[5] Concerns regarding whether these approaches will ever achieve a sufficient level of accuracy to effectively measure performance impairment have been raised.[1]

In contrast to neuropsychological testing technologies that are designed for acute clinical assessment, performance testing technologies are designed for repeated measurement of an individual's performance under standardized testing conditions. Clinical evaluations of performance on these tests can be based on population norms (as is the case with many neuropsychological testing technologies) or on deviations from individually determined performance standards established through repeated measurements of an individual's performance (i.e., change from baseline performance). Most performance testing technologies have emerged from laboratory-based research that has occurred over the past three decades (e.g., see Heishman and Myers, Chapter 5). The development and evaluation of performance testing technologies have proliferated in parallel with the availability of the personal computer, and a wide array of tests and systems are available for which significant information regarding reliability and validity exists. The major advantages of performance testing technologies for the detection of performance impairment are the wide variety of options that are available (i.e., the face validity of performance testing can be addressed through careful selection and modification of existing performance tests), the immediate availability of results, and the non-invasive manner in which tests can be administered (relative to biological sample testing). Disadvantages include the lack of specificity with regard to test results (i.e., many factors can alter test performance), and the cost of technology development and implementation. The high costs of performance testing technology development and implementation stem, in part, from a lack of information regarding the optimal use of performance tests in occupational settings. In addition, while the reliability and validity of performance tests have been repeatedly demonstrated in controlled laboratory settings, little evidence regarding the reliability and validity of these procedures in applied settings has been published in peer-reviewed journals. As such, the utility of these procedures has not been clearly established.

The focus of this chapter is on issues associated with the use of performance testing technologies for the detection of drug-induced impairment. Since performance tests are not selectively sensitive to the effects of drugs alone, discussion will focus on the detection of the effects of risk factors, including drug use, sleep deprivation, or adverse physical or mental health, on performance. It is important to note, however, that while this chapter specifically addresses performance testing as a means of impairment detection, no direct or implied recommendation for exclusive development of performance testing technologies for impairment testing is suggested. It is likely that no single technology will be universally effective in all settings or situations. A combination of technologies, based on the availability of resources needed to support those technologies, will likely enhance the effectiveness of any impairment testing system.[1,6]

6.2 ISSUES IN THE SELECTION AND IMPLEMENTATION OF PERFORMANCE TESTING TECHNOLOGIES

The presence of risk factors, such as adverse physical and emotional health, use of behaviorally active drugs/medication, and sleep deprivation, may compromise performance safety and productivity. However, the presence of such risk factors may or may not have implications for how an individual will perform his or her work. An important consideration in the selection of an impairment testing technology is the purpose for which such testing is intended.[7] Impairment testing can be designed to detect the influence of risk factors on performance, regardless of whether or not the effects are related to the individual's work performance. However, impairment testing can also be designed to detect deviations from optimal work performance, regardless of the presence or absence of risk factors.

While the presence of risk factors may or may not have a direct effect on job performance under normal day-to-day operating conditions, it is often assumed that these factors can have an adverse impact on an individual's performance when there is a change from the normal conditions associated with job performance (e.g., the ability to respond safely and effectively to an emergency). If so, the detection of any change in normal performance (e.g., altered performance during a computerized assessment task) signals a change in an individual's capacity that could have adverse implications for job performance. If detection of risk factors is the objective of impairment testing, finding a technology that is reliable and sensitive to many risk factors may be a useful strategy, and concerns regarding reliability and validity in this pursuit become of paramount importance.

On the other hand, detection of the effects of risk factors on performance may have little to say about the likelihood with which an individual will effectively perform an appointed task. From this perspective, risk factors are relevant only if they have adverse effects on normal job performance (i.e., job performance is the relevant metric for impairment testing, not performance on assessment tasks). If the objective of impairment testing is to assess the normal job performance, considerations of the relationship between performance during impairment testing and job performance become a primary concern, and criterion validity issues must be carefully considered. Job simulation tests, such as video-disc simulators for emergency rooms,[8] are examples of performance tests designed to maximize the assessment of on-the-job performance.[2] One advantage of this approach is that employees more easily accept and comply with impairment testing when the ecological or face validity of the testing procedures is apparent.[9] On the other hand, the development costs of simulations can be substantial.

Although it is important to decide on the purpose(s) for performance impairment testing, practical issues must also be considered. Several reviews of practical considerations associated with the selection and implementation of impairment testing technologies have been published, and many details may be obtained from these sources.[4,9–11] However, one primary consideration is the manner in which performance tests will be administered. Performance assessment measures can be administered by trained observers, such as is the common practice with law enforcement personnel who administer field sobriety tests designed to detect the influence of drugs on driving ability, by computers under standardized conditions, or by some combination of these two approaches. The use of trained observers to administer performance impairment tests provides maximum flexibility and minimizes the amount of training and practice required of the test population. However, there are no well-validated observation systems that are currently available, and the reliability of testers will always be a concern, unless reliability and validity assessment can be incorporated into the standard testing protocol. In addition, the recurring personnel costs associated with such testing procedures can be substantial, given the need for repeated test administration.

Automation provides a solution for many of the concerns associated with trained observers. When trained observers are not available, time for testing is limited, or immediate results are needed, automated performance test administration procedures should be considered. It is also possible to standardize the presentation of stimulus materials and data collection with automated testing devices, thereby enhancing the reliability of the testing procedure. Initial development and start-up costs, which are based on the number of testing sites required and the amount of back-up support that is needed, can be substantial, but other than maintenance are not recurring costs. However, clinical interpretation of test results is limited when testing is completely automated and evaluations are based strictly on algorithms that are established as part of the testing system. Even the most automated systems will benefit from human interface for maintenance and set-up support, in addition to data management and interpretation. Given the clear advantages with regard to cost and efficiency, this chapter focuses on automated performance testing technologies.

6.2.1 Selecting a Performance Testing System

When selecting a performance testing system, issues that could affect the practicality, accuracy, and general utility of the system include the specific performance tests that are included in the system, the availability of norms upon which performance can be evaluated (and upon which decisions regarding readiness to perform are based), the reliability and validity of the measures, the accuracy of the measurement, the user interface, and the administrative interface. The relevance of each of these issues is discussed, as are some of the specific questions that merit some consideration when evaluating performance testing systems.

6.2.1.1 Selection of Individual Tests

Performance on various tests is thought to reflect the involvement of selective and, in some cases, isolated dimensions of human capacity, such as sensory and motor ability, attention, and elements of cognition (Heishman and Myers, Chapter 5). Drug effects have also been shown to vary as a function of behavioral mechanisms sustaining performance, including reinforcement contingencies and stimulus context. The use of multiple tests sampling a wide variety of human capacities under a variety of conditions has proved most effective for differentiating among the effects of drugs on behavior.[12] A general description of individual tests is beyond the scope of this chapter, but such descriptions are available elsewhere.[4,12,13] It is important to note that the task parameters and behavioral mechanisms can vary among similar tests when used in different assessment systems; it is critical to consider these variables when interpreting the dimensions of performance being measured within an assessment system.

Sensory tests measure ability to differentiate between objects varying along a stimulus dimension, such as auditory or visual intensity or frequency, or light flicker rate. The critical flicker frequency test is a commonly used type of sensory test.

Motor ability tests focus on measures associated with motor control. The most common examples of motor tasks are finger tapping tests, tracking tests, and hand steadiness tests.

Attention tests include tests of focused attention, in which performance is measured for short durations (typically less than 10 min); selective attention, which involves responding to selected stimuli among a variety of distracting or irrelevant stimuli; divided attention, which requires attention to two or more tasks presented simultaneously; and sustained attention, in which some aspect of the previous three measures of attention is required over longer durations (typically 10 min or longer). Focused attention tests include measures of simple and choice reaction time, pursuit tracking, symbol substitution, encoding/decoding, time estimation, continuous performance (i.e., vigilance), visual monitoring, sequence comparisons, and visual monitoring. Clearly, performance on these tasks includes both sensory and motor components. Selective attention tasks include the Stroop test, Neisser tests, letter and number cancellation tests, dichotic listening tests, and switching or shifting attention tests.

Cognitive tests focus on measures of acquisition, memory, other performance that demonstrates effective use of language and logic, and measures of self-control or inhibition. Acquisition tests include serial and repeated acquisition, and associative learning. Memory tests include immediate and delayed free-recall and recognition tests, matching-to-sample and Sternberg tests, pattern comparison, sequence memory, selective reminding, text memory, the misplaced objects test, facial memory, and digit-span (i.e., digit-recall) or character-recall tests. Other language- or logic-based cognitive performance tests include spatial rotation, pattern matching, the Manikin test, logical reasoning, mental arithmetic, linguistic processing, vocabulary, and the Raven Progressive Matrices test. Measures of self-control include the card-perseveration and Stop/Go tests.

These tests have been used frequently for detection of the effects of risk factors on human performance. The greater the number of tests used in a system, the more comprehensive the assessment, and the more likely it will be that the adverse effects of any risk factor are detected. However, the cost of testing (i.e., test-taking time and training) is also directly related to the number of tests that are included. Many of these tests can be modified to simulate more carefully work-related activities (e.g., digit-recall tasks can be reformulated as telephone number–recall tasks) or incorporated into simulation tasks. Performance impairment test systems use varying combinations of these and other tests; however, there is no commonly agreed-upon strategy for selecting the number or diversity of tasks that are used in a test system. Selection of a system, or collection of tests, must be related to the needs of the testing organization and to the objectives of impairment testing.

6.2.1.2 Reliability and Validity

The selection of performance impairment test systems should also include a thorough consideration of the reliability and validity of the systems. Reliability refers to the consistency of results on the test across repeated testing, and validity refers to the effectiveness with which the test accomplishes its intended purpose, be that identification of the effects of risk factors or the detection of individuals who are at risk for reduced safety and/or productivity in the workplace.

Many performance impairment test systems are based on face validity, or the degree to which the tests appear to accomplish their intended purposes. While face validity is an important consideration with regard to the acceptance of a testing system by management and the workforce, it is, by itself, insufficient for demonstrating the evidence needed to ensure that the test system is indeed accomplishing its intended purposes. Few commercially available performance impairment systems provide adequate evidence of validity, and the evidence that is provided is often limited by the context under which the evidence was collected (i.e., does not generalize to different worksites — ecological validity). It is advised that information regarding the validity of performance testing systems be collected in a proactive manner when the systems are introduced, as there is not sufficient information available to justify even global statements regarding the validity of performance impairment testing systems at the present time.

6.2.1.3 Evaluation Norms

Another important consideration in the selection of an impairment testing system is whether norm-based decision criteria will be used to evaluate readiness to perform an assignment and, if so, whether such norms are currently available. It is important that such norms address both *decrements* and *improvements* in performance, as improved performance may also signal the influence of a risk factor. For example, stimulant medications may have minimal effect on performance of most tasks, but under test conditions requiring sustained attention, enhanced performance may be noted.[14] These same doses of stimulant medication may have important implications for more complex dimensions of human behavior,[15,16] so the detection of enhanced performance may signal an increased risk for detrimental effects on other more complex behaviors that are not directly measured during testing.

Two approaches to the establishment of norms have been proposed.[11] The first approach stresses the development of standards of performance that are universally applied to all individuals, and evaluation of test performance is based on whether an individual performs above or below a given standard. The second approach utilizes the results of prior performance of an individual to establish a baseline upon which to evaluate future performance.

The use of a fixed performance standard has appeal in that simple and consistent criteria may be uniformly applied to all individuals who are taking the test. If these criteria are closely linked with minimal standards of successful work performance, both workers and management can easily recognize and accept the utility of the testing procedure. However, a number of shortcomings with this strategy are also apparent. There are substantial individual differences in performance on most tests, and the routine performance of some individuals may fall below the standard criterion, regardless of risk factors. In addition, performance on tests may change over time, for example, through normal aging processes. An individual who has routinely met performance standards may, over time, exhibit gradually decreasing levels of proficiency that may eventually result in substandard performance. If standardized criteria are used, legal issues associated with discrimination must also be considered,[9] and the inclusion of the test during initial employment evaluations is recommended. The utility of minimal performance standards also presupposes that test performance is a valid indicator of effective work performance (as opposed to a valid indicator of the effect of a risk factor). The evidence needed to support such a supposition is rarely available. Under such conditions, the potential for misuse or abuse of performance test results must be considered.

Change from an individual's own baseline as determined by past performance is the more commonly used criterion for evaluation of the effects of risk factors on performance. Performance measures from previous tests can be evaluated with standardized algorithms to establish objective criteria for evaluating an individual's current or future performance on the same tests under similar test conditions. However, even when baseline measures are used, the establishment of criteria upon which to make decisions regarding whether changes from baseline performance are clinically relevant are oftentimes arbitrary. For example, if a user routinely completed 5.5 trials per minute during a test, what degree of change would be needed to be certain that the performance was influenced by some risk factor, rather than the result of chance variation in normal performance? Individualized variability criteria, which take into account a user's "normal" variance in performance, can be computed, as well, and used as a standard by which to evaluate change from baseline. The efficacy of this approach, however, presupposes that the user will provide samples of performance that are independent of the presence of any risk factor during baseline determinations; if baselines are established while an individual is using drugs, for example, the performance of the individual under the influence of a drug will become the norm. Additional research is needed to establish strategies for the development of effective standards of performance evaluation.[17]

Another complication of the baseline approach concerns the interpretation of relative performance among users. It is quite possible, when using baseline criteria, that the identification of a clinically significant decrement in performance from the normal baseline of one user may occur under conditions in which the level of performance of that user is higher than the performance of another user who is performing at baseline level. Interpretation of changes from baseline is a complicated process, and few standards are currently available.

One issue that is routinely associated with the degree of acceptability of testing programs to the workforce is the consequence of poor performance on a test.[9–11] The establishment of policies regarding the response of management to test failures requires careful consideration. Trice and Steele[9] suggest that coordination between performance testing and employee assistance programs will enhance the utility of both resources in the overall effort to reduce drug use by the workforce, and will enhance the acceptability of programs to both management and the workforce.

Questions have been raised about the feasibility of establishing evaluation norms that can be used across different populations and settings, or with similar tests used on different computer test systems. Certainly, situational factors influence performance on computerized performance tests. In addition, epidemiological factors, such as gender and age, have been demonstrated to influence performance on these tests. Due to mechanical and electronic differences across computer systems, as well as differences in software control techniques, it is perhaps impossible to provide norms that can be used across differing testing platforms. No universally accepted norms for the evaluation of task performance are currently available, and it is highly recommended that a scheduled evaluation of the validity of existing norms be planned in a proactive manner whenever these existing norms are used in new setting.

6.2.1.4 Administrative Interface

The ease and flexibility of the use of performance impairment test systems can be influenced by the interface between the software and test administrator. Characteristics that might be considered include the flexibility in organizing the tests to be delivered, making changes in test parameters, and in the manner in which data are presented, analyzed, and stored for future access.

Another consideration with regard to the administrative interface, as discussed previously, is the degree to which test delivery can be automated. The need for an administrator to be on site for test delivery has cost and efficiency implications. If the test is completely automated, procedures for maintaining accurate identification regarding test sessions (e.g., participant I.D., date, time, etc.) must be established.

6.2.1.5 User Interface

The cost of test delivery can also be influenced by the availability of user interfaces. The user interface can provide access to a variety of support resources to the user, including general instructions and support during training. If an instruction module is available, it should be designed to provide clear, complete, and standardized information and instructions concerning the operation of the test equipment and the completion of task components. One useful feature of an instruction module would be the inclusion of a section designed to assess whether users understood the instructions, particularly if these instructions are important determinants of user performance. This can be accomplished with a series of questions designed to provide additional information when users do not answer questions accurately. The training module should be designed to administer the tests and to provide feedback to users in a manner that enhances the development of stable and reliable performance.

6.2.2 Testing Platform

Hardware considerations for automated performance testing systems generally include the computer, software, monitor, and input devices. These features can be provided on multiple testing platforms, including personal computers, handheld personal digital assistants, Internet-based systems, or on platforms that are specially designed to simulate occupational contexts.

6.2.2.1 Personal Computers

Many government and commercial impairment testing systems can be implemented on standard commercially available personal computer platforms (e.g., PC, Macintosh). Despite software and hardware advancements that have minimized the differences across platforms, it is still important to consider carefully the hardware and software requirements needed to support a system, as these specifications may have important implications for the accuracy of stimulus presentation and the precision of performance measures. In addition, there may be differential costs associated with the hardware and software specifications. The speed of the computer processor is one important specification that requires careful consideration. Other concerns include the amount of memory that is needed to present the test and record the results, the manner in which the data are to be stored, the size and portability of the computer, and the video-display requirements. Some systems may also require additional components, such as joysticks, keyboards, mouse, touch-sensitive monitors, light pens and drawing boards, or response panels.

In general, the processor speeds and memory capacities of modern personal computers are sufficient to support most systems (e.g., milliseconds timing resolution and response monitoring requirements). However, running these systems on older computers having a slower processing speed and limited memory capacity could have a detrimental impact on the accuracy of the test, so caution is recommended.

There are a number of advantages associated with the use of personal computers for supporting performance testing systems. Given the ubiquity of personal computers, personal computers afford a fair amount of flexibility for equipment support and maintenance. If new equipment is acquired, personal computers can support a variety of services when not needed for performance testing. Finally, the availability of numerous personal computer vendors helps to assure reasonable prices and adequate product availability.

There are also some disadvantages associated with the use of personal computers. Desktop computers have limited mobility. Portable personal computers are typically more expensive, have more limited capabilities than desktop machines, and present greater security concerns. Data management can be more complicated if results from different testing occasions are required in a central database or if an individual is tested in multiple settings with different computers.

6.2.2.2 Handheld Personal Digital Assistants

Rapid advances in software and electronic capabilities of personal digital assistants have supported the proliferation of handheld data collection technologies.[18,19] Since these devices are typically less expensive than personal computers, the use of handheld personal digital assistants (PDA) for performance testing reduces the equipment cost of these systems. Like personal computers, these devices can support a variety of services when not needed for performance testing, particularly if each user is provided with his or her own device. The portability of the devices permits testing to occur in a greater variety of contexts and times, thereby enhancing the flexibility and reducing the cost of data collection.

There are disadvantages to the use of handheld devices, as well. Most importantly, the video display and response input capabilities of these devices are much more limited than for personal computers. Stimulus and response requirements are critical elements of many tasks and, as such, PDAs may limit the range of tasks that can be included in a performance testing system. Security concerns are even greater than those presented by portable computers, and data management can be an even greater challenge than with personal computers, given the limitations in data exchange options associated with these devices.

6.2.2.3 Web-Based Systems

Although not yet available, it is likely that Web-based performance testing systems will become available in the near future. Web-based systems will permit selected tasks to be presented on computers equipped with appropriate Web browser software. Hardware requirements include Internet access and appropriate memory and software to support Web-based applications. Depending on the design of the Web-based system, it is could be possible to tailor the specific tasks presented for the performance testing system from a menu of options. Alternatively, testing systems consisting of a standardized array of tasks can also be chosen. As such, the start-up costs of Web-based systems should be lower than with personal or handheld computer systems. Subject identification, date, and time can be recorded at the start of a test, and data from multiple subjects and test occasions can be stored in a central file for easy access to the data.

There are some clear disadvantages associated with Web-based systems, as well. The most important limitation is that the flexibility of the performance test systems is necessarily restricted to the range of tasks and associated parameters that are available through the Web-based software. While individualized software could be requested, it is likely that there will be additional time and monetary costs associated with each request. Second, stimulus presentation and response inputs may be variable across test sites unless standardized systems are used to access the Web-based software. It may also be difficult to use standardized norms to evaluate task performance, due to variable stimulus and response conditions that may exist across test sites. Finally, although the start-up costs may be reduced, there will be greater recurrent costs associated with repeated use of the Web-based software.

6.2.3 Test Implementation

In addition to considerations of impairment testing systems and the equipment and platform to administer the systems, the implementation of the testing system must also be considered. Test cost, frequency of administration, maintenance of stable patterns of performance (i.e., motivation), and worker acceptance are among the issues that merit consideration.[11] In addition, concerns regarding the legal status of performance test systems, the manner in which labor unions and arbitrators might view such test systems, and whether there is a potential for misuse of the test system could affect system implementation.[9]

6.2.3.1 Cost

Test costs include the initial expense of acquiring the test equipment and providing a test space, the time required to complete the test, and administrative costs (e.g., record keeping, test set-up, maintenance and replacement of equipment). However, test costs may be complicated by the presence of hidden factors, as well.[10] For example, cost of training the users may be substantial. Based on the consequences of test failure, lost work time may also be factored in, particularly under conditions in which the false positive rate (i.e., identification of the influence of a risk factor on a user's performance when none, in fact, exists) is high. There are additional costs associated with initial negotiations between management and workers concerning the appropriateness of a testing program and the consequences of test failure, and potential costs associated with litigation, should it occur.

6.2.3.2 Test Frequency

No clear landmarks exist for making decisions regarding test frequency. In general, tests are administered before an individual begins an assigned work activity. However, risk factors can emerge at any time, and are not limited to activities that occur before work activities begin. For example, the effects of fatigue, illness, and drug use can all occur after work has begun, and would not be measured by tests occurring only at the beginning of a work activity. In addition, it is not clear whether the frequency of test administration influences the reliability of test performance. If tests are administered on a regular basis, or if rest intervals (e.g., weekends) separate successive tests, motivational changes may influence performance.

6.2.3.3 Maintenance of Performance Stability

Repeated administration of tests, without contingencies designed to maintain motivation, invariably result in decrements in performance over time. Maintenance of motivated performance across repeated administration of a test is an important consideration during the implementation of an impairment testing system. It is generally assumed that under conditions in which access to assigned work activities, and financial compensation for that work, is contingent on suitable test performance, motivated performance is likely to be maintained across repeated testing.[10]

However, there have not been adequate investigations of this assumption, and it is likely that emotional behavior would also occur if access to work were denied as a result of poor performance on a test. The use of additional contingencies that target performance stability might be helpful, in addition to the seemingly punitive consequence of loss of work opportunities associated with poor performance. It has been suggested that the use of more complex or varied testing procedures may also help eliminate changes in motivation over time. Clearly, additional research on these issues is needed.

6.2.3.4 User Acceptance

Another important consideration with regard to the implementation of an impairment testing system is the acceptance of the test system by the workforce. Worker acceptance is influenced by the comfort in taking the tests, as well as by test relevance, or face validity, availability, and accuracy.[11] Comfort refers to the degree to which worker performance on these tests is acceptable under routine testing conditions, and may be inversely related to the likelihood of false-positive outcomes. Relevance, or face validity, is associated with the extent to which workers report that performance during the test will reflect performance of their assigned work tasks. Availability refers to the reliability of the test equipment — if the tests cannot be administered when scheduled, confidence in the accuracy of the test system is questioned. Accuracy refers to the extent to which the test results are related to risk factors. Workers receive direct or indirect feedback on test systems (i.e., pass or fail). Rates of false positives (failures given the absence of any risk factor) and false negatives (passes given worker recognition of the influence of a potential risk factor, such as drug use) influence worker estimates of test accuracy.

6.2.3.5 Legal Issues

No clear guidelines exist with regard to the legal status of performance impairment test systems. In comparison with employee selection criteria, Trice and Steele[9] suggest that the legality of these test systems may be related to the degree to which their use results in discriminatory outcomes. They cite Klein's[20] description of an 80% rule as a workable strategy for assessing discriminatory practices. If the pass rate obtained when testing of any race, sex, or ethnic group is less than 80% of the group with the highest pass rate, then the test system has an adverse impact. Trice and Steele[9] also indicate that the absence of information regarding a cause of test failure could have a negative impact on considerations of the legality of test systems, because under such conditions employees might feel unduly compelled to reveal details of their personal lives.

The status of performance impairment test systems with regard to fair-labor practices is also undetermined at the present time. Trice and Steele[9] suggest that since biological sample testing approaches to the detection of drug use have been ruled in the past to be a mandatory labor practice, and as such, require bargaining with labor or unions prior to implementation, performance test systems would likely be viewed in a similar manner. However, they also note that, because performance tests are less invasive than biological sample testing procedures and can be demonstrated to have greater job relatedness, employers could make the case that performance impairment test systems can be implemented unilaterally without bargaining.

6.2.3.6 Potential for Misuse of Test Systems

Misuse of performance impairment tests is related to the consequences of worker performance. Test systems can be implemented with the sole purpose of providing feedback to workers regarding their level of performance (i.e., no consequences associated with work activities are imposed). The objective of such testing procedures is to provide workers with information to use to adjust their own on-work and off-work behavior in an attempt to more accurately monitor their own levels of safety and productivity. For example, in describing a feasibility study of the implementation of a performance testing system, truck drivers adjusted their own rest behavior based on feedback they received during performance testing, even though that feedback was unrelated to drivers' work eligibility.[21] On the other hand, systems that use the results of performance on impairment tests to influence work eligibility (and possibly employment status) are more likely to involve some risk for test misuse.

No clear guidelines exist for the appropriate use of performance impairment test systems for work eligibility. There is general agreement that in situations in which worker or public safety is potentially influenced by a worker's performance, impairment test systems are justified. However, no clear criteria for identifying safety issues are available.[9] The use of such tests as a means of managing worker productivity is less universally accepted, and if used as an employee evaluation criterion, such tests should be given careful scrutiny.

6.3 APPLICATIONS OF IMPAIRMENT TESTING TECHNOLOGIES

Currently, application of laboratory-based performance assessment technologies occurs in at least three settings. The most frequent utilization of this technology is in the law enforcement setting. Law enforcement personnel have varying amounts of training and experience in the administration of performance tests and in the interpretation of the behavior of individuals during test performance. In addition, law enforcement personnel have limited opportunities to compare their own evaluations of performance on field sobriety tests with the results of drug assays from blood tests taken concurrently with the tests in order to monitor the accuracy of their evaluations. Under these conditions, the reliability and validity of the field sobriety test remain largely unknown, in spite of its widespread utilization. Results from recent assessments of the reliability and validity of performance-based drug evaluation programs, such as sobriety testing, are presented here.

A second application of laboratory-based performance assessment technologies has been in the field of fitness-for-duty assessment, primarily supported by military and other government agencies. A varied number of fitness-for-duty assessment batteries have been developed; several of these are reviewed here. A major strength of these fitness-for-duty assessment batteries is the availability of a substantial database on the reliability and validity with which these batteries can detect changes in performance related to a number of manipulations, including drug administration, sleep deprivation, and exposure to extreme environments.

A third application of laboratory-based performance assessment technologies has been in the field of readiness-to-perform assessment in workplace settings. Many of the approaches to readiness-to-perform assessment that are being used in workplace settings have evolved from strategies that are currently in use in government-sponsored performance assessment batteries or laboratory settings, but, in general, these approaches have been subjected to reliability and validity assessment with less consistency. Several assessment technologies that have been subjected to some reliability and validity assessment are described here.

6.3.1 Law Enforcement Applications: Drug Evaluation and Classification Program

6.3.1.1 Background

Motor vehicle accidents are the leading cause of death in the U.S. for people aged 1 to 34.[22] Studies investigating the prevalence rate of drugs other than alcohol in fatally injured drivers have reported varied results, ranging from 6 to 37%.[23–27] Among individuals stopped for reckless driving who were judged to be clinically intoxicated, urine drug testing indicated 85% were positive for cannabinoids, cocaine metabolites, or both.[28] These relatively high prevalence rates reinforce the general assumption that psychoactive drugs are capable of impairing driving,[29,30] although drug prevalence rates do not imply impaired driving.[31,32] Because certain drugs reliably degrade psychomotor and cognitive performance in the laboratory (Heishman and Myers, Chapter 5), many drug-related vehicular accidents and DUI/DWI arrests probably involve impaired behaviors critical for safe driving.

Currently, the only standardized procedure for detecting drug-induced impairment is the Drug Evaluation and Classification (DEC) program,[33] which is used by police departments throughout the nation. The DEC program consists of a standardized evaluation conducted by a trained police officer (Drug Recognition Examiner, DRE) and the toxicological analysis of a biological specimen. The evaluation involves a breath alcohol test, examination of the suspect's appearance, behavior, eye movement and nystagmus, field sobriety tests, vital signs, and questioning of the suspect. From the evaluation, the DRE concludes (1) if the suspect is behaviorally impaired such that he or she is unable to operate a motor vehicle safely, (2) if the impairment is drug-related, and (3) the drug class(es) likely causing the impairment. The toxicological analysis either confirms or refutes the DRE's drug class opinion.

Several field studies have indicated that DREs' opinions were confirmed by toxicological analysis in 74 to 92% of cases when DREs concluded suspects were impaired.[17,34–38] These studies attest to the validity of the DEC program as a measurement of drug-induced behavioral impairment in the field. However, the validity of the DEC evaluation has not been rigorously examined under controlled laboratory conditions. Heishman, Singleton, and Crouch[39,40] have examined the validity of the individual measures of the DEC evaluation in predicting whether research volunteers were administered various drugs of abuse. A synopsis of these studies is presented.

6.3.1.2 Method

Research volunteers were recruited from the community. Before the study, participants were given psychological and physical examinations to determine whether they were healthy and capable of participating in the study. At each test session, a single drug dose or placebo was administered under double-blind conditions. Sessions were separated by 48 to 72 h. In Study 1, participants received oral ethanol (0, 0.28, 0.52 g/kg); intranasal cocaine (4, 48, 96 mg/70 kg); and smoked marijuana (0, 1.75, 3.55% Δ^9-tetrahydrocannabinol [THC], 16 puffs). In Study 2, participants received oral alprazolam (0, 1, 2 mg); oral D-amphetamine (0, 12.5, 25 mg); codeine (0, 60, 120 mg); and smoked marijuana (0, 3.58% THC, 8 puffs). Dosing of the various drugs was staggered so that the DEC evaluation occurred during peak drug effect.

The DEC evaluation began with an ethanol breath test. DREs measured pulse and recorded information about physical defects, corrective lenses, appearance of the eyes, and visual impairment. DREs also assessed eye tracking and nystagmus, pupillary size, and condition of eyelids. The next segment involved examination of the eyes and performance of four field sobriety tests (FST). Subjects' eyes were tested for horizontal gaze nystagmus, vertical nystagmus, and convergence. The FST were Romberg Balance (RB), Walk and Turn (WT), One Leg Stand (OLS), and Finger to Nose (FN). The RB assessed body sway and tremor while subjects stood for 30 s with feet together, arms at sides, head tilted back, and eyes closed. The WT test required subjects to take nine heel-to-toe steps along a straight line marked on the floor, turn, and return with nine heel-to-toe steps. The OLS assessed balance by having subjects stand on one leg, with the other leg elevated in a stiff-leg manner 15 cm off the floor for 30 s. Subjects were given a brief rest between right and left leg testing. In the FN test, subjects stood as in the RB and brought the tip of the index finger of the left or right hand (as instructed) directly to the tip of the nose. DREs then measured pulse, blood pressure, and oral temperature.

The final portion involved further examination of the eyes. DREs estimated the diameter of each pupil to the nearest 0.5 mm under conditions of ambient room light, nearly total darkness, indirect light, and direct light. While illuminating the eyes under direct light from a penlight for 15 s, DREs assessed constriction of the pupils and fluctuation of pupillary diameter. Last, DREs measured pulse and assessed muscle tone, attitude, coordination, speech, breath odor, and facial appearance.

6.3.1.3 Results

The 76 variables derived from the DEC evaluation were first analyzed using stepwise discriminant analysis to determine the variables that best predicted the presence or absence of each drug. This subset of best-predictor variables was then subjected to a discriminant function analysis that predicted and classified whether subjects were dosed or not dosed with drug. The resulting data were classified as true positive, true negative, false positive, or false negative. These parameters were then used to calculate several measures of predictive accuracy of the DEC evaluation, including sensitivity, specificity, and efficiency.

In Study 1, the stepwise discriminant analysis resulted in a subset of 17 variables that were the best predictors of ethanol. The discriminant function comprising these 17 variables predicted the presence or absence of ethanol with extremely high accuracy. The model was equally accurate in predicting the presence (sensitivity = 94.4%) and absence of ethanol (specificity = 92.6%); overall predictive efficiency was 93.3%. The analysis also resulted in a subset of 17 variables that were the best predictors of dosing with cocaine. The discriminant function predicted the presence or absence of cocaine with high accuracy. The model had greater specificity (96.3%) than sensitivity (88.9%), and efficiency was 93.3%. The stepwise discriminant analysis resulted in a subset of 28 variables that best predicted the presence or absence of marijuana. The discriminant function comprising these 28 variables predicted the presence (sensitivity = 100%) and absence (specificity = 98.1%) of marijuana with extremely high accuracy; predictive efficiency was 98.8%.

In Study 2, the stepwise discriminant analysis resulted in a subset of seven variables that were the best predictors of alprazolam. The model was more accurate in predicting the absence of alprazolam (specificity = 96.7%) than its presence (sensitivity = 78.3%), and predictive efficiency was 90.4%. The analysis resulted in a subset of three variables that were the best predictors of dosing with D-amphetamine. As with alprazolam, the model's predictions had greater specificity (92.5%) than sensitivity (75.0%), and efficiency of the model was high (86.5%). The discriminant analysis resulted in a subset of two variables that were the best predictors of codeine. The model's predictions had much greater specificity (92.4%) than sensitivity (34.8%), and efficiency was moderate (73.2%). The discriminant analysis resulted in a subset of seven variables that were the best predictors of marijuana. The model predicted with greater accuracy the absence (specificity = 93.3%) of marijuana than its presence (sensitivity = 61.4%); predictive efficiency was 82.7%.

6.1.3.4 Conclusion

The validity of the DEC evaluation was examined by developing mathematical models based on discriminant functions that identified the subsets of variables that best predicted whether subjects were dosed with placebo or active drug. The data clearly indicated that a subset of variables of the DEC evaluation accurately predicted acute administration of various psychoactive drugs across several pharmacological classes, including alprazolam, D-amphetamine, marijuana, ethanol, cocaine, and to a lesser extent codeine. These findings suggest that predictions of impairment and drug use may be refined if DREs focused on a subset of variables associated with each drug class, rather than the entire DEC evaluation.

6.3.2 Government Application: Tests of Fitness for Duty

6.3.2.1 Background

Much of the early interest in the area of human performance testing was funded and manned by several branches of the U.S. Military. The successful military mission depends on optimal performance by its personnel. Hostile and hazardous environments may have subtle to profound influences on a soldier's performance.[41] The goal of military human performance research was to identify those environments and agents that cause a deterioration in ability, and to what degree. With this knowledge, military personnel could attempt to compensate for, or avoid, undesirable environments or agents. A comprehensive review of many assessment batteries used by government agencies, which includes a review of evidence related to the reliability and validity of the batteries, can be found elsewhere.[4,7]

6.3.2.2 Computerized Performance Test Batteries

Most government-sponsored computerized performance test batteries are compilations of computer performance tests that were originally developed and tested in controlled laboratory settings. The purpose of many of these tests is to determine the effects of risk factors on fitness for government duty, and to assess the efficacy of countermeasures designed to offset the performance effects of these risk factors.

Unified Tri-Service Cognitive Performance Assessment Battery

The Unified Tri-Service Cognitive Performance Assessment Battery (UTC-PAB) was constructed by the Tri-Service Working Group on Drug Dependent Degradation of Military Performance, which eventually became known as the Office of Military Performance Assessment Technology (OMPAT).[42] OMPAT, which was headed by Fred Hegge, included representatives from the U.S. Navy, Air Force, and Army. The group developed a standardized laboratory tool to assess cognitive performance using repeated measures in a tri-service chemical-defense biomedical drug-screening program.[43] All the tasks in the test battery were designed to run on standard MS DOS platform computers with graphical presentation and keyboard responding.

The UTC-PAB is a library of cognitive tests that can be modified into smaller subsets or batteries for a specific purpose. The original UTC-PAB consisted of 25 tasks that were chosen due to their construct validity, reliability, and sensitivity to levels of cognitive functioning. Several of the commonly known subsets or variations include the Testor's Workbench/Automated Neuropsychological Assessment Metrics (TWB/ANAM or ANAM) battery, the Naval Medical Research Institute Performance Assessment Battery (NMRI-PAB), the UTC-PAB/NATO AGARD STRES Battery, and the Criterion Task Set (CTS).[43]

The UTC-PAB's modular design offered the investigator the freedom of customized batteries by combining any number of the tasks, and in any order. This enabled researchers to utilize only those tasks that best suited the needs of each protocol or evaluation. Accuracy and response time were automatically measured and the data collection updated for any of the tasks that were selected. Numerous parameters of the individual tasks could be modified such as stimulus duration, intertrial interval, number of stimulus presentations, and length of the task. Instruction screens and help files could be modified as well. The default parameter settings for the UTC-PAB tasks were patterned from the North Atlantic Treaty Organization AGARD-STRES Battery.[44]

Table 6.1 contains the individual tasks of the UTC-PAB. These tasks measure a variety of human cognitive and psychomotor functioning, including focused attention, selective attention, divided attention, memory, and a variety of additional task components.[4,7]

Walter Reed Army Institute Performance Assessment Battery

The Walter Reed Army Institute Performance Assessment Battery (WRPAB) was designed by Dr. David Thorne, Fred Hegge, and colleagues at the Walter Reed Army Institute of Research, Division of Neuropsychiatry, Department of Behavioral Biology. This battery was also supported by OMPAT, but was designed to measure changes in performance over time as a function of acute perturbations (e.g., drugs, fatigue, sleep deprivation) as opposed to serving as a screening tool.[45]

Table 6.1 Task Components of the Unified Tri-Service Cognitive Performance Assessment Battery (UTC-PAB)

Focused Attention
Complex Reaction Time
Visual-Motor Tracking
Substitution (Symbol-Digit or Code)
Time Estimation
Continuous Performance
Sequence Comparison
Visual Monitoring
Selective Attention
Stroop
Nessier
Dichotic Listening
Divided Attention
Acquisition
Repeated Acquisition
Memory
Match/Nonmatch to Sample
Sternberg Memory
Pattern Comparison
Sequence Memory
Other Cognitive Performance
Spatial Rotation-Sequential
Pattern Matching
Manikin
Grammatical/Logical Reasoning
Arithmetic Computation
Serial Add/Subtract
Linguistic Processing

The WRPAB was designed to offer investigators a menu of individual cognitive, perceptual, and psychomotor tests from which investigators could choose specific tests to best support a given application. Table 6.2 lists the individual tasks of the WRPAB. These tasks assess focused attention, selective attention, acquisition, memory, and a variety of additional task components.[45] A user-friendly building routine allows for the development of smaller, individualized PABs. Options are available to adjust the software to match the testing equipment and for specifying the characteristics of the data output, and individual task parameters can be adjusted by using documentation that accompanies the software. The software operates on the MS DOS platform with graphic screen presentation on a local or remote monitor with responding performed on a standard keyboard.[45] Installation of a timer card may be necessary to ensure precise timing.

As mentioned earlier, the WRPAB is best suited for experiments with repeated measured designs involving treatments, dosages, or differing environments. Specific tasks in the WRPAB have been found to be sensitive to certain psychoactive drugs. Several government agencies have implemented the WRPAB as a research tool. For example, the National Institute on Drug Abuse Intramural Research Program has studied the effects of nicotine and nicotine replacement on smokers' and nonsmokers' cognitive abilities and attention processes using the Two-[46,47] and Six-Letter Search.[46] Cognitive abilities were also measured using the WRPAB Digit Recall and Logical Reasoning tasks.[46,47]

Table 6.2 Task Components of the Walter Reed Army Institute Performance Assessment Battery (WRPAB)

Focused Attention
Complex Reaction Time
Substitution (Symbol-Digit or Code)
Encoding/Decoding
Time Estimation
Selective Attention
Stroop
Nessier
Acquisition
Associative Learning
Memory
Match/Nonmatch to Sample
Sternberg Memory
Pattern Comparison
Sequence Memory
Other Cognitive Performance
Manikin
Grammatical/Logical Reasoning
Arithmetic Computation
Serial Add/Subtract

Naval Medical Research Institute Performance Assessment Battery

The Naval Medical Research Institute Performance Assessment Battery (NMRI-PAB) was developed to measure the effects of a wide variety of military environments upon the technically oriented tasks of Marine and Naval personnel. The battery's methodology was based on a tri-service methodology in an attempt to standardize measurement of human performance in military environments.[41] The NMRI-PAB, like the WRPAB and UTC-PAB, is a menu-driven, microcomputer-based assessment tool that comprises individual tasks.

The NMRI-PAB consists of eight individual tasks that measure different aspects of human functioning (Table 6.3). The software controller allows the experimenter to modify certain aspects of task presentation. The software collects detailed information about subject's accuracy and speed of responding. Since the NMRI-PAB is microcomputer based, multiple subjects can participate simultaneously and in different locations. The software runs on standard MS DOS platform with graphical screen presentation and keyboard responding. The design of this assessment tool allows for repeated measures testing. The individual tasks of the NMRI-PAB measure the following areas of human cognitive functioning, including focused attention, selective attention, memory, and a variety of additional task components.[4]

Advisory Group for Aerospace Research and Development–Standardized Test for Research with Environmental Stressors Battery

The Advisory Group for Aerospace Research and Development–Standardized Test for Research with Environmental Stressors Battery (AGARD-STRES) was developed to investigate the effects of environmental stress on human performance.[44] After receiving funding from the U.S. Air Force,

Table 6.3 Task Components of the Naval Medical Research Institute Performance Assessment Battery (NMRI-PAB)

Focused Attention

Continuous Performance

Selective Attention

Stroop

Memory

Match/Nonmatch to Sample
Sternberg Memory
Pattern Comparison

Other Cognitive Performance

Spatial Rotation-Sequential
Manikin
Grammatical/Logical Reasoning

the Advisory Group for Aerospace Research and Development (AGARD) set out to construct a standardized performance assessment battery using tests that had proved successful in stress research. The group utilized seven of the individual tests from the UTC-PAB.[44] The AGARD-STRES battery was designed to provide a standardized method of task presentation (e.g., the seven tests are presented in a predetermined order, and the task parameters are designed to remain constant) in order to more effectively compare performance on these tasks across subject populations and settings. The software runs on standard MS DOS platform with graphical screen presentation with keyboard input. This would facilitate standardization and allow researchers to compare all administrations of the battery equally. This assessment tool is well suited for repeated measures research.

Table 6.4 presents the individual tests of the AGARD-STRESS battery. Focused attention, divided attention, and memory categories of tasks are included in this battery, in addition to a variety of other tasks.

Table 6.4 Task Components of the Advisory Group for Aerospace Research and Development — Standardized Test for Research with Environmental Stressors Battery (AGARD-STRESS)

Focused Attention

Complex Reaction Time
Visual-Motor Tracking

Divided Attention: Memory

Sternberg Memory

Other Cognitive Performance

Spatial Rotation-Sequential
Grammatical/Logical Reasoning
Serial Add/Subtract

Table 6.5 Task Components of the Automated Neuropsychological Assessment Metrics (ANAM)

Focused Attention
Complex Reaction Time
Visual-Motor Tracking
Memory
Sternberg Memory
Character/Number Recall
Other Cognitive Performance
Spatial Rotation
Spatial Rotation-Sequential
Grammatical/Logical Reasoning
Serial Add/Subtract

Automated Neuropsychological Assessment Metrics

The Automated Neuropsychological Assessment Metrics assessment battery (ANAM) is a modified version of the AGARD STRES battery. The ANAM was developed primarily as a screening tool for assessing neuropsychological functioning and has been used in military and commercial aviation applications. This battery has added pursuit tracking, which requires a mouse for completion, and has eliminated tracking, dual task, and reaction time tasks from the AGARD STRES battery because these tasks engendered unsuitably variable performance. A tracking test, running memory test, the Walter Reed mood scale, and the Stanford sleepiness scale were substituted.

Table 6.5 presents the various tasks of the ANAM battery assess. Focused attention and memory categories of tasks are included in this battery, as well as a variety of additional task components.

The Spaceflight Cognitive Assessment Tool (S-CAT) is a variant of the ANAM that was compiled by NASA's Behavioral Health and Performance Group (BHPG) to assist in behavioral monitoring and assessment of flight crew health.[48] The battery was designed to assess memory, sustained concentration, working memory, and recall and was developed for use aboard the Space Station Mir and the International Space Station, as well as to support future prolonged space missions.

Another variant is the ANAM Readiness Evaluation System (ARES), a multiple-user cognitive testing system designed to run on PDAs using the Palm OS.[49] This system also incorporates many of the features of the ANAM. ARES is shipped with three standard test batteries. The NeuroCog battery is primarily used for monitoring the recovery of individuals with CNS damage. It is designed for use by neuropsychologists with ANAM interpretation experience. The ARES Commander is a self-monitoring battery that assesses concentration, working memory, and mental efficiency. The ARES Warrior is designed as a neurocognitive screening tool, which can be used by medical personnel during field operations. Custom batteries can also be created with provided support software.[49]

Neurobehavioral Evaluation System 2

The Neurobehavioral Evaluation System 2 (NES2) is a neurobehavioral evaluation system designed to facilitate screening of populations at risk of nervous system damage due to environmental agents. This evaluation system is administered on a microcomputer. Epidemiologic research influenced the sets of tests that were included in this battery. An expert committee convened by the World Health Organization (WHO) and the National Institute for Occupational Safety and Health (NIOSH) proposed a set of core tests for this battery. Many of the core tests that were

Table 6.6 Task Components of Neurobehavioral Evaluation System 2 (NES2)

Motor Ability Tests
Finger Tapping
Focused Attention
Simple Reaction Time
Substitution (Symbol-Digit or Code)
Continuous Performance
Selective Attention
Switching/Shifting Attention
Acquisition
Serial Acquisition
Associative Learning
Memory
Pattern Comparison
Character/Number Recall
Other Cognitive Performance
Pattern Matching
Grammatical/Logical Reasoning
Arithmetic Computation
Vocabulary

chosen are adaptations of preexisting clinical instruments that have been recognized as valuable tools in investigating neurotoxin exposure.[50]

Table 6.6 presents the individual tests of the NES2 battery. Motor ability, focused attention, selective attention, acquisition, and memory categories of tasks are included in this battery, in addition to a variety of other tasks. The battery is made up of separate tasks; performance on combinations of these tasks is potentially altered by exposure to neurotoxic agents such as pesticides, solvents, or carbon monoxide. Many of the tasks are suitable for repeated testing of any individual. Five of the tests are similar to the core tests of the WHO battery.[50]

The NES2 software was developed using IBM Advanced BASIC. The software is menu-driven and allows the interviewer to choose the individual tasks that are presented at any one session. The software was designed to run on IBM PC-compatible hardware with a standard DOS operating system. Response inputs occur through a joystick with a pair of push-buttons.[50]

Baker and colleagues[50] found that the validity and stability of three tests in the NES2 were comparable to five previously validated traditional interviewer-administered neuropsychological instruments. High correlations were reported between individual trials of the same interviewer-administered task. Stability on four of the computerized tests was supported by high correlations between scores when research subjects were tested on four separate days.

Automated Portable Test System

The Performance Evaluation Tests for Environmental Research Program (PETER), jointly sponsored by the U.S. Navy and NASA, attempted to identify measures of human cognitive, perceptual, and motor abilities that would be sensitive to environmental perturbations that are associated with decrements in safety and productivity. An extensive collection of literature yielded more than 140

Table 6.7 Task Components of the Automated Portable Test System (APTS)

Motor Ability Tests
Finger Tapping
Focused Attention
Simple Reaction Time
Complex Reaction Time
Substitution (Symbol-Digit or Code)
Time Estimation
Continuous Performance
Sequence Comparison
Visual Monitoring
Selective Attention
Stroop
Neisser
Acquisition
Associative Learning
Memory
Sternberg Memory
Pattern Comparison
Sequence Memory
Character/Number Recall
Other Cognitive Performance
Spatial Rotation
Spatial Rotation-Sequential
Pattern Matching
Manikin
Grammatical/Logical Reasoning
Arithmetic Computation
Serial Add/Subtract
Linguistic Processing
Spatial Visualization

tests that were rated for reliability and sensitivity. The PETER Program incorporated those tasks that were most suitable for repeated-measures applications. Inclusion criteria were met if a task's intertrial correlations were unchanging and variances were homogenous across baselines.[51]

The Automated Portable Test System (APTS) evaluation system is an outgrowth of the work of the PETER Program. The PETER Program had identified tests that were reliable, stable, and sensitive to environmental and toxic stressors. Kennedy and colleagues[52] adopted and computerized a core set of 18 tasks from the PETER Program's recommended list of performance tasks suitable for repeated measures application. Those tasks are listed in Table 6.7.

The APTS was designed for portability works on IBM PC compatible systems running on a standard MS DOS operating system.[53] The battery measures abilities of motor function, focused attention, selective attention, acquisition, and memory, as well as spatial perception and reasoning, mathematical calculation, and other language skills.[4,7] Similar to most of the computerized performance assessment batteries, additions and deletions of individual components have occurred as the battery has matured and been used in different applications.

Table 6.8 Task Components of the Memory Assessment Clinics Battery (MAC)

Focused Attention	
	Complex Reaction Time
Divided Attention	
Acquisition	
	Associative Learning
Memory	
	Match/Nonmatch to Sample
	Selective Reminding
	Text Memory
	Misplaced Objects
	Facial Memory
	Character/Number Recall

Memory Assessment Clinics Battery

The Memory Assessment Clinics Battery (MAC) was designed to assess the effects of pharmacological treatments on simulated memory tasks.[54] Intended to study potentially cognitive-enhancing pharmaceutical compounds, the battery is also used to assess age-related memory differences in ongoing clinical trials. Initial testing of the MAC Battery was administered on an AT&T 6300 computer utilizing color graphic presentation, laser-disk technology, and touch-screen responding along with other custom-made manipulanda.

The battery mimics real-life memory and recognition demands, such as remembering a 7- or 10-digit telephone number, or associating a name with a face. Table 6.8 presents the individual tasks of the MAC battery. Focused attention, divided attention, acquisition, and memory categories of tasks are included in this battery.

Synwork

Many performance batteries involve the administration of varied tasks, each of which requires the focused application of a limited number of cognitive or motor skills, in a sequential manner. One concern that has repeatedly been raised regarding the use of sequential laboratory tests as a system for measuring performance impairment is that such systems do not assess all human capabilities, including some that are critically dependent for job performance. For example, while performance tests may assess specific abilities, such as reaction time or learning ability, it may be unusual in job settings for such activities to be required in a sequential manner. Elsmore and colleagues[55] contend that real-world human behaviors or operations may consist of two or more of these attributes and abilities occurring concurrently. Effective job performance may require the ability to engage in multiple tasks in a simultaneous or continuous manner, adjusting between task requirements as priorities change. It is unclear whether such higher-order performance requirements are effectively assessed in sequential performance test systems.

In contrast to PAB-like tasks involving the sequential presentation of individual performance tasks, Synwork attempts to emulate the simultaneous or continuous task demands of real-world jobs by requiring subjects to perform four individual tasks presented concurrently in one of four quadrants of a screen.[55] The tasks are presented on a standard IBM PC compatible computer with DOS operating platform. Subjects interact with the software by manipulating a standard mouse. The individual tasks of the Synwork software measure attention and working memory (Sternberg Memory Task); mathematical calculations (Arithmetic task); spatial perception and reasoning

(Visual Monitoring); and auditory perception and reasoning (Auditory Monitoring). A more detailed account of the Synwork software can be found in Elsmore et al.[56]

Elsmore and colleagues,[55] while examining the impairing effects of sleep deprivation, demonstrated that subjects find Synwork to be more interesting and demanding than a sequentially administered PAB-like version, but performance engendered by Synwork is less sensitive to the effects of sleep deprivation than the same tasks presented simultaneously.

Psychomotor Vigilance Task

The Walter Reed Army Institute of Research's Department of Behavioral Biology has developed a field-deployable version of a commercial Psychomotor Vigilance Task (PVT) that has been widely used in sleep research. The software runs on handheld PDAs running the Palm Operating System (Palm OS). It is modeled after the simple reaction time task of Wilkinson and Houghton,[57] as modified by Dinges and Powell.[58] The Palm OS version incorporates additional stimulus, feedback, control, and data options developed by Dr. Thorne. In laboratory studies, performance on the PDA task has been shown to be sensitive to time-on-task fatigue effects, sleep deprivation, and circadian variation.[18] Field studies have utilized the PVT to measure the efficacy of caffeine gum as a sleep loss countermeasure.

MiniCog

A Palm OS-based cognitive testing system, called MiniCog, is currently under development by the National Space Biomedical Research Institute's (NSBRI) neurobehavioral and psychosocial factors team. It will contain cognitive tasks that assess attention (vigilance, divided attention, and filtering), motor control, verbal and spatial working memory, and verbal and spatial reasoning. The development team has designed this testing system for both spaceflight and ground-based research. MiniCog project development is currently obtaining norms from healthy subjects in a laboratory setting.[19]

6.3.3 Occupational Application: Readiness To Perform Tests

6.3.3.1 Background

Given the complex nature of many commercial work environments, as well as the reciprocal interactions between employers and employees, factors associated with the development and implementation of performance impairment test systems in commercial environments become equally complex. In addition to the selection of test systems that are reliable and valid indicators of performance impairment, it is equally important to consider issues associated with worker acceptance of the testing system, time associated with the test, and the economic implications of use and non-use of impairment test systems. Substantial research into the use of impairment testing systems has been conducted over the past decade; however, the vast majority of this work is available only in company reports and/or technical monographs; with few exceptions (e.g., Delta), little information is available in peer-reviewed scientific publications.

6.3.3.2 Performance Tests in Applied Settings

Four applications of laboratory-based performance impairment test systems are described. These systems have been chosen to be presented for two reasons. First, they provide examples of the use of test systems for the measurement of performance impairment in commercial settings. Second, some information regarding the reliability and validity of these systems is available.

NovaScan, Nova Technology, Inc.

The NovaScan is a testing paradigm, rather than a fixed performance test, in that the system represents a method of presenting selected tests in a manner that standardizes the attentional requirements of the test user. The paradigm also allows for measurement of elements of attention allocation. The testing paradigm is designed to present any combination of a subset of 30 individual tasks originally developed and validated through the UTC-PAB project, described above. The tasks that are presented can be selected based on the specific needs of the test application (e.g., different combinations of tests have been used for different commercial applications, based on the specific needs/interests of the company employing the NovaScan). The resulting test system is designed to assess a variety of job-related skills, as well as generic attentional processes associated with the completion of the tasks, in a time-efficient manner.

The NovaScan is presented on a PC-compatible computer equipped with standard memory and visual capabilities, and is run on a DOS-based operating system. A customized response apparatus, including a joystick, control keys, and a keypad, is recommended. Trials of the tasks chosen to be included in the test system are displayed on the computer monitor in a random manner, thereby eliminating the need for the user to focus attention among simultaneously presented tests. However, divided attention components can be added, if needed. The length of the test (i.e., number of trials presented) can be adjusted based on the demands of the test environment. Performance is evaluated in an automated fashion using a change-from-baseline approach, and the test can be administered in an automated or supervisor-controlled manner.

The NovaScan has received substantial testing in a number of laboratory and applied settings. Performance on the NovaScan has been demonstrated to be sensitive to the effects of alcohol, marijuana, diazepam, amphetamine, scopolamine, and an over-the-counter antihistamine.[6,59,60] In addition, epidemiological differences in performance associated with gender, age, and occupation have been considered. Variations of the testing paradigm have been used in a number of commercial settings.

Delta, Essex Corporation

Delta, a commercial performance impairment testing system produced by the Essex Corporation, was derived from the Automated Portable Test System (APTS) evaluation system, which, in turn, was based on the work of the Performance Evaluation Tests for Environmental Research Program (PETER), a jointly sponsored U.S. Navy and NASA program designed to identify measures of human cognitive, perceptual, and motor abilities that would be sensitive to environmental perturbations that are associated with decrements in safety and productivity.

The Delta system contains many of the same tests contained in the APTS system, including those that monitor motor function, reaction time, attention and working memory, learning and memory, spatial perception and reasoning, mathematical calculation, and language (Table 6.1). More complete descriptions of the psychometric and validity studies supporting the utility of this testing system are available elsewhere.[61,62]

Performance on the Delta system has been demonstrated to be sensitive to the effects of alcohol, amphetamine, scopolamine, chemoradiotherapy, and hypoxia.[63–66] The Delta test system has been used in a number of applied settings, including airplane and tank operator training sites.[61,62]

Performance-on-Line, SEDICorp

Performance-on-Line is a software-based cognitive and psychomotor divided-attention task designed to evaluate tunnel vision, a rapid change in visual system activity in response to stress, that at elevated levels is associated with driving risk.[67] The task was derived from the hardware-based Simulated Evaluation of Driver Impairment (SEDI) distributed by SEDICorp. SEDI was found to generate performance that was highly reliable and sensitive to the effects of alcohol and marijuana.[68,69] SEDI used numeric displays that were novel to some subjects, and the memory-intensive instructions were found to be difficult to remember for some individuals. The hardware-based SEDI was also costly, and subjects frequently reported eye-muscle fatigue after its use.[70]

The Performance-on-Line software was designed to include language-free graphics and instructions that were not memory-intensive. Central and peripheral targets that are presented simultaneously require independent visual discrimination and responding. The software is designed to run on any computer using a DOS operating system. It supports a color graphic display and utilizes keyboard response inputs. The test is self administered, provides on-screen instructions, and has five independent levels of difficulty. An administrative interface allows for parametric modifications, such as whether or not performance feedback is provided to participants. The data are stored in formatted files that allow for easy use with other commercial spreadsheet or data analysis programs.[70] The Performance-on-Line software predicts driving performance[71] and engenders behavior that is sensitive to the effects of sleep deprivation, alcohol, and other drugs.[72]

CogScreen-Aeromedical Edition

In the late 1980s the Federal Aviation Administration (FAA) supported the development of a computer-based cognitive screening tool, CogScreen.[4] The goal of the FAA was to create a testing system that was sensitive to changes in cognitive function. If left unnoticed, cognitive dysfunction may result in poor pilot judgment or slow reaction time in critical operational situations.[73] Several phases of task selection and normative data collection yielded a cognitive testing system comprised of 11 tasks.[4] The current version, CogScreen-Aeromedical Edition (CogScreen-AE), is used during the medical re-certification evaluation of aviators suspected and/or known to have neurological or psychiatric conditions. This cognitive testing system detects changes in attention, immediate- and short-term memory, visual perceptual functions, sequencing functions, logical problem solving, calculation skills, reaction time, simultaneous information processing abilities, and executive functions.

6.3.4 Occupational Applications: Simulation

6.3.4.1 Background

An occupational simulation is a representation that approximates the actual operating conditions of a job.[2] Different scenarios can be used to represent specific sets of conditions developed for the purpose of assessing discrete sets of occupational skills within specified contexts.[74] Although initially developed for training purposes, they have evolved as tools for assessing skills for educational or formal certification purposes and are being used more frequently for evaluating occupational fitness. Simulation has most often been used to evaluate workers' ability to use machinery or drive vehicles. It has been more challenging to assess the job performance of other professionals, such as lawyers, doctors, and managers, with computer-based simulation, because their tasks are varied and complex. Recent developments in the use of actors in defined roles have expanded the use of simulation in a broader array of professions.

In those cases where simulation is possible, it can offer some important advantages. Simulation allows participants to perform job functions under a range of circumstances without risk of injury or adverse economic consequences. For example, within a given scenario, it is possible to monitor performance within contexts that approach or reach catastrophe (e.g., pilot response to problems during flight; account representative management of competition). Safety is an important attribute of simulation. A second advantage of simulation is that it permits the repeated assessment with specified scenarios, thereby supporting the assessment of reliability. High reliability is a necessary attribute for any effective performance assessment method, a threat when assessment is conducted in natural settings. A third advantage is that simulation can provide consistency in assessment procedures, which, in turn, allows for the comparison of performance across individuals or across worksites when individuals or groups are measured repeatedly over time. A simulated assessment exercise can also be recorded and played back. This provides an opportunity for participants to repeatedly observe their own performance within the context of a given scenario. Another advantage of simulation is that it supports assessment in rare or unusual contexts. The true measure of an employee may lie in performance during the low-probability real-world conditions with major safety or economic implications. Simulation provides a means to evaluate performance in low-probability but significant contexts. A final advantage of simulation is that the complexity and difficulty can be systematically altered within a given scenario. Employee ability to maintain effectiveness and efficiency as complications escalate is an important measure of performance capacity.

There are important limitations to simulation that deserve consideration, as well. As with all assessment strategies, validity should be questioned. Clearly, performance assessment that takes place in the occupational setting while work is actually performed is the most valid approach. Simulations can make employees feel as if they are operating under normal conditions; however, it is also clear that job performance expressed in a simulator is not "real." With regard to capturing the workplace context, simulators are still superior to computerized performance batteries. Nonetheless, performance assessment using computerized batteries can offer a greater degree of control over contextual variables that can influence performance, and can provide more precise measurement of specific functions, such as cognition, reaction time, divided attention, and memory, than is possible during simulation. Simulation provides a gross measure of overall job performance, whereas computerized batteries offer precise assessment of more elementary dimensions of performance. As simulators try to incorporate key elements of the workplace context, they become vulnerable to unknown confounding due to these contextual representations.

6.3.4.2 Simulations in Experimental Settings

Howland and colleagues[75] used maritime simulators that replicated merchant ship operation to test the effects of low-dose alcohol exposure in two separate scenarios. Maritime cadets were randomly assigned to receive either 0.00 (placebo) or 0.04 g% blood alcohol concentration, or BAC (a relatively low dose equivalent to two to three commercial cocktails). Significant alcohol-induced impairment was observed on simulated power plant operation and piloting.[76] The testing of simulated ship operation the day after random dosing at 0.10 g% BAC (five or more commercial cocktails) is ongoing. These experimental studies using a single occupational model are consistent with the adverse associations of heavy alcohol use derived from large-scale cross-sectional surveys of worker performance.[77] Simulation picked up subtle effects of low-dose alcohol sedation on work performance that are not visible in surveys. Furthermore, the merchant ship experiments could not have been conducted ethically without the use of simulators.

Automobile and truck simulators have also been used in randomized studies to demonstrate the impairing effects of various doses of alcohol.[78–80] Similar studies have been conducted using flight simulators.[81–85] In addition, both types of simulators have been used to assess the effects of marijuana, nicotine, and other sedative medications.[86–88] Simulations have also been used to examine other environmental perturbations, including sleep deprivation and elevated carbon dioxide levels.[89,90]

6.4 CONCLUSION

This chapter focused on issues associated with the use of performance testing technologies for the detection of performance impairment. While the application of this technology remains largely untested, the evidence presented in this chapter strongly suggests that this technology shows promise as a component of performance impairment testing systems. A substantial database regarding the reliability and validity of performance tests for measuring the effects of risk factors on human performance has been established, and initial efforts at developing performance testing systems made effective use of this database. Limitations with regard to the predictive validity of these tests continue to be addressed in modifications to existing testing systems, as well in the development of more sophisticated simulation testing systems. Issues regarding the selection and implementation of performance testing systems have been addressed in recent publications.[4,9–11] Clearly, careful and systematic evaluations of the use of these systems in applied settings are warranted.

It is important to note, however, that while this chapter specifically addressed performance testing as means of impairment detection, there is no evidence to suggest that performance testing systems are more effective than other impairment testing systems. Trice and Steele[9] suggest that performance testing systems may have practical advantages over more common biological sample testing systems, including potentially being more widely accepted by the workforce, requiring less invasive testing requirements, and interfacing more efficiently with existing employee assistance programs, but no evidence to support such claims is available, due to the limited information regarding the use of these systems. It is likely that no single technology will be universally effective in all settings, or even on one setting across all individuals over time. The combination of technologies, based on the availability of resources needed to support those technologies, will likely enhance the effectiveness of any impairment testing system.

ACKNOWLEDGMENT

Mr. Taylor and Dr. Heishman were supported by the NIH Intramural Research Program, NIDA.

REFERENCES

1. Normand, J., Lempert, R.O., and O'Brien, C.P., *Under the Influence? Drugs and the American Work Force,* National Academy Press, Washington, D.C., 1994, chap. 6.
2. Howland, J., Mangione, T.W., and Laramie, A., Simulation for measurement of occupational performance, unpublished data, 2004.
3. Finkle, B.S., Blanke, R.V., and Walsh, M.J., Technical, Scientific and Procedural Issues of Employee Drug Testing, U.S. Department of Health and Human Services, Washington, D.C., 1990.
4. Kane, R.L. and Kay, G.G., Computerized assessment in neuropsychology: a review of tests and test batteries, *Neuropsychol. Rev.*, 3, 1, 1992.
5. Murphy, K.R., *Honesty in the Workplace*, Brooks Cole, Pacific Grove, CA, 1993.
6. Kelly, T.H. et al., Performance-based testing for drugs of abuse: dose and time profiles of marijuana, amphetamine, alcohol and diazepam, *J. Anal. Toxicol.*, 17, 264, 1993.
7. Gilliland, K. and Schlegel, R.E., Readiness to Perform Testing: A Critical Analysis of the Concept and Current Practices, U.S. Department of Transportation, National Technical Information Service, Springfield, VA, 1993.
8. Gerber, B., Simulating reality, *Training*, 27, 41, 1990.
9. Trice, H.M. and Steele, P.D., Impairment testing: issues and convergence with employee assistance programs, *J. Drug Issues*, 25, 471, 1995.
10. Gilliland, K. and Schlegel, R.E., Readiness-to-perform testing and the worker, *Ergon. Des.*, January, 14, 1995.
11. Miller, J.C., Fit for duty? Performance testing tools for assessing public safety and health workers' readiness for work, *Ergon. Des.*, April, 11, 1996.
12. Heishman, S.J., Taylor, R.C., and Henningfield, J.E., Nicotine and smoking: a review of effects on human performance, *Exp. Clin. Psychopharmacol.*, 2, 345, 1994.
13. Zacny, J.P., A review of the effects of opioids on psychomotor and cognitive functioning in humans, *Exp. Clin. Psychopharmacol.*, 3, 432, 1995.

14. Fischman, M.W., Cocaine and the amphetamines, in *Psychopharmacology: The Third Generation of Progress*, Meltzer, H.Y., Ed., Raven Press, New York, 1987, 1543.
15. Fischman, M.W., Kelly, T.H., and Foltin, R.W., Residential laboratory research: a multidimensional evaluation of the effects of drugs on behavior, in Drugs in the Workplace: Research and Evaluation Data, Vol. II, NIDA Research Monograph 100, Gust, S.W., Walsh, J.M., Thomas, L.B., and Crouch, D.J., Eds., U.S. Government Printing Office, Washington, D.C., 1991, 113.
16. Kelly, T.H., Foltin, R.W., and Fischman, M.W., Effects of alcohol on human behavior: implications for the workplace, in Drugs in the Workplace: Research and Evaluation Data, Vol. II, NIDA Research Monograph 100, Gust, S.W., Walsh, J.M., Thomas, L.B., and Crouch, D.J., Eds., U.S. Government Printing Office, Washington, D.C., 1991, 129.
17. Preusser, D.F., Ulmer, R.G., and Preusser, C.W., Evaluation of the impact of the drug evaluation and classification program on enforcement and adjudication, National Highway Traffic Safety Administration, DOT HS 808 058, U.S. Department of Transportation, Washington, D.C., 1992.
18. Thorne, D.R. et al., The Walter Reed Palm-held Psychomotor Vigilance Test, *Sleep*, 26(Suppl.), 182, 2002.
19. Kosslyn, S., Quick assessment of basic cognitive function: blood pressure cuffs for the mind. Technical Summary of Neurobehavioral and Psychosocial Factors Team Project, National Space Biomedical Research Institute, Houston, TX, 2002.
20. Klein, A., The current legal status of employment tests, *Los Angel. Lawyer*, July/August, 35, 1987.
21. Miller, J.C., Kim, H.T., and Parseghian, Z., Feasibility of Carrier-Based Fitness-for-Duty Testing of Commercial Drivers: Final Report, ESI-TR-94-003, Evaluation Systems, El Cajon, CA, 1994.
22. Morbidity and Mortality Weekly Report, Update: alcohol-related traffic fatalities — United States, 1982–1993, *Morb. Mortal. Wkly. Rep.*, 43, 861, 1994.
23. Terhune, K.W. et al., The Incidence and Role of Drugs in Fatally Injured Drivers, National Highway Traffic Safety Administration, U.S. Department of Transportation, DOT HS 808 065, Washington, D.C., 1992.
24. Williams, A.F. et al., Drugs in fatally injured young male drivers, *Public Health Rep.*, 100, 19, 1985.
25. Soderstrom, C.A. et al., Marijuana and alcohol use among 1023 trauma patients, *Arch. Surg.*, 123, 733, 1988.
26. Budd, R.D., Muto, J.J., and Wong, J.K., Drugs of abuse found in fatally injured drivers in Los Angeles County, *Drug Alcohol Depend.*, 23, 153, 1989.
27. Marzuk, P.M. et al., Prevalence of recent cocaine use among motor vehicle fatalities in New York City, *J. Am. Med. Assoc.*, 263, 250, 1990.
28. Brookoff, D. et al., Testing reckless drivers for cocaine and marijuana, *N. Engl. J. Med.*, 331, 518, 1994.
29. O'Hanlon, J.F. and de Gier, J.J., *Drugs and Driving*, Taylor & Francis, London, 1986.
30. Marowitz, L.A., Drug arrests and drunk driving, *Alcohol Drugs Driving*, 11, 1, 1995.
31. Consensus Development Panel, Drug concentrations and driving impairment, *J. Am. Med. Assoc.*, 254, 2618, 1985.
32. Bates, M.N. and Blakely, T.A., Role of cannabis in motor vehicle crashes, *Epidemiol. Rev.*, 21, 222, 1999.
33. National Highway Traffic Safety Administration, Drug Evaluation and Classification Program, U.S. Department of Transportation, Washington, D.C., 1991.
34. Preusser Research Group, Inc., Drug Evaluation and Classification Program: History and Growth, National Highway Traffic Safety Administration, Letter Report, U.S. Department of Transportation, Washington, D.C., 1995.
35. Compton, R.P., Field Evaluation of the Los Angeles Police Department Drug Detection Procedure, National Highway Traffic Safety Administration, Report DOT HS 807 012, U.S. Department of Transportation, Washington, D.C., 1986.
36. Adler, E.V. and Burns, M., Drug Recognition Expert (DRE) Validation Study, Final Report to Governor's Office of Highway Safety, State of Arizona, 1994.
37. Kunsman, G.W. et al., Phencyclidine blood concentrations in DRE cases, *J. Anal. Toxicol.*, 21, 498, 1997.
38. Tomaszewski, C. et al., Urine toxicology screens in drivers suspected of driving while impaired from drugs, *Clin. Toxicol.*, 34, 37, 1996.
39. Heishman, S.J., Singleton, E.G., and Crouch, D.J., Laboratory validation study of Drug Evaluation and Classification program: ethanol, cocaine, and marijuana, *J. Anal. Toxicol.*, 468, 1996.

40. Heishman, S.J., Singleton, E.G., and Crouch, D.J., Laboratory validation study of Drug Evaluation and Classification program: alprazolam, *d*-amphetamine, codeine, and marijuana, *J. Anal. Toxicol.*, 22, 503, 1998.
41. Thomas, J.R. and Schrot, J., Naval Medical Research Institute Performance Assessment Battery (NMRI PAB) Documentation, Naval Medical Research Institute (NMRI 88-7), Bethesda, MD, 1988.
42. Hegge, F.W. et al., The Unified Tri-Service Cognitive Performance Assessment Battery (UTC-PAB), 11: Hardware Software Design and Specification, U.S. Army Medical Research and Development Command, Fort Detrick, MD, 1985.
43. Reeves, D., Schlegel, R., and Gililand, K., The UTCIPAB and the NATO AGARD STRES Battery: Results from Standardization Studies, Medical Defense Biosciences Review, Aberdeen, MD, 1991.
44. Santucci, G. et al., AGARDograph #308, Human Performance Assessment Methods, North Atlantic Treaty Organization Advisory Group for Aerospace Research and Development, Working Group 12, Seine, France, 1989.
45. Thorne, D. et al., The Walter Reed Performance Assessment Battery, *Neurobehav. Toxicol. Teratol.*, 7, 415, 1985.
46. Snyder, F.R. and Henningfield, J.E., Effects of nicotine administration following 12 h of tobacco deprivation: assessment on computerized performance tasks, *Psychopharmacology*, 97, 17, 1989.
47. Heishman, S.J., Synder, F.R., and Henningfield, J.E., Performance, subjective and physiological effects of nicotine in non-smokers, *Drug Alcohol Depend.*, 34, 11, 1993.
48. Flynn, C. et al., Spaceflight Cognitive Assessment Tool for Lunar-Mars Life Support Test Project Phase III Test, in *Isolation: NASA Experiments in Closed-Environment Living,* Vol. 104, Lane, S.W., Sauer, R., and Feeback, D.L., Eds., Unicelt, Inc., San Diego, 2002, 155.
49. Elsmore, T.F., Reeves, D.L., and Reeves, A.N., ANAM™ for Palm OS Handheld Computers: The ARES® Test System for Palm OS Handheld Computers, unpublished data, 2004.
50. Baker, E.L. et al., A computer-based neurobehavioral evaluation system for occupational and environmental epidemiology: methodology and validation studies, *Neurobehav. Toxicol. Teratol.*, 7, 369, 1985.
51. Bittner, A.C., Jr. et al., Performance Evaluation Tests for Environmental Research (PETER): evaluation of 114 measures, *Percep. Mot. Skills*, 63, 683, 1986.
52. Kennedy, R.S. et al., Development of an automated performance test system for environmental and behavioral toxicology studies, *Percep. Mot. Skills*, 65, 947, 1987.
53. Kennedy, R.S. et al., Psychology of computer use: IX. Menu of self administered microcomputer-based neurotoxicology tests, *Percep. Mot. Skills*, 68, 1255, 1989.
54. Larrabee, G.J. and Crook, T., A computerized everyday memory battery for assessing treatment effects, *Psychopharmacol. Bull.*, 24, 695, 1988.
55. Elsmore, T.F. et al., A Comparison of the Effects of Sleep Deprivation on Synthetic Work Performance and a Conventional Performance Assessment Battery, Naval Health Research Center, San Diego, CA/Naval Medical Research and Development Command (Report No. 95-6), Bethesda, MD, 1995.
56. Elsmore, T.F. et al., Performance Assessment Under Operational Conditions Using a Computer-Based Synthetic Work Task, U.S. Army Research Institute of Environmental Medicine, Natick, MA, 1991.
57. Wilkinson, R.T. and Houghton, D., Field test of arousal: a portable reaction timer with data storage, *Hum. Factors*, 224, 487, 1982.
58. Dinges, D.F. and Powell, J.W., Microcomputer analyses of performance on a portable, simple visual RT task during sustained operations, *Behav. Res. Methods Instrum. Comput.*, 17, 652, 1985.
59. NTI, Inc., The Effects of Alcohol and Fatigue on an FAA Readiness-To-Perform Test, U.S. Department of Transportation/Federal Aviation Administration document DOT/FAA/AM-95/24, Office of Aviation Medicine, Washington, D.C., 1995.
60. O'Donnell, R.D., *The NOVASCAN™ Test Paradigm: Theoretical Basis and Validation*, Nova Technologies, Inc, Dayton, OH, 1992.
61. Turnage, J.J. and Kennedy, R.S., The development and use of a computerized human performance test battery for repeated-measures applications, *Hum. Perform.*, 5, 265, 1992.
62. Turnage, J.J. et al., Development of microcomputer-based mental acuity tests, *Ergonomics*, 35, 1271, 1992.
63. Kennedy, R.S. et al., Indexing cognitive tests to alcohol dosage and comparison to standardized field sobriety tests, *J. Stud. Alcohol*, 55, 615, 1994.

64. Parth, P. et al., Motor and cognitive testing of bone marrow transplant patients after chemoradiotherapy, *Percep. Mot. Skills*, 68, 1227, 1989.
65. Kennedy, R.S. et al., Differential effects of scopolamine and amphetamine on microcomputer-based performance tests, *Aviat. Space Environ. Med.*, 61, 615, 1990.
66. Kennedy, R.S. et al., Cognitive performance deficits occasioned by a simulated climb of Mount Everest: Operation Everest II, *Aviat. Space Environ. Med.*, 60, 99, 1989.
67. Mills, K.C., Tunnel vision: lifeline or killer? Some research on why training to "keep your cool" is valuable, *Law Order*, 11, 80, 2000.
68. Mills, K.C. and Bisgrove, E.Z., Cognitive impairment and perceived risk from alcohol: laboratory, self-report and field assessments, *J. Stud. Alcohol*, 44, 26, 1983.
69. Perez-Reyes, M. et al., Interaction between marihuana and ethanol: effects on psychomotor performance, *Alcohol. Clin. Exp. Res.*, 12, 269, 1988.
70. Mills, K.C., Parkman, K.M., and Spruill, S.E., A PC-based software test for measuring alcohol and drug effects in human subjects, *Alcohol. Clin. Exp. Res.*, 20, 1582, 1996.
71. Mills, K.C. et al., Prediction of driving performance through computerized testing: high-risk-driver assessment and training, Transportation Research Record 1689, Transportation Research Board, National Research Council, Washington, D.C., 1999.
72. Mills, K.C. et al., The influence of stimulants, sedatives and fatigue on tunnel vision: risk factors for driving and piloting, *Hum. Factors*, 43, 310, 2001.
73. Engelberg, A.C., Gibbons, H.L., and Doege, T.C., A review of the medical standards for civilian airmen: synopsis of a two-year study, *J. Am. Med. Assoc.,* 225, 1589, 1986.
74. National Research Council, *Simulated Voyages: Using Simulation Technology to Train and License Mariners,* National Academy Press, Washington, D.C., 1996.
75. Howland, J. et al., Effects of low-dose alcohol exposure on simulated merchant ship piloting by maritime cadets, *Accid. Anal. Prevent.*, 33, 257, 2001.
76. Howland, J. et al., Effects of low-dose alcohol exposure on simulated merchant ship power plant operation by maritime cadets, *Addiction*, 95, 719, 2000.
77. Mangione, T.W. et al., Employee drinking practices and work performance, *J. Stud. Alcohol*, 60, 261, 1999.
78. Laurell, H., Effects of small doses of alcohol on driver performance in emergency traffic situation, *Accid. Anal. Prevent.*, 9, 191, 1977.
79. Liguori, A. et al., Alcohol effects on mood, equilibrium, and simulated driving, *Alcohol. Clin. Exp. Res.*, 23, 815, 1999.
80. Tornos, J. and Laurell, H., Acute and hangover effects of alcohol on simulated driving performance, *Blutalkohol*, 28, 24, 1991.
81. Morrow, D., Alcohol, age, and piloting; judgement, mood, and actual performance, *Int. J. Addict.*, 26, 669, 1991.
82. Morrow, D., Leirer, V., and Yesavage, J., The influence of alcohol and aging on radio communication during flight, *Aviat. Space Environ. Med.*, 61, 12, 1990.
83. Ross, L.E. and Mundt, J.C., Multiattribute modeling analysis of the effects of low blood alcohol level on pilot performance, *Hum. Factors*, 30, 293, 1988.
84. Yesavage, J., Dolhert, N., and Taylor, J., Flight simulator performance of younger and older aircraft pilots: effects of age and alcohol, *J. Am. Geriat. Soc.*, 42, 577, 1994.
85. Yesavage, J. and Leirer, V., Hangover effects on aircraft pilots 14 hours after alcohol ingestion: a preliminary report, *Am. J. Psychiatry*, 143, 1546, 1986.
86. Mumenthaler, M.S. et al., Influence of nicotine on simulator flight performance in non-smokers, *Psychopharmacology*, 140, 38, 1998.
87. Vermeeren, A. and O'Hanlon, J.F., Fexofenadine's affects, alone and with alcohol, on driving and psychomotor performance, *J. Allerg. Clin. Immunol.*, 101, 306, 1998.
88. Weiler, J.M. et al., Effects of fexofenadine, diphenhydramine, and alcohol on driving performance, *Ann. Intern. Med.*, 132, 354, 2000.
89. Collins, W.E., Performance effects of alcohol intoxication and hangover at ground level and at simulated altitude, *Aviat. Space Environ. Med.*, 51, 327, 1980.
90. Traffinder, N.J. et al., Effect of sleep deprivation on surgeons' dexterity on laparoscopy simulator, *Lancet*, 352, 1191, 1998.

CHAPTER 7

Pupillometry and Eye Tracking as Predictive Measures of Drug Abuse

Wallace B. Pickworth, Ph.D.[1] **and Rudy Murillo, B.A.**[2]
[1] Battelle Centers for Public Health Research and Evaluation, Baltimore, Maryland
[2] Clinical Pharmacology and Therapeutics Branch, National Institute on Drug Abuse, National Institutes of Health, Department of Health and Human Services, Baltimore, Maryland

CONTENTS

7.1 INTRODUCTION

Measurements of pupillary diameter, eye tracking, and the pupillary response to a flash of light are readily available, non-invasive indices of central nervous system function. Recently, such parameters have been used by law enforcement personnel, employers, and primary care and emergency room physicians to make a rapid and initial assessment of recent drug ingestion. In this chapter, the physiological basis for the control of pupil size and the light reflex and the instruments used to measure pupillary responses are briefly reviewed. The results of a residential, within-subject study of the effects of various drugs of abuse on pupillary size and the light reflex are described. A summary of the literature on the effects of abused drugs on pupillary measures is given. An outpatient study analyzing the effects of polydrug use on pupillary responses is also presented. The advent of new classes of pupillometers that measure eye position and gaze is also included. These new instruments hold great promise for revealing subjective effects of drugs and drug withdrawal through a psychophysiologic measure. The chapter concludes with a discussion of the utility and limitations of pupillometry in the detection of abused drugs.

7.2 PHYSIOLOGICAL BASIS OF PUPIL SIZE AND THE LIGHT REFLEX

7.2.1 Pupil Size

The human pupil ranges in diameter from 1.5 mm at full miosis to 8.0 mm at full mydriasis. The most powerful determinant of pupil size is the ambient light level. Pupil size is also influenced by several factors including subject age, iris pigmentation, gender, state of arousal, and time of day.[1] Newborns have very small pupils because the pupillary dilator muscle develops well after birth. Pupil size is maximal during adolescence and decreases in older age. People with a lightly pigmented iris (blue eyes) generally have larger pupils than those with a heavily pigmented iris (brown eyes). Pupil diameter tends to decrease over the course of the day.[2] About 17% of the population have pupils of unequal size (aniscoria), but differences exceeding 0.5 mm occur in only about 4% of the population.

7.2.2 Instrumentation

Pupil size can be estimated from direct observation. A variety of cards and scales are available whereby the experimenter compares the size of the pupil to standard patterns and scales. The simplest and most often used card is the Haab pupil gauge. This consists of a card with black circles graduated in size between 2 and 10 mm in 0.5-mm increments. The card is held on the temporal side of the eye out of the subject's vision (to reduce accommodation miosis). Pupil size can be determined to an accuracy of 0.2 mm. A disadvantage of this method is the inability to make measurements in the dark and the possibility that the subject's eyes will react to the test or its administration.

The Polaroid close-up camera has been used to photograph the eye of subjects before and after the administration of opiates and other psychoactive drugs.[3,4] Pupil size can be estimated to within 0.1 mm by means of calipers and a magnified scale that is concomitantly photographed. Disadvantages of this method are the possibility that the flash used in the photography can reduce pupil size, the expense of the film, and the possibility that the subject may focus on the camera, thereby inducing accommodation miosis. Recently, digital cameras have been used to determine pupil size.[5]

Sequential photographs can be used to monitor pupil size over an extended time. If the pupil is illuminated with infrared light and infrared-sensitive film is used, recordings can be made in total darkness. Although this method was used in seminal studies of the pupillary light reflex and other dynamic applications,[6,7] it is seldom used today because of the high cost of film, processing time, and limited temporal resolution.

Other pupillometers usually employ infrared illumination of the eye and a television or computer. These instruments sample pupil diameter at rates up to 60 images per second. Pupillometers offer the advantage of accurate sampling across a wide range of ambient light. They can record pupil diameter over extended times, enabling the investigator to quantify dynamic aspects of the light reflex and fluctuations of pupil size (hippus). These instruments are extensively used to determine the effects of drugs, fatigue, stress, autonomic reactivity, and level of anesthesia. Instruments produced by Eye Dynamics (Torrance, CA) and Pulse Medical Instruments (Bethesda, MD) use short programmed trials to evaluate pupil diameter, light reflex measures, and saccadic or smooth pursuit eye tracking.

Modern pupillometers have the added ability to track eye position and movement. Pupillometers such as the I-Portal (Neuro Kinetics, Inc, Pittsburgh, PA), the Eye Link II (SR Research, Ontario, CA), and the EyeTrace 300X (Applied Science Laboratories, Bedford, MA) have sampling speeds of up to 600 samples/second. Their ability to track eye position and gaze fixation enables these pupillometers to be used to study components of drug abuse, such as drug seeking, stimulus relevance, and cue reactivity, which cannot be assessed with conventional pupillometry. One experiment of particular interest would be to study the time it takes drug users to find illicit drugs or drug paraphernalia within a matrix of control objects using eye tracking technology. In the following section aspects of the pupillary light reflex measured with modern pupillometers are discussed.

7.2.3 Light Reflex

When the retinal rods and cones are stimulated with light in the visual wavelength, there is constriction of the pupil. A major factor in determining the intensity of the reflex is the adaptation state of the retina because the rate of change of retinal illumination evokes the response. Other factors influence the light reflex. The retinal area that is stimulated is differentially sensitive; the fovea and macular areas are most sensitive and the periphery is least sensitive. The subject's state of arousal[8] and anxiety[9] and the wavelength of the stimulus light and its direction all may influence the reflex.[10,11]

As shown in Figure 7.1, there are several components of the light reflex that may be evaluated with dynamic pupillometers. From studies in cats, monkeys, and rabbits, Lowenstein and

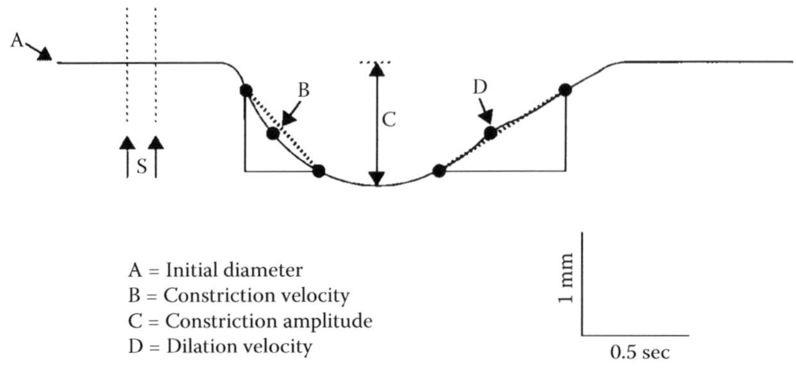

Figure 7.1 Pupil diameter before (A) and after a light stimulus (S). Constriction (B) and dilation (D) velocities are determined from a least square fit of the slope. Amplitude of constriction (C) represents the maximal difference in diameter before and after the flash.

Lowenfeld[12] identified the components of the light reflex that were controlled by parasympathetic and sympathetic innervation of the smooth muscles controlling pupil diameter. They concluded that the parasympathetic nervous system must be intact to observe the light reflex; the sympathetic nervous system influences the shape of the reflex. For example, in the absence of sympathetic innervation, the constriction velocity is increased and the dilation velocity is decreased. Conversely, in situations of increased sympathetic tone, the constriction is sluggish and incomplete, and the pupil slowly returns to its baseline size. The effects of abused drugs on these and other components of the light reflex were studied in the experiment described below.

7.3 LABORATORY STUDY OF PUPILLARY EFFECTS OF ABUSED DRUGS IN HUMANS

In an effort to understand and quantify the effects of several classes of abused drugs on human pupillary response, a study, briefly described below, was conducted on the residential unit of the Intramural Research Program of the National Institute on Drug Abuse (NIDA). Further methodological details and results are published elsewhere.[13]

7.3.1 Methods

7.3.1.1 Subjects

Eight healthy male subjects with a mean age of 34.1 years volunteered for this study. During their participation in the study, they resided on a clinical research unit. The subjects had extensive histories of illicit drug use that included recent ingestion (within the past 2 years) of opiates, marijuana, stimulants, alcohol, and sedative-hypnotics, although they were not dependent on any drug (except nicotine).

7.3.1.2 Study Design

All the subjects received each of the treatments. Neither the subjects nor the technician knew the identity of the treatment at the time of the experiment. The treatments were randomly presented a minimum of 48 hr apart. On study days subjects swallowed three opaque capsules, drank a large cold tonic drink (480 ml, in 15 min) with 2 ml 95% ethanol floating on top, and smoked a cigarette (either marijuana or placebo) according to a paced puffing procedure: 8 puffs per cigarette, 20-s puff retention, 40-s interpuff interval.[14] On any experimental day all of the dosage forms could have been a placebo (no active drugs) or one of the dosage forms could have contained an active drug. The active drug conditions were marijuana 1.3 and 3.9% THC; ethanol 0.3 and 1.0 g/kg; hydromorphone (Dilaudid) 1 and 3 mg; pentobarbital 150 and 450 mg; and amphetamine 10 and 30 mg. Drugs were administered at the same time each day (9:45 A.M.).

7.3.1.3 Pupillary Measures

Measures of pupillary diameter and parameters of the light reflex were made using a Pupilscan (Fairville Medical Optics) handheld pupillometer.[15] The sampling rate was 10 diameters (in pixels)/s; the light reflex was evoked with a 0.1-s, 20-Lumen/ft^2, 565-nm (green) stimulus light. Initial (prestimulus) pupil diameter and the following parameters of the light reflex were derived from the data collected on a personal computer: constriction and dilation velocities and the amplitude of constriction.[2,16] Pupillary measures were collected from the left eye before drug administration and at 30, 105, 180, and 300 min after the drug.

7.3.1.4 Subjective Measures

Subjective effects of the experimental drugs were estimated from scores on several standardized tests and computer-delivered 100-mm visual analog scales that measured drug symptoms, "strength" and "liking." The 100-mm scale was anchored with the terms "not at all" (0 mm) and "extremely" (100 mm). The subjects rated subjective effects at about the same times of the pupillary measures.

7.3.1.5 Performance Measures

Before beginning the experimental series, subjects trained to a consistent level of performance on several tests of cognitive performance including the Digit Symbol Substitution Test (DSST). In the DSST a random digit appeared on the computer screen. The subject used the numeric keypad of the computer to reproduce a geometric pattern (three keystrokes) that was uniquely associated with the displayed digit. The dependent measure used was the number of correct responses during the 2-min task.[17] In the circular lights task the subject pushed lighted buttons on a wall-mounted board. At the start of the task, one of the 33 buttons was illuminated. Pushing that button added a point to the score and lighted another button at a random position. The score was the total number of points (hits) in the 1-min task.[18]

7.3.1.6 Statistical Analyses

Repeated measures analyses of variance (ANOVA)[19] were conducted on the pupillary, subjective, and performance variables. The main factors were drug (12 levels) and time (5 or 6 levels). Using *a priori* tests, data points after drug administration were compared to baseline values and placebo values. The pupillary effects were correlated with subjective effects (visual analog rating of "high" and "strong") and performance effects (DSST, number correct; circular lights, hits) by means of the Pearson's product-moment correlation.

7.3.2 Results

7.3.2.1 Pupillary Measures

Pupil Diameter

The experimental drugs caused significant changes in pupillary diameter measured before the presentation of the light flash (Figure 7.2). One-way ANOVAs on the peak change indicated

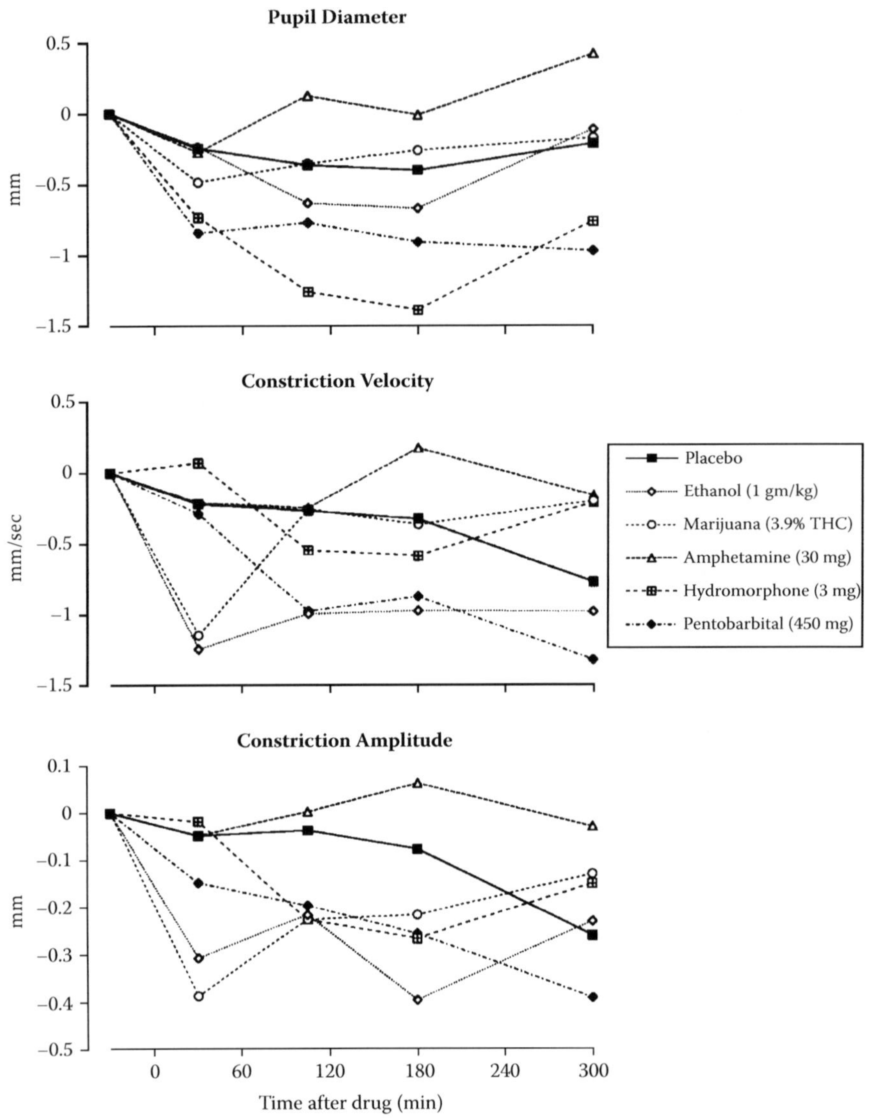

Figure 7.2 After high doses of the experimental drugs, changes (from baseline) in initial (prestimulus) pupil diameter, constriction velocity, and constriction amplitude varied as a function of the drug condition and time.

significant differences among the treatment conditions. A two-way ANOVA indicated significant differences among drug conditions and time of measurement, as well as a significant drug by time interaction. As shown in Table 7.1, high doses of ethanol, marijuana, hydromorphone, and pentobarbital decreased pupil size, whereas amphetamine caused an increase. Although the changes were statistically significant, their magnitude was not large. Pupil size decreased by 0.7, 0.5, 1.4, and 1.0 mm after the high doses of ethanol, marijuana, hydromorphone, and pentobarbital, respectively. The maximal increase after the high dose of amphetamine averaged 0.4 mm.

Constriction Amplitude

The constriction amplitude of the light reflex differed significantly among the treatment conditions (Figure 7.2). A two-way ANOVA indicated significant differences among drug conditions

Table 7.1 Pupillary Effects of Experimental Drugs

Drug	Dose	Pupil Diameter	Constriction Amplitude	Constriction Velocity	Dilation Velocity
Ethanol	1 g/kg	↓	↓	↓	NC
Marijuana	cigarette 3.9% THC	↓	↓	↓	↓
Hydromorphone	3 mg	↓	↓	↓	NC
Pentobarbital	450 mg	↓	↓	NC	NC
Amphetamine	30 mg	↑	NC	NC	NC

Note: Arrows indicate direction of significant changes from baseline values; NC indicates there was no significant change.

and time of measurement, as well as a significant drug by time interaction. As summarized in Table 7.1, constriction amplitude was significantly decreased by high doses of ethanol, marijuana, and hydromorphone. The magnitude of the effect was small and the maximal changes occurred at the time of the maximal change in pupillary size.

Constriction Velocity

The velocity of pupillary constriction changed significantly as a function of the drug treatment (Figure 7.2). A two-way ANOVA indicated significant differences among drug conditions and time of measurement, as well as a significant drug by time interaction. As shown in Table 7.1, constriction velocity decreased after high doses of ethanol, marijuana, hydromorphone, and pentobarbital. The high doses of marijuana, hydromorphone, and pentobarbital reduced the constriction velocity by 1.2, 0.6, and 1.3 mm/s, respectively, changes that represented reductions of 26, 14, and 27% of control velocities.

Dilation Velocity

As summarized in Table 7.1, only the high dose of marijuana significantly changed (reduced) the velocity of dilation of the pupil during the recovery phase of the light reflex.

7.3.2.2 Subjective Measures

Visual analog scale scores on the strength of drug effect were significantly different as a function of drug condition and time of measurement (Figure 7.3). There was also a significant drug by time interaction (Figure 7.3). Similarly, scores on the drug liking visual analog scale differed significantly among the drug conditions. These data indicate the subjects perceived the high doses of the experimental drugs as being strong and being liked. The positive endorsement of questions of drug liking and strength by experienced drug users indicate that such drugs have a high abuse potential.[20]

7.3.2.3 Performance Measures

Digit Symbol Substitution Task

ANOVAs on the number of correct responses on the DDST indicated there were significant differences among drug conditions, time of measurement, and a significant drug by time interaction (Figure 7.4). Performance was significantly impaired after high doses of marijuana, ethanol, pentobarbital, and hydromorphone.

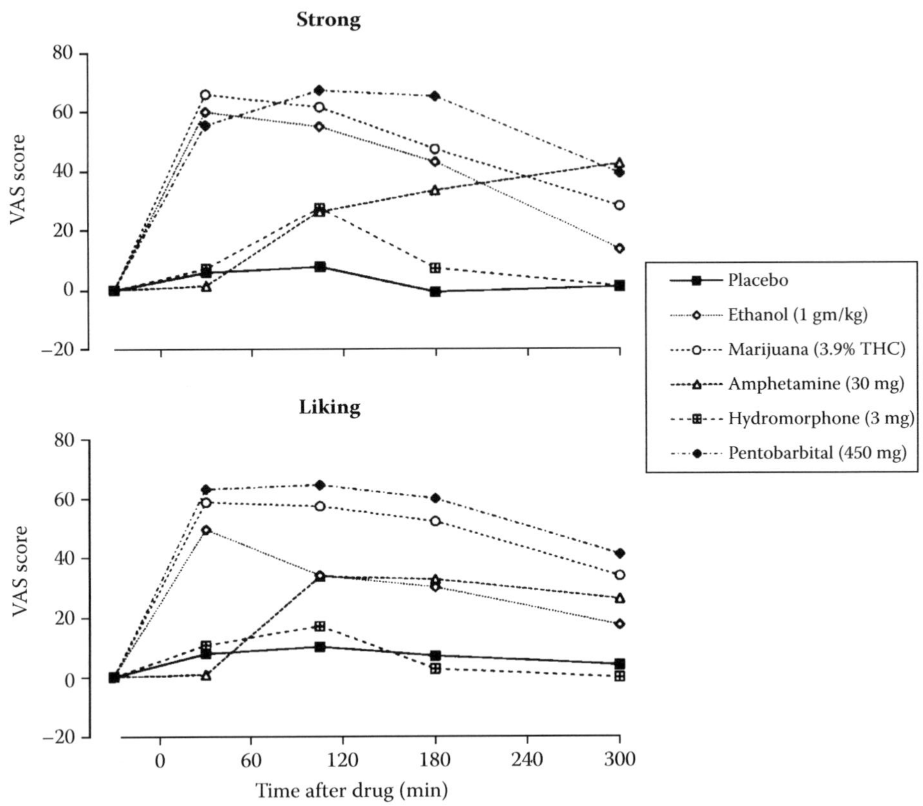

Figure 7.3 High doses of the experimental drugs increased scores (from baseline levels) on drug strength and drug liking. The effects varied as a function of the drug administered and the time after administration.

Circular Lights Task

High doses of ethanol and pentobarbital significantly decreased the number of hits on the circular lights task (Figure 7.4). The other experimental drugs caused no significant change in this measure of performance.

7.3.2.4 Correlational Analyses

A visual comparison of the pupillary, subjective, and performance effects of the experimental drug (Figures 7.2 through 7.4) indicates that in most instances the maximal change in each parameter occurred at the same time. Furthermore, the time of maximal effect was related to the dosage form. For example, smoked marijuana produced maximal subjective and performance effects 30 min after drug administration, whereas the capsules (pentobarbital, hydromorphone, and amphetamine) produced significant maximal changes 120 min or longer after drug administration. Correlational analyses were performed to determine if performance and subjective changes varied as a function of pupillary change. Correlations between the change in pupil diameter and the changes in the subjective and performance measures (total of 176 correlations) were statistically significant in only 15 cases (7 at the high dose condition). Furthermore, only 3 of the significant correlations in the high dose conditions occurred during the time of the maximal pupillary change. These results indicate there is a very weak relationship among the pupillary, performance, and subjective effects of these experimental drugs. Furthermore, pupillary changes, even under ideal laboratory conditions,

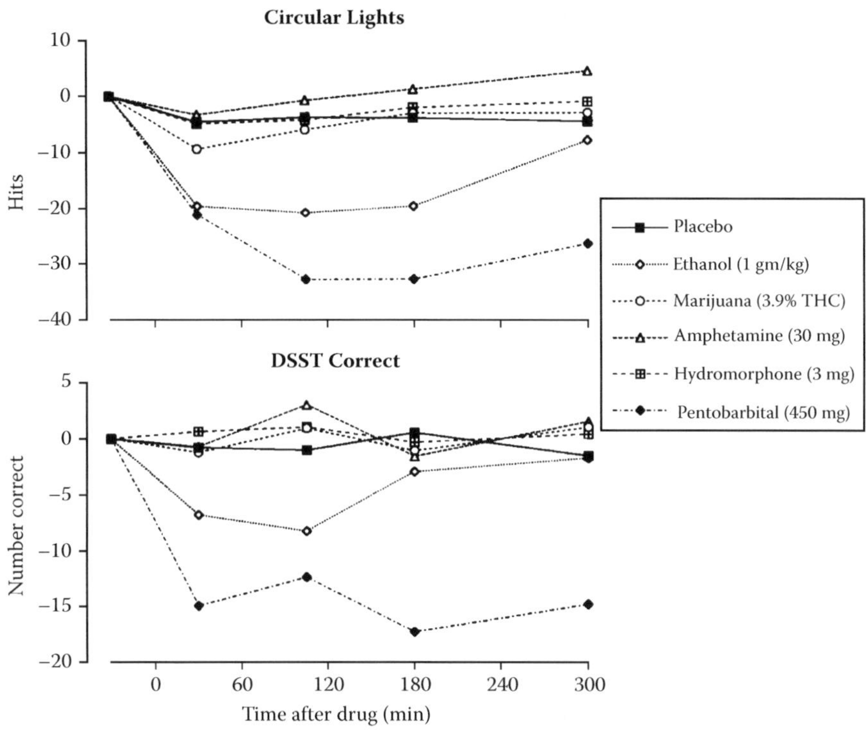

Figure 7.4 High doses of the experimental drugs caused changes (from baseline) in performance on the circular lights and DSST tasks. The effects varied as a function of the administered drug and the time after administration.

do not predict changes in performance of experimental tasks. However, as discussed below, changes in pupillary measures may be useful in predicting performance in the workplace environment.

7.4 EFFECTS OF ABUSED DRUGS ON PUPILLARY MEASURES

7.4.1 Opiates

In early clinical studies, it was shown that morphine caused miosis and morphine withdrawal caused mydriasis.[21] In humans, most opiates caused pupillary constriction and diminished the constriction and dilation velocities of the light reflex.[22] The results of the above study confirm that hydromorphone, a potent orally active opiate, decreased pupil size and diminished the constriction velocity and amplitude of the light reflex. Buprenorphine, a partial opiate agonist, also decreased pupil size, constriction and dilation velocities, and the constriction amplitude of the light reflex.[23,24] On buprenorphine withdrawal there was a significant increase in pupil size and parameters of the light reflex.[16] Mixed agonists-antagonists caused less constriction than full agonists. For example, cyclazocine caused a small but reliable miotic response in human volunteers.[25]

7.4.2 Stimulants

As was demonstrated in the experiment above and elsewhere, amphetamine[26] and its derivatives and cocaine[26,27] significantly increased pupil size through an activation of the sympathetic nerve innervation of the iris. Evidence from an animal study indicated that amphetamine-induced mydriasis is partially mediated through actions in the brain where it inhibits the parasympathetic output of the oculomotor nucleus.[28] Tennant[29] also reported that cocaine and amphetamine-type stimulants increased pupil diameter and diminished the pupil reaction to light.

7.4.3 Barbiturates

In the laboratory experiment described above, pentobarbital (450 mg) caused a small but significant decrease in pupil size and a reduction in the constriction velocity of the light reflex. The maximal effect was measured 300 min after oral drug administration. Nystagmus (rhythmical oscillation of the eyeballs) and ptosis (drooping of the upper eyelid) are the eye signs that are most often attributed to ingestion of barbiturates, benzodiazepines, ethanol, and other CNS depressants.[26,30,31]

7.4.4 Ethanol

As shown in the above experimental results, ethanol caused a small but significant decrease in pupil size and a reduction in the response to a flash of light. In a review of the effects of abused drugs on pupillary and ocular measures, Tennant[29] reported that ethanol caused no change in pupil size but diminished the light reflex. Nystagmus is a well-known sign of ethanol intoxication.[26]

7.4.5 Marijuana

The high dose of marijuana decreased pupil diameter in all subjects in the experiment described above. The peak response occurred 30 min after smoking. There were significant decreases in the constriction and dilation velocities of the light reflex. Tennant[29] reported that marijuana obtunded the light reflex without changes in pupil size. In a subsequent study, marijuana smoking obtunded the light reflex and caused decrements in smooth pursuit eye tracking.[32]

7.4.6 Hallucinogens

Both indoleamine (e.g., lysergic acid diethylamide, LSD; psilocybin) and phenethylamine hallucinogens (e.g., mescaline) increased pupil diameter.[26] There have been no systematic studies of the effects of these drugs on dynamic measures of the light reflex. Phencyclidine (PCP) does not cause marked changes in pupil size or light reflex. However, subjects intoxicated with PCP often show horizontal and vertical nystagmus.[26]

7.4.7 Nicotine

Cigarette smoking has been reported to increase pupil size during the time the cigarette is being smoked.[33] Pupil size returned to baseline values within 45 s after smoking a single cigarette. Pupil diameter of smokers was smaller (mean = 5.1 mm) than that of nonsmokers (mean = 6.0 mm), suggesting that chronic cigarette smoking may persistently decrease pupil size.[34]

7.4.8 Club Drugs

MDMA (3,4-methylenedioxymethamphetamine), otherwise known as "ecstasy," causes significant mydriasis.[35,36] Mas et al.[35] reported significant mydriasis (increases of 3.5 mm) in subjects given doses above 50 mg. Ketamine, also known as "Special K," also causes mydriasis.[37] Other drugs such as gamma hydroxybutyrate (GHB) and flunitrazepam, Rophynol ("Roofie"), are more difficult to study using pupillometry because they tend to render the users unconscious, although flunitrazepam has been found to cause mydriasis.[38] More research must be done to understand more fully the pupillary effects of this relatively new class of abused drugs.

7.5 PUPILLARY EFFECTS OF CONCOMITANT DRUG USE

Although a high percentage of drug users tend to abuse more than one drug at a time, no studies had analyzed the pupillary effects of polydrug use. In a recent study[39] we measured the pupillary effects of polydrug use in an outpatient population undergoing methadone treatment. The purpose of this study was to determine if pupillary changes occurred when subjects co-administered illicit drugs while they were maintained on methadone or buprenorphine.

7.5.1 Methods

7.5.1.1 Participants

Patients (n = 37) already enrolled in studies at the NIDA Archway Clinic were invited to participate. The subject population included 21 males and 16 females; 68% of the participants were African Americans and 32% were Caucasian. The average age of the participants was 41.9 years. The participants had extensive drug abuse histories that included current opioid dependence, chronic cocaine use, and frequent use of other illicit drugs. Most (n = 35) were maintained on methadone in doses that ranged from 70 to 100 mg/day; two participants were maintained on buprenorphine (16 mg/day).

7.5.1.2 Study Design

After agreeing to participate, and signing an informed consent form, the operation of the pupillometer, FIT 2000 (Pulse Medical Instruments [PMI], Rockville, MD), was explained and demonstrated to the research volunteers. They were allowed to practice the test sequence in the presence of the administrator until they obtained a successful test sequence. This single exposure was the only supervised orientation the participants received.

Participants used the pupillometer three occasions each week, on days when they provided a urine sample for drug testing. Urine was analyzed on-site for: amphetamines, barbiturates, benzodiazepines, cocaine, marijuana metabolites, phencyclidine, and opiates. Subjects were compensated for successful pupillary tests with a $2 coupon redeemable at a fast food restaurant chain.

7.5.1.3 Study Measures

On study days, room lights were kept at a constant illumination. The participant stood comfortably in front of the instrument and looked through the viewing lens with one eye (left) while the other eye was open at all times. The pupillary test sequence was initiated when the participant pressed a start button. A green LED target quickly moved horizontally across the viewing screen. Saccadic velocity (SV) data were collected at a rate of 750 Hz during this phase. The target then paused in the middle of the viewing field, and a series of light flashes ensued. Initial pupillary diameter (ID) (measured before the flashes), constriction amplitude (CA), and constriction latency (CL) were collected at a rate of 60 Hz. If the instrument lost eye tracking or for any reason that data could not be collected, a low tone sounded, a fault message was given, and the test was aborted. After a fault message the participant could re-initiate a test sequence. A successful test sequence lasted about 30 s. Subjects repeated the test sequence until they obtained a successful result.

7.5.1.4 Statistical Analyses

The data were analyzed to determine the feasibility for use in this patient population. The number and percentage of successful and unsuccessful (faults) tests were summarized for each participant. Pupillary data from days when there was no evidence of other recent drug use (urine negative for abused drugs) were compared to days when there was evidence of recent drug use (urine positive). These comparisons were done using both within-subject and between-subject tests. A drug-free baseline was determined for subjects who provided negative urine on more than 10 days. The four parameters were used to determine the goodness-of-fit calculation as follows:

$$\text{Index} = \left(\frac{\mu_{ID} - ID}{\sigma_{ID}}\right)^2 + \left(\frac{\mu_{CL} - CL}{\sigma_{CL}}\right)^2 + \left(\frac{\mu_{CA} - CA}{\sigma_{CA}}\right)^2 + \left(\frac{\mu_{SV} - SV}{\sigma_{SV}}\right)^2$$

where ID, CL, CA, and SV are the value of the parameters on any particular pupillary screening, μ represents the mean baseline value, and σ is the baseline standard deviation of each parameter. After a baseline was established for each participant (FIT index), a chi square analysis with 4 degrees of freedom was calculated for subsequent drug-positive days. This result was referenced against the critical chi square values table ($p < 0.1$, $\chi^2 = 7.78$, $p < 0.01$, $\chi^2 = 13.28$). These calculations yielded the probability that the particular reading differed from the established baseline. Finally, pupillary parameters in participants who always gave negative urine were compared to those who always gave positive urine to determine if there was more stability of measures among those who only ingested the treatment medication.

7.5.2 Results

7.5.2.1 Fault Analyses

The overall success rate for correct use of the pupillometer by participants ($n = 37$) was 92.9%; that is, nearly every time participants attempted a trial they were eventually successful. The success rate (percentage obtaining a successful sequence on the first try of each study day) in participants after minimal experience (2 weeks or about 6 exposures) was 72%, and if the four participants who had trouble obtaining stability were eliminated, the overall success rate further increased to 81%. Thus, even minimally trained patients maintained on methadone[4] or buprenorphine,[16] drugs known to produce miosis, obtained reliable pupillary measures.

7.5.2.2 Pupillary Reactions on Drug-Positive and Drug-Negative Days

Shown in Table 7.2 are the mean and standard deviation of the four parameters collected on subjects ($n = 6$) on days (minimum of 10) when their urine was negative for drugs of abuse compared to days when their urine was positive for abused drugs. Although the mean values are similar, the variability increased (larger standard deviation) for ID, CL, and SV on urine-positive days. The variability in the measures obtained for constriction amplitude was similar regardless of the presence of illicit drugs in the urine.

Table 7.2 Participants (n = 6) with >10 Days When Urine Was Positive or Negative for the Presence of Illicit Drugs

	Urine Negative	Urine Positive
Pupil diameter (ID) (mm)	5.7 ± 0.51	5.9 ± 0.68
Constriction amplitude (CA) (mm)	0.8 ± 0.12	0.8 ± 0.3
Constriction latency (CL) (mm/s)	297.9 ± 12.1	301.5 ± 14.6
Saccadic velocity (SV) (mm/s)	80.9 ± 7.22	82.8 ± 11.1

Note: Values shown are mean ± standard deviation of the four FIT parameters.

Table 7.3 Comparison of Pupillary Measures in Participants (n = 4) with Urine Samples Consistently Negative for Illicit Drugs and Participants (n = 20) with Consistently Positive Urines

	Urine Negative	Urine Positive
Pupil diameter (ID) (mm)	5.2 ± 0.31	5.9 ± 0.81
Constriction amplitude (CA) (mm)	0.9 ± 0.14	0.7 ± 0.13
Constriction latency (CL) (ms)	301.2 ± 9.86	314 ± 22.9
Saccadic velocity (SV)(mm/s)	75.0 ± 6.46	76.0 ± 10.1

Note: Values shown are mean ± standard deviation of the four FIT parameters.

7.5.2.3 Comparison of Individuals Always Positive or Negative for Illicit Drugs

Many of the participants (n = 20) were never able to provide ten or more drug-free urine samples, and a few (n = 4) always gave urine samples that were drug negative. The data from these subjects were not useful for the comparisons illustrated in Table 7.2, but examination of the variation of the parameters in Table 7.3 revealed a similar pattern. Specifically, the standard deviation of the mean of ID, SV, and CL was larger in the group with the positive urine samples.

7.5.2.4 Fit Equation

Participants with 10 or more clean days were analyzed using the FIT equation. A baseline was established from pupillary data on days when the urine was negative for illicit drugs. The pupillary measures from days when the urine was positive for drugs were inserted into the FIT equation to determine probabilities between $p < 0.1$ and $p < 0.01$. For example, one participant had baseline values of 5.35 (± 0.68), 0.97 (± 0.12), 281.52 (± 8.0), and 78.2 (± 9.8) for ID, CA, CL, and SV, respectively. On a day when the urine was positive for cocaine and methamphetamines, the values for the four parameters were 6.31, 0.79, 305.1, and 91.23. When inserted into the equation this generated a FIT index of 14.69, a value well above the critical values for $p < 0.1$ (7.78) and $p < 0.01$ (13.28). Using this methodology, concomitant drug use was detected 29% of the time at the $p < 0.1$ level. There was a high variability of detection among participants. At the $p < 0.1$ level, drug-positive urines were detected 53% of the time in three participants. However, in another three participants, detection averaged only 10%.

7.6 UTILITY AND LIMITATIONS OF PUPILLARY TESTING FOR ABUSED DRUGS

In some circumstances the use of pupillometry in drug detection appears reasonable. However, based on the experimental evidence cited above and a review of the literature, there are reservations about the use of pupillometry to detect recent ingestion of abused drugs. Several areas of concern and the limitations of the methodology are discussed below.

7.6.1 Subject Variability

The size of the pupil and its responsiveness to a light stimulus vary considerably across subjects. Normal pupil diameter ranges between 2 and 8 mm in the extremes of ambient light. In conditions of controlled, low-level (4 ft cd) ambient light, pupil size ranged from 3.5 to 8 mm, and there were similarly large variations in constriction and dilation velocities of the light reflex.[2] Fosnaugh et al.[2] recorded pupil measures on 4 consecutive days and found very little within-subject variation in pupil size and parameters of the light reflex. These findings have practical and theoretical importance. The wide variability between subjects indicates that a single examination of the pupils and the light reflex is unlikely to be highly predictive of recent drug ingestion. On the other hand, the small within-subject, day-to-day variability indicates that a relatively small change in pupil measures in an individual may be an indicator of recent drug ingestion. These suggestions emphasize the importance of having verifiable, drug-free baseline data (both mean and variation are important) for individuals enrolled in testing programs. As demonstrated in the polydrug study, a baseline with minimal variation is the best way to assure detection of differences.

7.6.2 Conditions of Measurement

The ambient light present when pupillary measures are made clearly influences the values obtained. For example, Fosnaugh et al.[2] determined the effects of ambient light on pupil size and measures of the light reflex. As ambient light varied between less than 0.1 and 200 ft cd, pupil size decreased from 6.5 to 2.5 mm; constriction and dilation velocities decreased from 6.0 to 1.5 mm/sc and from 2.5 to 1.5 mm/s, respectively. The ranges in the Fosnaugh et al.[2] experiment are similar to those reported elsewhere.[11,40] In the high ambient light conditions pupil diameter and constriction and dilation velocities increased when an opaque patch was placed over the contralateral eye.[2] These findings indicate that the design of pupillometers should incorporate features to assure that the ambient light is constant and that the subject consistently opens (or closes) the contralateral eye as the measures are made. In pupillometers where the subject is required to focus or gaze at a near object, accommodation-induced miosis will change pupil size and may diminish the sensitivity of the pupil to a light flash.

7.6.3 Effect of Fatigue, Disease, and Legal Drugs

Fatigue tends to decrease pupil size and diminish the response to light through diminished inhibition of the Edinger Westphal nucleus.[6] Subjects with diabetes mellitus have smaller pupils and a sluggish light reflex.[41] Schizophrenia and other psychiatric diagnoses are associated with sluggish pupillary response to a light flash and other pupillary abnormalities.[42] The light reflex is obtunded in anxious subjects.[9]

The ingestion of many widely used drugs changes pupillary diameter and the responsiveness to light.[26,30,43] For example, the following drug classes increase pupil size: anticholinergics (e.g., atropine, scopolamine), sympathomimetics (e.g., epinephrine, ephedrine), and antihistamines (diphenhydramine). Other drug classes decrease pupil diameter: cholinomimetics (physostigmine, pilocarpine), sympatholytics (e.g., reserpine, guanethidine, alpha-methyldopa), and chlorpromazine. The wide range of drugs that affect pupillary measures represents a challenge to the application of pupillometry in the detection of illegal drugs.

7.7 CONCLUSIONS

The proposal that pupillary measures could be used to distinguish classes of drugs likely to impair automobile driving performance[29] stimulated interest in the use of pupillometry for drug detection applications. More recently pupillometry has been applied to other fitness-for-duty applications on the assumption that small changes in static and dynamic indices of pupillary functions predict CNS impairment. The impairment may be induced by fatigue, disease, or stress. The literature was reviewed and the results of the controlled, clinical studies presented in this chapter indicate that several classes of commonly abused drugs have specific, dose-related effects of pupil size and measures of the light reflex. The application of pupillometry for the detection of drugs of abuse is theoretically possible, but the practical utility is limited. Because of the large between-subject variation in pupillary measures, one must know baseline values and ordinary variations for the tested subject. This limits the use of the technique to workplace, military, or institutional applications. The profound influence of ambient light on pupillary measures dictates that the conditions under which measures are made be carefully controlled. Other drugs, fatigue, and some diseases also influence measures of the light reflex and may increase the number of false-positive readings. Finally, the magnitude of the effects of the drugs studied are small and transient and often do not exceed the within-subject variability. These considerations challenge the use of pupillometry as a drug detection application.

ACKNOWLEDGMENTS

Mr. Ed Hotchkiss (PMI) provided the pupillometer used in the Archway study and collaborated in analyzing results. We are grateful for the help of Ed Bunker and Reginald Fant for their efforts in the previous edition of this chapter and to the students who contributed to these studies: Heide York, Michelle Fank, and Sharifeh Farasat. This research was supported, in part, by the NIH Intramural Research Program, NIDA.

REFERENCES

1. Alexandridis, E., *The Pupil*, Springer-Verlag, New York, 1985.
2. Fosnaugh, J.S., Bunker, E.B., and Pickworth, W.B., Daily variation and effects of ambient light and circadian factors on the human light reflex, *Meth. Find. Clin. Exp. Pharmacol.*, 14, 545, 1992.
3. Marquardt, W.G., Martin, W.R., and Jasinski, D.R., The use of the Polaroid CU camera in pupillography, *Int. J. Addict.*, 2, 301, 1967.
4. Jasinski, D.R. and Martin, W.R., Evaluation of a new photographic method for assessing pupil diameters, *Clin. Pharmacol. Ther.,* 8, 271, 1967.
5. Greenwald, M.K., Johanson, C.E., and Schuster, C.R., Opioid reinforcement in heroin-dependent volunteers during outpatient buprenorphine maintenance, *Drug Alcohol Depend.,* 56, 191, 1999.
6. Lowenstein, O. and Lowenfeld, I.E., The pupil, in *The Eye*, Davson, H., Ed., Academic Press, New York, 1969, 255.
7. Lowenstein, O. and Lowenfeld, I., Electronic pupillography, *Arch. Ophthalmol.*, 59, 352, 1958.
8. Newman, J. and Boughton, R., Pupillometric assessment of excessive daytime sleepiness in narcolepsy-cataplexy, *Sleep,* 14, 121, 1991.
9. Bakes, A., Bradshaw, C.M., and Szabadi, E., Attenuation of the pupillary light reflex in anxious patients, *Br. J. Clin. Pharmacol.,* 30, 377, 1990.
10. Zinn, K.M., *The Pupil,* Charles C Thomas, Springfield, IL, 1972.
11. Ellis, C.J., The pupillary light reflex in normal subjects, *Br. J. Ophthalmology*, 65, 754, 1981.
12. Lowenstein, O. and Lowenfeld, I.E., Mutual role of sympathetic and parasympathetic in shaping of the pupillary reflex to light, *Arch. Neurology Psychiatry* (Chicago), 64, 341, 1950.
13. Pickworth, W.B., Rohrer, M.S., and Fant, R.V., Effects of abused drugs on psychomotor performance, *Exp. Clin. Pharmacol.*, 5, 3, 1997.
14. Heishman, S.J., Stitzer, M.L., and Bigelow, G.E., Alcohol and marijuana: comparative dose effect profiles in humans, *Pharmacol. Biochem. Behav.*, 31, 649, 1988.
15. Radzius, A. et al., A portable pupilometer system for measuring pupillary size and light reflex, *Behav. Res. Method Instrum. Comput.*, 21, 611, 1989.
16. Pickworth, W.B., Lee, H., and Fudala, P.J., Buprenorphine-induced pupillary effects in human volunteers, *Life Sci.,* 47, 1269, 1990.
17. Heishman, S.J. et al., Acute and residual effects of marijuana: profiles of plasma THC levels, physiologic, subjective and performance measures, *Pharmacol. Biochem. Behav.*, 37, 561, 1990.
18. Pickworth, W.B. et al., Acetaminophen fails to inhibit ethanol-induced subjective effects in human volunteers, *Pharmacol. Biochem. Behav.*, 41, 189, 1991.
19. Winer, B.J., Brown, D.R., and Michels, K.M., *Statistical Principles in Experimental Design,* 3rd ed., McGraw-Hill, New York, 1991.

20. Jasinski, D.R., Johnson, R.E., and Henningfield, J.E., Abuse liability assessment in human subjects, *Trends Pharmacol. Sci.*, 5, 196, 1984.
21. Himmelsbach, C.K., The morphine abstinence syndrome, its nature and treatment, *Ann. Intern. Med.*, 15, 829, 1941.
22. Pickworth, W.B. et al., Opiate-induced pupillary effects in humans, *Meth. Find. Exp. Clin. Pharmacol.*, 11, 759, 1989.
23. Pickworth, W.B. et al., Intravenous buprenorphine reduces pupil size and the light reflex in humans, *Life Sci.*, 49, 129, 1991.
24. Pickworth, W. B. et al., Subjective and physiologic effects of intravenous buprenorphine in humans, *Clin. Pharmacol. Ther.*, 53, 570, 1993.
25. Pickworth, W.B et al., A laboratory study of hydromorphone and cyclazocine on smoking behavior in residential polydrug users, *Pharmacol. Biochem. Behav.*, 77, 711, 2004.
26. Urey, J.C., Some ocular manifestations of systemic drug abuse, *J. Am. Optometr. Assoc.*, 62, 832, 1991.
27. Rothman, R.B. et al., Lack of evidence for context-dependent cocaine-induced sensitization in humans: preliminary studies, *Pharmacol. Biochem. Behav.*, 49, 583, 1994.
28. Sharpe, L.G., Pickworth, W.B., and Martin, W.R., Actions of amphetamine and antagonists on pupil diameter in the chronic sympathectomized dog, *Psychopharmacology*, 53, 115, 1977.
29. Tennant, F., The rapid eye test to detect drug abuse, *Postgrad. Med.*, 84, 108, 1988.
30. Koetting, J.F., The use of drugs for behavior modification as it relates to the practice of optometry. Part 2, *J. Am. Optometr. Assoc.*, 48, 213, 1977.
31. McLane, N.J. and Carroll, D.M., Ocular manifestations of drug abuse, *Surv. Ophthalmol.*, 30, 298, 1986.
32. Fant, R.V. et al., Acute and residual effects of marijuana in humans, *Pharmacol. Biochem. Behav.*, 60, 4, 1998.
33. Roberts, J.D. and Adams, A.J., Short term effects of smoking on ocular accommodation and pupil size, *J. Am. Optometr. Assoc.*, 40, 528, 1969.
34. Pickworth, W.B. et al., Effects of mecamylamine on spontaneous EEG and performance in smokers and non-smokers, *Pharmacol. Biochem. Behav.*, 56, 81, 1997.
35. Mas, M. et al., Cardiovascular and neuroendocrine effects and pharmacokinetics of 3,4-methylenedioxymethamphetamine in humans, *J. Pharmacol. Exp. Ther.*, 290, 136, 1999.
36. Torre, R. et al., Pharmacology of MDMA in humans, *Ann. N.Y. Acad. Sci.*, 914, 225, 2000.
37. Pun, M.S. et al., Ketamine anaesthesia for paediatric ophthalmology surgery, *Br. J. Ophthalmol.*, 87, 535, 2003.
38. Raymon, L.P., Steele, B.W., and Walls, H.C., Benzodiazepines in Miami-Dade County, Florida driving under the influence (DUI) cases (1995–1998) with an emphasis on Rohypnol: GC-MS confirmation, patterns of use, psychomotor impairment, and results of Florida legislation, *J. Anal. Toxicol.*, 23, 490, 1999.
39. Murillo, R. et al., Pupillometry in the detection of concomitant drug use in opioid maintained patients, *Methods Find. Exp. Clin. Pharmacol.*, 26, 271, 2004.
40. Taniguchi, H. et al., Pupillary light reflex in healthy subjects, *Kobe J. Med. Sci.*, 34, 189, 1988.
41. Lanting, P. et al., The cause of increased pupillary light reflex latencies in diabetic patients: the relationship between pupillary light reflex and visual evoked potential latencies, *EEG Clin. Neurophysiol.*, 78, 111, 1991.
42. Steinhauer, S.R. and Hakerem, G., The pupillary response in cognitive psychophysiology and schizophrenia, in Psychophysiology and Experimental Psychopathology: A Tribute to Samuel Sutton, Friedman, D. and Bruder, G., Eds., *Ann. N.Y. Acad. Sci.*, 658, 182, 1992.
43. Turner, P., The human pupil as a model for clinical pharmacological investigations, *J. R. Coll. Physicians* (London), 9, 165, 1975.

CHAPTER 8

Abuse of Marketed Medications

Kenzie L. Preston, Ph.D.,[1] David H. Epstein, Ph.D.,[1] John P. Schmittner, M.D.,[1] and Sharon L. Walsh, Ph.D.[2]

[1] Clinical Pharmacology and Therapeutics Branch, National Institute on Drug Abuse, National Institutes of Health, Department of Health and Human Services, Baltimore, Maryland

[2] Department of Behavioral Science, Center on Drug and Alcohol Research, University of Kentucky College of Medicine, Lexington, Kentucky

CONTENTS

8.1 OVERVIEW OF THE PROBLEM

The abuse* of marketed medications has been at the forefront of public awareness in recent years, mostly due to widespread reports concerning OxyContin and hydrocodone.[1] While these are highly regulated, prescription-only medications with recognized potential for abuse, even some over-the-counter (OTC) medications have become problematic, either because of their own effects (e.g., ephedrine) or because they are used in the manufacture of other abused substances (e.g., pseudoephedrine, used to make methamphetamine).[2,3]

The increase in concern seems to reflect a true increase in incidence. The numbers of new nonmedical users of the four major classes of prescription-type drugs (narcotic pain relievers, tranquilizers, stimulants, and sedatives) increased between 1991 and 2001.[4] There were substantially more new users for narcotic pain relievers than for the other three drug categories — an increase from 628,000 initiates in 1990 to 2.4 million in 2001.[5] This increase in new users was accompanied by a 76% increase between 1997 and 2000 in the number of primary treatment admissions for narcotic-analgesic abuse.[6] Initiation of nonmedical tranquilizer use also increased steadily during the 1990s, from 373,000 initiates in 1990 to 1.1 million in 2001.[5]

With reports of increasing abuse has come increasing tension between the need to prevent diversion (illicit use of marketed medication) and the need to keep effective medications available. This tension has been most visible in the realm of opioid analgesics. The need for adequate treatment of pain (e.g., References 7 through 9) coexists uneasily with some state and federal regulatory policies, and with prosecutions of physicians by the Drug Enforcement Agency (DEA) for reported overprescribing; these efforts at control may deter *appropriate* prescribing.[10–12] A similar effect has been suggested with regard to state-legislated triplicate-prescription requirements and the appropriate prescription of benzodiazepines for agitation and anxiety.[13] Scheduled analgesics are also understocked at some pharmacies, especially in nonwhite neighborhoods.[14] Underavailability or underprescription of effective medication, resulting in inadequate treatment, may itself be a type of misuse of medication. For the sake of optimal patient care, an appropriate balance must be struck between the opposing needs for availability and control.

It is appropriate to recognize that some medications are more susceptible to abuse than others. If two medications are equally effective for a given indication, the one with lower abuse liability† would obviously be preferred. Information on abuse liability is necessary for the appropriate regulation of medications and provides a basis for education of physicians, patients, and the public. In this chapter we describe the control of marketed medications, abuse-liability assessment procedures for premarketing testing in laboratory animals and humans, considerations of the formulation properties, and postmarketing surveillance of abuse. Finally, we provide three "case studies" of marketed medications that have been abused.

8.2 CONTROL OF MARKETED MEDICATIONS

In the U.S., substances can be "scheduled" (controlled) under federal law if they are found to have the potential for abuse. Medications being proposed for approval by the U.S. Food and Drug Administration (FDA) may be required to undergo abuse-liability testing and scheduling review. Compounds deemed to have some liability for abuse can be scheduled at one of five levels reflecting how stringently their manufacture and distribution will be regulated. Compounds with high abuse liability and no medically recognized use in the U.S. are placed in Schedule I. (Some Schedule I compounds are used medically in other countries; for example, heroin is approved for analgesia in

* Throughout this chapter, the term *abuse* is used in its broadest sense, referring to any nonmedical or not-as-prescribed use.
† The term *abuse liability*, although standard in behavioral pharmacology, may have unintended implications to clinicians, for whom the word *liability* can connote a threat of litigation. In some contexts, *abuse potential* may be preferable.

England.[15]) Compounds whose medical utility is recognized are placed in one of the other four schedules (II to V), with higher numbers reflecting less stringent control.

Scheduling serves as a warning to physicians and patients that a particular medication has the potential to be abused. However, the primary purpose of scheduling is to deter diversion and to provide a mechanism for detection if diversion should occur. To that end, requirements for many aspects of the manufacture and distribution of controlled substances are defined in the Controlled Substances Act.[16] The drugs in each schedule are listed, along with the requirements for labeling and packaging, security, storage, record maintenance, manufacturing quotas, and registration requirements both for persons who manufacture, distribute, dispense, import, or export the substances and for places where the substances are manufactured, distributed, dispensed, imported, or exported. Also regulated are the issuance of prescriptions by physicians, dispensing by pharmacists, and prescription labeling, filing, and refilling. For example, prescriptions for drugs in Schedule II cannot be refilled; prescriptions for drugs in Schedules III and IV cannot be refilled more than five times.

Eight criteria for a drug's scheduling, or exemption from scheduling, are outlined in Section 811 of the Controlled Substances Act:[17] (1) its actual or relative potential for abuse; (2) scientific evidence of its pharmacological effect, if known; (3) the state of current scientific knowledge regarding the substance; (4) its history and current pattern of abuse; (5) the scope, duration, and significance of abuse; (6) what, if any, risk there is to the public health; (7) its psychological or physiological dependence liability; (8) whether the substance is an immediate precursor of a substance already controlled.

Several of these factors (such as 1, 2, 3, and 7) are amenable to premarketing abuse-liability testing. Most abuse-liability testing is targeted to assess the pharmacological entity without regard to its formulation. The past decade has demonstrated that new formulations of old medications add a potentially dangerous twist to assessment of abuse liability.

8.3 PREMARKETING ABUSE-LIABILITY TESTING

8.3.1 Assessment of Pharmacological Entity

Standardized experimental procedures have been developed to evaluate pharmacological entities according to actual or relative potential for abuse, pharmacological effects, and psychological or physiological dependence liability. One indicator of abuse potential is the extent to which a drug produces reinforcing effects. This is typically estimated in self-administration studies by use of operant-conditioning paradigms that measure the ability of the drug to act as a reinforcer in laboratory animals or sometimes humans. Methods for measuring discriminative-stimulus and subjective effects have been developed to estimate the extent of similarity of the pharmacologic profile of novel compounds to prototypic compounds of a drug class that are already scheduled. In drug-discrimination studies, laboratory animals or human subjects are trained to discriminate the presence or absence of a prototypic drug, and novel drugs are tested for their ability to substitute for the prototypic drug. Subjective-effects studies are conducted with human participants. A novel drug is administered over a range of doses, and its subjective effects are measured on a battery of questionnaires and compared to those of prototypic drugs of abuse. In physical-dependence studies, the test drug is administered repeatedly and then withdrawn; physiological, behavioral, and, in the case of humans, subjective effects are measured. The capacity to produce physical dependence not only can increase the likelihood of abuse but also can increase the adverse consequences of abuse, although physical dependence alone is neither necessary nor sufficient for abuse potential.

The toxicity of abused substances is considered because misuse has the potential to create public-health problems and because the presence or absence of toxic effects can limit abuse liability. Toxicity data can be obtained in studies designed specifically for that purpose as well as from studies of other pharmacological effects such as those listed above.

8.3.1.1 Self-Administration

The self-administration paradigm is a model of drug abuse widely used to assess the reinforcing efficacy of drugs. In this model, research subjects, usually laboratory animals, are given access to a drug under controlled experimental conditions, and their drug-taking behavior is evaluated. A drug is considered to be reinforcing if the frequency of a designated behavioral response (e.g., a lever press) is increased when drug delivery is contingent on the performance of that response in comparison to the frequency of responses in the absence of the drug. The capacity of a drug to reinforce behavior and, thus, maintain self-administration under experimental conditions is associated with a significant likelihood of abuse by human drug abusers. Since the early 1960s, hundreds of drugs have been tested in operant self-administration paradigms. Drug self-administration has been demonstrated by various routes of administration (intravenous, oral, intragastric, intracranial, intracerebroventricular, intramuscular, and inhalation) and in a wide variety of species (pigeons, mice, rats, cats, dogs, non-human primates, and humans) (for review see Reference 18). The self-administration paradigm is complex; only a brief summary of methods is outlined below. For a more detailed discussion, interested readers are referred to one of the numerous reviews on this topic.[18–20]

To establish a drug's relative reinforcing efficacy in a self-administration paradigm, a number of procedures can be used: response-rate analysis, concurrent or second-order schedules, progressive-ratio (PR) schedules, and discrete-trial choice.[20] The most widely used method, response-rate analysis, employs an operant schedule of reinforcement that defines the work requirement for, or the temporal availability of, the drug, such as a fixed-ratio schedule (FR schedule; a given number of responses is required to obtain the reinforcer) or a fixed-interval schedule (FI schedule; the reinforcer is contingent on the first response emitted after a fixed time interval). Dependent measures typically include the rate of responding (responses/time), temporal response pattern, and the number of drug administrations per session. Duration of access to the drug is an important variable that can be manipulated. Access is typically confined to a limited and predetermined time period (e.g., a 3-h session) in which multiple small unit doses may be obtained. Using fixed access periods, FR and FI schedules generate reliable and reproducible patterns of responding for most drugs.

Self-administration studies can be initiated in one of two ways: direct self-administration or substitution. In the direct self-administration procedure, inexperienced subjects are given access to a test drug, and the extent to which self-administration is initiated and maintained is measured and can be compared to the rate of behavior observed when placebo and/or other drugs are available. In the more commonly used substitution procedure, self-administration of a standard or prototypic abused drug is established first; the test drug is then substituted for the standard drug, and changes in self-administration behavior are measured.

While self-administration has proved very useful in abuse-liability assessment, several issues must be considered when interpreting the results. One is the reliance on response rate as an index of reinforcing efficacy or reinforcement strength.[21] Drugs produce a constellation of effects, only a portion of which may be directly related to their reinforcing efficacy. Drug self-administered at the beginning of an experimental session can alter the subject's ability to make the required responses for self-administration later in the session. Thus, nonspecific behavioral effects must be ruled out. One control for nonspecific effects is to incorporate another operant task (such as responding for food) within the experimental session. Another approach is to use more complex schedules of reinforcement (such as second-order and concurrent schedules) (see Reference 20). Another complexity stems from the nonlinear relationship between dose and response rate or drug delivery. The dose–response function generated from self-administration studies is typically shaped as an inverted U. The relationship between dose and response rate or drug delivery is positive at low doses (thus forming the ascending limb of the dose–response curve) and negative at high doses (thus forming the descending limb). In some cases where there is an inverse relationship between unit dose (i.e., dose per injection) and the number of drug deliveries, the total intake of drug can actually be constant across the descending limb of the dose–response curve.[22,23] Consequently, response rate *per se* may not be a valid index of relative reinforcing strength or efficacy.

Alternatives to response-rate analysis include the progressive-ratio (PR) paradigm and the choice procedure. In the progressive-ratio paradigm, subjects are initially trained to complete a low requirement (e.g., FR-1) for the delivery of a given dose of drug, and then the response requirement is systematically increased until the subject fails to complete it. The last response requirement completed before cessation of responding is known as the "breakpoint"; this serves as the primary measure of the relative strength of the reinforcer. In general, there is an orderly relationship between PR breakpoint and drug dose. In the choice procedure, subjects are trained to respond on at least two separate manipulanda, each associated with its own distinctive conditioned stimulus (e.g., different colored lights). The subject is initially trained on a simple task in which a choice is made between two discriminable drug stimuli such as saline vs. a dose of cocaine. During subsequent testing, the subject is first given an opportunity to sample each choice, and then is required to make a preference choice between the two available manipulanda. In this task, the measure of reinforcing efficacy is the number of drug choices made in a given session and may be expressed as the total percentage of choices for a given drug.

Despite the numerous complexities of self-administration procedures, the data generated from these studies are invaluable for predicting the abuse liability of drugs. When self-administration studies are conducted with the appropriate experimental controls, orderly relationships can be obtained both across and within drug classes. For example, for drugs within the same class, those with higher abuse liability engender more self-administration behavior in the laboratory than related drugs with lower abuse liability. Based on the vast published self-administration literature and epidemiologic reports of drug abuse, self-administration behavior is considered a reliable and strong predictor of the abuse liability of drugs in humans.[18,24,25]

Self-administration is predominantly used in the animal laboratory, although our review of the literature suggests that an increasing number of self-administration studies are being conducted with human volunteers. As more of the parameters are worked out, it is likely that human self-administration studies will gain even wider use in abuse-liability assessment.

8.3.1.2 Drug Discrimination

Drug discrimination is an experimental paradigm used to classify drugs based on their interoceptive stimulus effects (i.e., effects occurring within the subject) using a behavioral criterion.[26] The drug-discrimination paradigm and the types of data it generates have been reviewed in detail.[27–30] The paradigm has been used extensively to study pharmacology and to assess abuse liability in humans and nonhumans.[31–34] In drug-discrimination studies, differential reinforcement is used to establish discriminative control by two or more drugs: subjects are trained to emit one response in the presence of a training drug and to emit an alternate response in the absence of the training drug, while other environmental conditions are held constant. For example, in one training session, a drug dose is administered and responses on only one of two (or more) levers produce reinforcer delivery. In another training session, vehicle or no drug is administered, and responses on an alternate lever produce reinforcer delivery. Repeated reinforcement of correct identifications generally leads to stable discrimination.

After the discrimination is acquired, generalization or substitution testing with novel drug stimuli can be conducted. Doses of a test drug are administered in place of the training drug, and the distribution of responses on the drug-appropriate or vehicle-appropriate lever is recorded. If the novel drug produces predominantly drug-appropriate responses (usually 80% or greater), the novel drug is said to substitute completely and, thus, produce stimuli like those of the training drug. If the novel drug produces responses predominantly on the vehicle or no drug-appropriate lever, the novel drug is characterized as not substituting for the training drug. Intermediate degrees of responding are characterized as partial substitution. Drugs within the same pharmacological class that share interoceptive effects can be differentiated from drugs in other pharmacological classes; even within drug classes, discrimination procedures can differentiate among drugs having activity at different receptor subtypes.[27]

While drug discrimination has been predominantly used in animal studies, it is also used with humans.[35] The procedures used to study drug discrimination in humans are quite similar to those used in laboratory animals, but adapted to the unique capabilities of humans. In the discrimination-training phase, training drugs are paired with letter codes as identifying labels. Drugs are given under double-blind conditions and are not identifiable by appearance or volume, and money typically serves as the reinforcer for correct responses. Most human studies include the concurrent collection of questionnaire data on subjective effects, which has been invaluable in evaluating the interrelationship of behavioral discrimination and subjective effects.

Drug discrimination is not a direct measure of reinforcing efficacy. Although virtually all abused drugs can be trained as discriminative stimuli, most psychoactive drugs, including those that are not self-administered, are discriminable from vehicle or no drug.[35] Thus, discriminability in and of itself is not evidence of abuse liability; rather abuse liability may be inferred from the relative similarity of a drug's stimulus effects to those of a known standard or prototypical abused drug. However, there is substantial concordance between discriminative stimulus effects and subjective effects in humans[35,36] and self-administration behavior in laboratory animals.[27]

An important caveat in interpreting drug-discrimination data is that results must be considered in the context of the training drug. For example, in subjects trained to discriminate cocaine from saline, D-amphetamine fully substitutes for cocaine while pentobarbital and morphine do not, even though all four drugs have significant abuse potential.[37,38] Training dose is critical; with higher training doses, generalization dose–response curves tend to be shifted to the right so that higher doses of test drug are needed to produce full substitution. A drug with partial-agonist properties may substitute for a low training dose but fail to substitute for a higher training dose of a full agonist.[27] Lower training doses generally produce less pharmacologic specificity than higher training doses, increasing the likelihood of generalization between pharmacologically dissimilar drugs.[30]

8.3.1.3 Subjective Effects

Subjective-effect measures have been recognized as a critical element in abuse-liability assessment in humans for several decades.[39,40] Subjective effects are feelings, perceptions, and moods personally experienced by an individual. Drugs of abuse produce characteristic subjective effects or interoceptive stimuli that are perceived as positive and desirable to some individuals; drugs that produce these positive mood effects are often described as euphoriants.[40] Because subjective effects are not accessible to observers for public validation, they can only be obtained through self-reports from the individual experiencing them. Subjective-effect measures in the form of questionnaires have been developed to determine whether a drug produces perceptible effects and to determine the quantitative and qualitative characteristics the drug user experiences. They may be used to collect individual self-reports that are consistent across individuals, studies, and situations, can be combined across subjects, can provide reliable and replicable data, and are meaningful to outside observers. Such questionnaires are scientifically useful for assessing a drug's pharmacologic properties, including time course and potency, and can be used to measure the degree of similarity between a test drug and a known standard for abuse-liability assessment. In general, the critical element is the assessment of whether participants like the effects of the drug. Abuse-liability studies, however, usually incorporate multiple questionnaires in order to gather a comprehensive profile of a drug's subjective effects.

The most commonly used questionnaires are scales of global drug effects, subscales of the Addiction Research Center Inventory (ARCI), Profile of Mood States (POMS), Adjective Rating Scales, and the Drug-Class Questionnaire. On measures of global drug effects, participants are asked to integrate the different aspects of a drug's effects and to rate the "overall strength" of those effects, the participants' "liking" of the drug, and the degree to which the drug produces any "good" effects or "bad" effects. The ARCI is a 550-item true/false questionnaire that was developed empirically to assess a range of physical, emotive, and subjective effects of drugs from several pharmacological classes.[41,42] The ARCI can be tailored to study a particular drug by including only those subscales that are appropriate. The most frequently used scales in abuse-liability studies of acute drug effects are the Morphine-Benzedrine Group (MBG; an index of euphoria), the Pentobarbital-Chlorpromazine-Alcohol Group (PCAG; an index of apathetic sedation), and the Lysergic Acid Diethylamide Group (LSD; an index of dysphoria or somatic discomfort). Increases in the MBG scale, or euphoria scale as it is sometimes called, are associated with significant abuse potential. The Profile of Mood States (POMS) questionnaire is a 65- or 72-item standardized adjective rating scale developed to measure changes in mood in psychiatric populations.[43] The POMS does not contain drug-liking or euphoria scales; its utility in abuse-liability assessment derives from determinations of similarity to a standard drug of abuse and from identification of possible aversive effects.[44] Adjective rating scales are questionnaires on which participants rate symptoms describing global drug effects (e.g., high, strength of drug effect), mood effects (e.g., anxious, depressed), and physical symptoms (e.g., itchy, nausea). In the Drug-Class Questionnaire, participants are asked to indicate which among a list of drugs/drug classes was most similar to the test drug. Experienced abusers can reliably distinguish placebo from active drug and can reliably distinguish among the major drug classes when tested with adequate doses.[45]

Subjective-effect studies require consideration of several experimental factors and control procedures. Participants must be able to comprehend and respond appropriately to questionnaires. Drugs should be administered under double-blind conditions to avoid the introduction of bias into participants' reports. The participants' prior drug exposure could influence responding; most studies assessing abuse potential have used participants with histories of illicit drug use, though a number of studies have been conducted in healthy volunteers without histories of drug abuse.[40,44–47]

Subjective measures can be used to qualitatively characterize the effects of the drug, and these tend to be consistent across drug classes. Each of the major pharmacological classes has been characterized using the questionnaires described above. Drugs of different pharmacological classes generally produce profiles of subjective effects that are unique to that class of drugs and that are recognizable to individuals. This can be of value to the extent that pharmacological class predicts abuse liability. It can also be useful when testing novel drug classes, for example, when testing drugs that act at newly identified receptors and for which no prototypic drugs are known.

As one might expect, global subjective-effect measures such as "liking" and "disliking" tend not to differentiate between different pharmacological classes of drugs, although they do provide quantitative information regarding the overall magnitude of drug effects. Actually, "liking" has especially good concordance with rates of abuse (i.e., highly abused drugs produce dose-related increases in ratings of liking while nonabused drugs do not[40]) and is therefore probably the single most important subjective-effect measure in human abuse-liability assessment.

8.3.1.4 Physical-Dependence Capacity

Repeated administration of some drugs can result in tolerance and physical dependence. With the development of tolerance, the effect of a drug decreases if the dose is held constant. Tolerance to the desired effect often leads to escalation of the doses self-administered by abusers. Use of higher doses in turn increases the risk of adverse effects, such as physiological toxicity, psychomotor impairment, and physical dependence. Physical dependence becomes evident when reduction or termination of drug administration is followed by withdrawal signs and symptoms, which can manifest as physiological, psychological, and/or behavioral changes. The biological mechanisms of tolerance and physical dependence have been reviewed elsewhere (see, for example, References 48 and 49).

Physical dependence is no longer considered necessary or sufficient for abuse potential.[45,50] Nonetheless, physical dependence can contribute to the perpetuation of drug use (as dependent individuals seek drugs to avoid unpleasant withdrawal) and to the cost to the public health, in terms of both human suffering and the expense of medical treatment associated with withdrawal. Physical dependence, and the consequent abstinence syndrome, is significant for some drug classes such as opiates, barbiturates, and benzodiazepines, but less prominent with other highly abusable drugs including cocaine and the amphetamines. In addition, alleviation of the symptoms associated with physical dependence and withdrawal is not effective as a sole treatment for drug dependence.[50]

Physical-dependence capacity can be determined by direct addiction, substitution, or suppression studies. In direct-addiction studies, a test drug is administered repeatedly over time; doses are initially low and then gradually increased as tolerance develops to toxic effects. After subjects have been stabilized at a specified dose, tolerance and other effects of chronic drug administration are evaluated; methods for evaluating tolerance have been described in detail elsewhere.[20,51] Physical dependence can then be documented by abrupt discontinuation of drug administration or by administration of a selective antagonist for the appropriate receptor type (e.g., naloxone during chronic administration of an opioid). Subjects are observed for signs of an abstinence syndrome. With human subjects, self-report measures can also be included to gain qualitative information about the characteristics of the abstinence syndrome, including dysphoric effects. Drug-seeking behavior can also be monitored, either by recording requests for test drug or other medication during the withdrawal period (for example, see Reference 52), or by giving subjects the opportunity to self-administer the drug.[53,54]

The substitution and suppression procedures, variations on direct addiction, have also been used to evaluate physical-dependence capacity. These procedures have chiefly been used with the opioids[45,52] and are described only briefly here. In suppression studies, subjects are initially made physically dependent on a prototypical opioid agonist, for example, morphine administered in four injections/day. In test sessions, agonist administration is abruptly withdrawn, and at the peak of withdrawal (e.g., approximately 30 h after the last morphine dose) test medications are administered and evaluated for their ability to suppress withdrawal. The ability of opioid agonists to suppress the abstinence syndrome was documented using this methodology. In substitution studies, the maintenance drug is replaced with doses of test drug or placebo. The ability of the test drug to prevent the onset of the withdrawal syndrome is assessed over a specified period of time (for example, 24 h). This procedure enables crossover studies with multiple drugs or multiple dose levels of a test drug; subjects are restabilized on the maintenance medication between experimental test sessions.

8.3.2 Assessment of Preparation

8.3.2.1 Pharmacokinetics

The abuse liability of a drug is influenced by its pharmacokinetic properties and the numerous factors that determine its distribution, metabolism, and excretion. One important factor is the speed with which a drug is delivered to the central nervous system. In general, abuse potential is enhanced by speeding the delivery of drug to the brain, and this closely corresponds with the rate of rising drug concentration in arterial blood (see also Reference 55). Increased speed of delivery shortens the interval between drug administration and the perceived onset of the drug's pharmacodynamic effects, a behavioral feature considered critical to abuse potential.[56] Routes of drug administration that provide a more rapid delivery are associated with greater abuse liability. Because route of administration largely determines the speed of delivery, one of the simplest means of modifying the speed of drug delivery is to change the route of administration. For most drugs the rank order for routes of administration from fastest to slowest delivery are typically as follows: inhalation (e.g., smoking) > intravenous > intramuscular ≈ subcutaneous > intranasal > oral. Cocaine is an example of a drug with abuse potential that increases across routes of administration, with oral having the lowest dependence potential and intravenous and smoked having the highest.[57–62] The relationship between speed of onset and abuse potential has also been shown for pentobarbital and diazepam.[63,64] There are some exceptions to these rules; these include drugs that are themselves inactive but produce active metabolites (i.e., prodrugs) and drugs with particularly poor bioavailability when administered by a specific route.

8.3.2.2 Capacity to Be Made into More Abusable Preparation

Because faster onset of action is associated with higher potential for abuse, abuse-liability assessment should include consideration of whether a formulation can be altered to increase the speed of onset. There are numerous examples of abuse of a medication by a route other than that intended by the manufacturer. The sustained-release oral form of oxycodone, designed to deliver an initial rapid dose followed by slow release, has been widely abused by chewing the tablet, thus releasing the entire content of the tablet at once.[65] There is also evidence for intravenous use of sublingual buprenorphine tablets.[66] Transdermal systems developed to deliver medication slowly for extended periods of time have been prime targets for misuse,[67] as discussed below in the case study of fentanyl.

A wide range of possible uses and misuses must be considered in both the development of formulations and in regulatory decisions. Formulations need to be tested as they might be used, not just as they are meant to be used. While it is possible to develop formulations that lower the abuse potential of a pharmacological constituent, every effort must be made to challenge the formulation to substantiate such a claim.

8.3.2.3 Availability

The availability of a marketed medication is a key determinant of its abuse liability. A highly abusable medication may have a low rate of abuse if it can only be obtained, for example, in hospital settings. Even within hospital settings, the degree to which availability and, thus, opportunity play a role in incidence of abuse is illustrated by the greater incidence of substance abuse among anesthesiologists than among other physician groups.[68,69] Increasing the availability of a medication with a low rate of abuse can substantially increase the incidence of abuse. Two examples of this phenomenon are described below in the case studies: abuse of both fentanyl (an agonist opioid with high abuse liability) and butorphanol (an agonist-antagonist opioid with moderate abuse liability) increased when each drug was approved for prescribed use in outpatients, despite the use of formulations that might have been expected to minimize abuse liability.

Even drugs with low potential for abuse can have periodic increases in abuse if they are widely available, as discussed below in the case study of the OTC cough suppressant dextromethorphan. Other examples include anticholinergics[70,71] and antihistamines.[72] Abuse of these drugs tends to be mostly limited to particular populations — patient populations in the case of anticholinergics, and youth in the case of dextromethorphan. That the abuse liability of a drug may differ across populations, and that different populations may abuse a drug for different reasons, are possibilities that need consideration when selecting participants and outcome measures for abuse-liability studies. Abuse-liability testing has come to focus on assessment of euphoriant effects in experienced drug abusers rather than patterns of use in the clinical populations for whom the drug is intended or in other populations,[73] and while this approach is probably appropriate in most cases,[74] it does not always suffice (as illustrated below in the case studies).

In summarizing the relationship between availability and abuse, we need to recognize that there is no formula to predict exactly how much abuse will occur, and that the relationship may wax and wane over time, as discussed below in the case studies. Still, there are a few "rules of thumb." Given equal availability, drugs that produce more positive mood effects are more likely to be abused than those with less positive effects. However, all psychoactive drugs, even those with minimal positive mood effects, have the potential for abuse, even if only for their mood-altering effects.

Increasing the availability of a drug will likely increase the absolute numbers of abuse incidents. Finally, acute toxicity has the opposing effects of decreasing the likelihood of abuse while increasing the adverse consequences if abuse should occur.

8.4 POSTMARKETING SURVEILLANCE

Postmarketing surveillance is a continuation of the risk assessment conducted during drug development.[75–78] Postmarketing surveillance is necessary because the number of patients exposed to a new drug during premarket testing is usually too small to detect low-incidence adverse events and determine statistically whether those events are caused by the new drug. In addition, patients selected to participate in clinical trials often have more limited ranges of medical conditions and concomitant medications than those who are prescribed the medication after marketing. In the U.S., the FDA maintains the MedWatch program to collect adverse-event reports on marketed medications and to provide safety information for health-care professionals and the public.[79] Pharmaceutical companies often establish their own monitoring programs for adverse events.

Surveillance systems also exist for drug abuse (for review, see Reference 80). Through the Substance Abuse and Mental Health Services Administration (SAMHSA) of the Department of Health and Human Services, the U.S. federal government maintains the Drug Abuse Warning Network (DAWN),[81] which monitors trends in drug-related emergency-department visits and deaths (although the quality of these data has been questioned[82]). SAMHSA also conducts several surveys on drug use and treatment.[83] One SAMHSA survey, the National Survey on Drug Use & Health, formerly called the National Household Survey of Drug Abuse (NHSDA/NSDUH), is administered annually to a statistically representative sample to collect data on the use of illicit drugs, the nonmedical use of licit drugs, and the use of alcohol and tobacco products. Another SAMHSA survey, the Drug and Alcohol Services Information System (DASIS), collects data on treatment facilities for substance abuse, including services offered, numbers of individuals treated, and the characteristics of individuals admitted to treatment. Two of the data sets within DASIS are the Treatment Episode Data Set (TEDS) and the National Survey of Substance Abuse Treatment Services (N-SSATS, formerly known as UFDS). TEDS has demographic and drug-history information about individuals admitted to treatment, primarily by providers receiving public funding. N-SSATS is an annual census of U.S. treatment facilities registered with SAMHSA and contains information on their location, organization, structure, services, and utilization.

While these surveys are very informative about national trends in drug use, they probably have limited utility as early-warning systems for abuse of newly marketed medications. Ideally, detection of an emerging abuse problem would occur before the numbers of affected individuals grew large enough to be measurable on national surveys. More directed postmarketing surveillance has been used to monitor for diversion and abuse for two recently marketed medications, tramadol and sibutramine.[80] The tramadol surveillance program included spontaneous reports to the manufacturer and adverse-event data from MedWatch, but also used a key-informant network of treatment researchers who completed quarterly questionnaires. Proactive surveillance via the informant network increased the detection of cases of physical dependence, diversion, and abuse compared to the spontaneous-reporting systems.[84–86] In the sibutramine surveillance program, an anonymous questionnaire was completed by individuals in community- and university-based treatment programs every 6 months for 3 years.[80,87] The questionnaire requested information on experiences with sibutramine, phentermine (a scheduled anorectic agent), and a drug with a fabricated name. Early detection of clinically important diversion or abuse of a marketed medication through postmarketing surveillance could enable reconsideration of scheduling decisions before serious problems develop.

8.5 CASE STUDIES

In practice, the regulatory status of a marketed drug rarely emerges in a tidy way from experimentally obtained abuse-liability data. In this section, we examine the histories of three drugs (butorphanol, fentanyl, and dextromethorphan) chosen because the prediction of abuse liability for each drug has been imperfect for different reasons. For each drug, we reviewed three types of information: abuse-liability studies in laboratory animals and humans; case reports and news items concerning diversion, abuse, addiction, or overdose; and news items and official documents concerning changes in regulatory or commercial status. Sources included papers found through the Medline and PsycInfo databases (1966 through 2003) supplemented with references cited in the papers themselves; items from the popular press found through the Lexis/Nexis database (early 1970s through 2003); and the Web sites of the FDA and the DEA.

For each drug, the prevalence of abuse was partly attributable to its absolute availability — for example, the over-the-counter status of dextromethorphan (DXM) or the expansion of fentanyl and butorphanol from inpatient to outpatient use. But the pattern of abuse for each drug was distinctive and probably could not have been predicted from the available experimental abuse-liability data.

8.5.1 Butorphanol

Table 8.1 shows a selective timeline of the evaluation, abuse, and regulation of butorphanol, an opioid with mixed activity at mu and kappa receptors. The most salient aspects of the drug's recent history can be summed up in terms of two questions:

Who abused it? Most of the reports have concerned patients experiencing iatrogenic physical dependence, especially after 1991, when the drug was approved for outpatient use in a nasal-spray formulation. Reports seemed especially to increase when the drug was marketed for a new indication, migraine — a disorder with recurrent symptoms and the possibility of rapid rebound of symptoms if medication is overused.[88] Anecdotally, the modal pattern of abuse seemed to be escalation of use in patients with legitimate prescriptions,[89] even though some patients reported that the acute effects of the drug were extremely unpleasant.[90] There have been very few reports of diversion or abuse by nonpatients, and essentially no reports of use for euphoriant properties or for the avoidance of withdrawal from other opiates such as heroin.

Why was this pattern not predicted? Published abuse-liability studies with butorphanol have generally been conducted in experienced abusers of mu-agonist opioids, and have generally focused on whether butorphanol produces liking or euphoria and on whether it has morphine-like properties. The absence of such findings may have contributed to the nonscheduled status of the drug (until it was placed in Schedule IV in 1997). One review article[91] summarizes "data on file" at Bristol Laboratories from 1978 as follows: "During Phase III clinical trials, [injectable] butorphanol was administered chronically at therapeutic doses to patients for as long as 9 months and then abruptly terminated. No withdrawal symptoms or compulsive drug-seeking behavior were precipitated." The patient population is unspecified; it seems unlikely that it consisted largely of patients with migraine or that they had the opportunity to self-administer the drug more frequently or in larger doses. Similarly, the later clinical trials supporting the nasal-spray formulation[92,93] did not include patients with migraine and would not have been able to detect a cycle of rebound headache and dose escalation.

Comments. The clearest lesson from the butorphanol experience is that when a drug is introduced to a new population, it is important to determine whether extant abuse-liability studies will generalize to that population. If not, then clinical trials should be designed to detect signs of abuse in that population, and careful postmarketing surveillance should occur. The goal is not to prevent patient access to necessary medications, but to ensure that providers and patients have adequate information about the risks of such medications.

Table 8.1 Butorphanol Timeline

Year	Animal Data	Human Lab Data/Clinical Trials	Case Reports/Case Series/Surveys	News Items	Regulatory/Commercial Developments
1975		s.c.: Doses up to 8 mg do not precipitate morphine withdrawal; doses over 8 mg psychotomimetic[119]			
1976–1978		s.c.: Lower abuse potential than codeine or propoxyphene; no increase in liking w/doses 4–48 mg/day over a month, unlike pentazocine[120–122]			
1978		i.m.: No drug-seeking noted in participants in Bristol Labs Phase III trials after abrupt termination of drug[91]			i.m.: FDA's Drug Abuse Advisory Committee (DAAC) votes 12–2 to schedule butorphanol; recommendation not followed; scheduled in only one state (Oklahoma)[89]
1980					i.m.: FDA maintains position against scheduling due to absence of evidence of abuse; DAAC votes 9–4 in support of FDA[89]
1981	In rats, produces only mild withdrawal syndrome (similar to other partial agonists), but tends to precipitate withdrawal from morphine[123]				
1982	Baboons self-administer butorphanol, as well as nalbuphine and pentazocine (finding published 4 years after presentation)[124]				

1983			i.m.: Case report of diversion from hospital in Michigan[125]		DAAC votes 10–2 against scheduling of theoretical oral form; FDA considers diversion reports not of great significance[89]
1984	Physical dependence clearly shown in rats[94]		i.m.: 5 male teens in Mississippi using i.v. with antihistamine to get high; minor withdrawal syndrome; 1 fatal OD[126]		
1985			i.m.: Frequent diversion in hospitals;[127,128] some patients escalating use[129]		i.m.: Some hospitals indicate having tightened controls to Schedule II–IV level; some exclude drug from formulary[127]
1988		i.m.: In 3-choice discrimination in methadone patients: butorphanol more like naloxone than saline or hydromorphone; very little abuse liability[133]			
1989	In morphine-maintained rhesus monkeys: butorphanol discriminated as saline, not as naltrexone[132]				
ca. late 1980s			Nasal spray: 18 healthy volunteers in Bristol-Myers "first time in humans" study; withdrawal not seen when drug discontinued after 16 days[92]		
1990		i.m.: Very little abuse liability in methadone patients[133]	Nasal spray: Bristol-Myers clinical trial in post-Caesarian-section pain; no assessment of abuse liability or withdrawal[93]		

Continued

Table 8.1 Butorphanol Timeline *(Continued)*

Year	Animal Data	Human Lab Data/Clinical Trials	Case Reports/Case Series/Surveys	News Items	Regulatory/Commercial Developments
1991	In rats, naloxone-induced withdrawal is just as severe for butorphanol as for morphine[95]	Nasal spray: Very little abuse liability in male opioid abusers[134] i.m.: In 2-choice discrimination: butorphanol more like hydromorphone than like saline; withdrawal both morphine-like and kappa-like; but subjects choose sedative, not more butorphanol, for relief; increases liking, but not MBG; sometimes identified as barbiturate[135]			Nasal spray: FDA approves nonscheduled, despite DAAC concerns (e.g., that clinical trials were insensitive to abuse liability)[89]
1992					Nasal spray advertised for use in migraine; no published clinical trials on spray in migraine; Texas increases control amid reports of spray users unable to stop[89]
1993–1994			Nasal spray: Chicago-area neurologist writes that of his 24 migraine patients, 13 had had ADRs; "extremely stoned," "stuporous"; 6 said it was worst experience of their lives; no withdrawal mentioned[90]		Nasal spray: MedWatch reports increase[89]

1994	In cynomolgus monkeys, butorphanol acts only as an agonist[136]	i.m.: Male postaddicts; 3-choice discrimination: on VAS scales: increases high, liking, good, and not bad, but on ARCI, increased PCAG, not MBG; drug class: ID'd as sedative, not opiate; conclusion: more kappa than mu effects[137] i.v.: Healthy volunteers; on VAS, increases sedated (also liking, but not dose-related); on ARCI, increases PCAG and LSD; main difference from effects in opiate abusers: psychomotor impairment[138]	Nasal spray: Review of headache treatments acknowledges possibility of symptom rebound and dependence with overuse of analgesics, including spray[88]		
1995				Nasal spray: In August, suicide by gunshot during withdrawal (not widely reported until 1997)[139]	FDA survey: 39 of 47 states report diversion or abuse; 7 have tried to schedule butorphanol; more than half have special controls at hospitals; most-abused form is nasal spray. FDA leaves regulation to states[89] Nasal spray: In April, Bristol-Myers asks FDA to control[140]
1996					Nasal spray: Chicago-area pharmacists are said to dilute it to limit its abuse liability[89]
1997		i.v.: In healthy volunteers, butorphanol-induced ratings of "elated" (though not liking) actually increase during cold-water pain[96]		Nasal spray: Reports of addiction associated with rebound migraine[139] *Neurology* publishes historical review[89] coauthored by father of 1995 suicide	Nasal spray: FDA recommends scheduling to DEA, but decides against sending Dear Doctor letter[141] DEA places butorphanol in Schedule IV
1998		i.m.: Disliked by heroin/opiate abusers[142,143]		Nasal spray: Wrongful-death suits filed[144]	

Continued

Table 8.1 Butorphanol Timeline *(Continued)*

Year	Animal Data	Human Lab Data/Clinical Trials	Case Reports/Case Series/Surveys	News Items	Regulatory/Commercial Developments
2000		i.m.: Opioid chippers; hydromorphone vs. not hydromorphone discrimination; with these instructions, butorphanol does not substitute for hydromorphone at any dose; VAS: increases both good and bad, not liking; no effects on ARCI[145]		Nasal spray: Scattered news reports of addiction continue[146]	
2001		i.m.: Heroin chippers; butorphanol compared with a selective kappa agonist (enadoline) and a selective mu agonist (hydromorphine) and was more mu-like than kappa-like on most measures[147]		Nasal spray: First news report of recreational use: fatal OD in teen girl[148]	Nasal spray: FDA gives Mylan abbreviated NDA for generic
2002		i.m.: Methadone-maintained humans; trained on "naloxone vs. placebo vs. novel" discrimination; butorphanol produces 70% naloxone responding, 29% novel responding[149]		Nasal spray: Another news report of an addicted provider[150]	Nasal spray: FDA approves generic form Roxane

Note: Abbreviations used in tables: ADR, Adverse Drug Reaction; ARCI, Addiction Research Center Inventory; DAAC, Drug Abuse Advisory Committee; DEA, Drug Enforcement Administration; DO, dextrorphan (active metabolite of dextromethorphan); DSM-IIIR, *Diagnostic and Statistical Manual*, 3rd ed. revised; DXM, dextromethorphan; FDA, Food and Drug Administration; ID, identification; i.m., intramuscular; i.v., intravenous; NDA, New Drug Application; OD, overdose; OTC, over the counter; PCP, phencyclidine; s.c., subcutaneous; VAS, Visual Analog Scales; WHO, World Health Organization.

One of the risks of butorphanol, its physical-dependence potential, emerged in animal studies[94,95] more clearly than in human abuse-liability studies. It is also interesting to note that the human experimental data that seem most consistent with marketing experience did not appear until 1997, when it was shown that the modest euphoriant effects of butorphanol are more prominent in the presence of a painful stimulus (a finding opposite to what has been observed with most morphine-like drugs).[96] Each of these findings shows, of course, that relevant abuse-liability data are easiest to pick out in hindsight. Still, future marketing and regulatory decisions may benefit from increased attention to the multiplicity of ways in which a drug could be prone to abuse.

8.5.2 Fentanyl

Table 8.2 shows a selective timeline of the evaluation, abuse, and regulation of fentanyl, a potent agonist at mu-opioid receptors. Again, the most salient aspects of the drug's recent history can be summed up with two questions.

Who abused it? In contrast to butorphanol, fentanyl has been abused primarily by nonpatients who had access to the drug. There have been numerous reports (far too many to include in the timeline) of diversion and abuse of fentanyl for its euphoriant properties. Until 1990, these reports usually involved health-care providers with access to the intravenous formulation in hospital settings. After 1990, when a transdermal-patch formulation became available to outpatients, abuse spread to a much broader population. Yet only a very small proportion of the reports concerned patients for whom legitimate prescriptions had been written — again in contrast to butorphanol. The modal pattern of abuse was through illegitimate access to patches (taken from trash cans, removed from nursing-home patients, or, in one twice-published case,[97,98] removed from a dead body), followed by inhalation, ingestion, or injection of their contents.[99–103]

Why was this pattern not predicted? The highly euphorogenic nature of fentanyl was actually clear in abuse-liability studies as early as 1965,[104] and the drug was accordingly placed in Schedule II of the 1970 Controlled Substances Act; this was the most restrictive possible placement that still permitted medical use. What was apparently not foreseen, when the patch formulation was approved for outpatient use in 1990, was that its slow-release properties would be defeated by individuals seeking intoxication. The published literature appears to contain no abuse-liability studies for the patch formulation.

Comments. The obvious lesson of the fentanyl experience is that abuse-liability studies must take into account the possibility that an intended slow-release system will be subverted by users. How to respond to this possibility is a difficult question. Sometimes it may be possible to develop a formulation that is more difficult to subvert, such as a subcutaneous implant. But it is also important that the drug be available in formulations that patients need, such as the fentanyl lozenge approved in 1998 for breakthrough pain in patients with cancer — despite the likelihood that these formulations will be abused. (There has already been a newspaper report implicating fentanyl lozenges in the death of a man who used three lozenges simultaneously.[105]) Higher scheduling of fentanyl would make the drug completely unavailable for medical use. The regulatory response to fentanyl abuse at the federal level has been to maintain close FDA monitoring of advertising claims, commercial manufacture of new formulations, and imports through Internet pharmacies. Additional measures, such as tighter prescription tracking, have been considered by individual states such as Florida.

As mentioned above, most reports of fentanyl abuse have not involved iatrogenic addiction in patients. As with butorphanol, the human experimental data most consistent with this did not appear until 1996, when it was shown that the euphoriant effects of fentanyl are blunted in the presence of a painful stimulus.[106] Clearly, however, low incidence of iatrogenic addiction or abuse may not predict the likelihood of abuse in nonpatient populations.

Earlier in the chapter, we pointed out that the relationship between drug availability and abuse may wax and wane over time. In the case of fentanyl, this can be seen in the differing results of

Table 8.2 Fentanyl Timeline

Year	Human Lab Data/Clinical Trials	Case Reports/Case Series/Surveys	News Items	Regulatory/Commercial Developments
1965	i.v.: In postaddicts, more euphorogenic than morphine[104]			
early 1970s				i.v.: Sublimaze and Innovar introduced in U.S.; for hospital use only; on Schedule II
mid-1970s		i.v.: Abuse reported among health-care providers[151]		
1980s			i.v.: Scattered reports of diversion by health-care providers;[152,153] also some reports of illicitly manufactured powder[154]	
1989			Lozenge: Some controversy over appropriateness of "lollipop" formulation during multisite trials[155]	
1990				Patch: FDA approves Duragesic; no abuse-liability studies for patch in published literature
1991–1993		Patch: Scattered reports of misuse and ODs[103,156]	Illicit fentanyl: Many reports of fatal ODs on powder sold as "Tango & Cash";[157] referred to as a "serial killer"[108,158]	
1992				Illicit fentanyl: Bill introduced in Congress to equate possession penalties with those for heroin possession[159]
1993				Lozenge: FDA approves Oralet for hospital use
1994			Lozenge: More controversy over appropriateness of "lollipop" formulation[160–162]	Patch: FDA sends Dear Doctor letter
1995			i.v.: Medical student in New York City dies from self-injected fentanyl[163]	
1996	i.v.: In healthy volunteers, euphoriant effects blunted during pain[106]			
1997				Lozenge: FDA DAAC recommends approving Actiq for outpatient use
1998				Lozenge: FDA approves Actiq for outpatient use
2000–2003		Patch: Another case series on abuse and OD[164]	Patch: More stories on diversion and OD[165–167] Lozenge: Fatal OD with use of 3 simultaneously[105]	

Note: See Table 8.1 for abbreviations.

two published analyses. In the first analysis, from 1990 to 1996, fentanyl prescriptions increased 1168% while an index of overdose admissions (DAWN mentions of fentanyl, including both licitly and illicitly manufactured fentanyl) actually decreased 59%.[107] But in the second analysis, from 1994 to 2001, both measures increased, with the largest relative increase in DAWN mentions occurring in 1997.[1] This pattern may be partly attributable to negative news coverage of both illicit and diverted fentanyl, which, based on our Lexis/Nexis search, peaked from 1991 through 1993, then declined from 1994 to 1999, perhaps permitting some "forgetting" of the drug's risks. Negative publicity, or lack thereof, is likely to have complex effects on a drug's abuse liability; according to one newspaper report, when police used bullhorns to warn of the lethal potency of a batch of illicitly manufactured fentanyl being sold under the name Tango & Cash, local attempts to purchase the drug actually increased.[108]

Among the other trends we noticed in press coverage of fentanyl was that, although reports of overdoses from illicitly manufactured fentanyl tended to be lurid (often referring to the drug or its manufacturers as "serial killers"), this line of reportage rarely influenced the tone of stories about pharmaceutically used formulations. Even as reports of street-fentanyl fatalities peaked in the early 1990s, several newspapers ran positive pieces on the therapeutic potential of the fentanyl patch. Although there are several different ways in which this can be viewed, it is probably encouraging that abuse of fentanyl in one form did not automatically lead to the derogation of other forms.

8.5.3 Dextromethorphan

Table 8.3 shows a selective timeline of the evaluation, abuse, and regulation of DXM, a nonnarcotic cough suppressant with activity at sigma and PCP receptors. Unlike butorphanol and fentanyl, it has never been scheduled in the Controlled Substances Act, and it is available without a prescription in various over-the-counter formulations.

Who abused it? Most reports of abuse have involved teenagers either specifically seeking a dissociative/hallucinogenic experience or simply seeking any intoxicating effect. The pattern of abuse has generally been sporadic since the introduction of DXM in the 1950s, but reports of abuse have been more frequent and widespread since the mid-1990s, coinciding with the more rapid spread of information on the Internet.

Why was this pattern not predicted? As with butorphanol, initial abuse-liability studies were generally conducted in experienced abusers of mu-agonist opioids, and generally focused on whether DXM produced liking or euphoria and on whether it had morphine-like properties.[109,110] Participants in the first study[109] seemed completely insensitive to the acute dissociative effects of large single oral doses (up to 800 mg), and even when larger doses were used (up to 1800 mg), no dissociative effects emerged, perhaps because the outcome instruments had not been designed to detect them. The primary effect of single doses was drowsiness. Only chronic dosing produced strong effects, described as "confusion" and "loss of memory"; the participants found these effects frightening. The second study[110] found slightly stronger evidence for acute effects, such as increases on the PCAG (sedation) and LSD (dysphoria) scales of the ARCI, but again no measures were used that would have specifically identified dissociative effects, and the participants did not report liking the drug.

Comments. The clearest lesson from the DXM experience is that when designing an abuse-liability study, it is important to consider all possible effects that can make a drug abusable, bearing in mind that effects to which a particular study sample is insensitive or averse may be desired effects in others.

In the case of DXM, however, the desirability of the intoxicating effects appears to be confined largely to individuals in their teens and twenties — an observation consistent with the finding that the use of hallucinogens peaks at age 19 and then declines rapidly, regardless of birth cohort.[111] As a result of the drug's limited appeal, outbreaks of abuse have usually been self-limiting. This may be among the reasons that DXM remains unscheduled by the DEA and retains its over-the-

Table 8.3 Dextromethorphan (DXM) Timeline

Year	Animal Data	Human Lab Data/Clinical Trials	Case Reports/Case Series/Surveys	News Items	Regulatory/Commercial Developments
before 1956					Romilar tablets (DXM-only preparation) not controlled, but require prescription in U.S.[168]
1956					FDA moves Romilar tablets from prescription status to OTC[168]
1962		s.c. and oral: No acute subjective effects in postaddict prisoners; chronic subjective effects all aversive; also, no effects of active metabolite DO[109]			
1964–1969			Sporadic abuse outside U.S.[169–171]		
1970					DXM exempted from Controlled Substances Act[17]
1971		s.c. and oral: Acute psychotomimetic effects in postaddict prisoners, but no increase in VAS liking or ARCI MBG; drug ID: barbiturate or amphetamine; subjective effects: similar to nalorphine[110]			
ca. 1973					Romilar taken off market after increase in abuse[172]
1976					DO removed from Schedule II
1982					WHO concludes no evidence to warrant control[173]
1986					DXM made prescription-only in Sweden after reports of teen abuse there[174]

1988			First known fatal ODs, in Sweden: one suicide, one possible abuse[175]		
1990			Case of Robitussin-drinking dependence in U.S. meeting DSM-IIIR criteria; patient's initial attempts to seek help are met with disbelief (pharmacist says that getting high on cough syrup is impossible)[176]		Hearings by Pennsylvania drug board, then FDA; PA board was asked to put DXM on PA's Schedule V (limiting it to pharmacy or physician dispensing and to patients over 18); FDA reviews reports of abuse from several states; decides to leave control to states[177]
1991	In rats: DO induces PCP-like behavior, but DXM does not[178]				
1992			Two case reports of DXM-associated mania[179,180]	First newspaper mention of recreational use in U.S., in advice column[181]	
1993			Case report of mania[182] Abuse by two teenage boys in southern U.S.[183]	*Harper's* piece says abuse of DXM cough syrup is well known among teens but rarely written about[184]	
1994	In rats, DXM itself has PCP-like discriminative-stimulus effects[185]			Another advice-column mention[186] November: William White's DXM FAQ appears on Web[115]	
1995			Case report of massive long-term ingestion of cough syrup[187]	News report that DXM-syrup fad among teens is already declining in popularity;[188] another advice-column mention[189]	
1996			School survey in rural Pennsylvania: DXM-cough-syrup abuse fairly well known, first heard of in 1987[190] Two cases of mania with daily use[191]		Drixoral Cough Caps apparently discontinued

Continued

Table 8.3 Dextromethorphan (DXM) Timeline *(Continued)*

Year	Animal Data	Human Lab Data/Clinical Trials	Case Reports/Case Series/Surveys	News Items	Regulatory/Commercial Developments
1997–1998	In rats, DXM has sedative effects and DO has PCP-like effects[192]		Abuse in Korea[193,194] Two nonfatal ODs in California[195]	A few more news reports on abuse of cough syrups (e.g., [196]) and sale of DXM by mail order (e.g.,[197])	
1999	In rats and rhesus monkeys, "DXM has some PCP-like effects, but they are produced more reliably by DO"[198]		Retrospective case series of ODs in Switzerland[199] and Texas; increase shown in Texas[200]	Reports on sales of pure DXM over Internet[201]	DEA official says that upswing in DXM abuse is "out of our realm [of jurisdiction]"[202]
2000		Oral: In 9 detoxified alcoholics and 10 healthy controls, DXM (2 mg/kg) has ethanol-like effects, with higher scores in controls[203]		More OD reports in news, concerning both OTC formulations and pure DXM; Web sites criticized[204–207]	FDA official says that DXM is not approved for use outside marketed formulations[208]
2001				Fatal OD on Coricidin[209] Suspicion that teens are distilling pure DXM from cough syrup[210]	Local efforts to move DXM preparations behind the counter[211]

2002		Oral: In 10 methadone-maintained inpatients, DXM (120, 240, and 480 mg/day for 4 days each to reduce methadone tolerance) induced some drowsiness; no changes in subjective effects or ARCI; several patients reported intoxication at the highest dose[212]	Poisoning in a youth who tried to extract DXM from cough syrup with "Agent Lemon" procedure[213]	More local reports of abuse by teens, e.g., in New Hampshire;[214] increase shown in ODs near Chicago[215]	Failed bill in North Dakota to ban sale of cough medicine to minors;[216] more pharmacists move DXM behind the counter[217]
2003			Case of liver toxicity from abuse of Coricidin, due to acetaminophen[114]	More ODs, at least one fatal;[218] another acetaminophen poisoning from abuse of an OTC preparation[113]	Bill in Texas to ban sale of cough medicine to minors and outlaw abuse; in committee;[219] Palo Alto high-school resource officer on one-man "crusade" to make pharmacy chains change shelf placement of DXM products;[220] pharmacist in Iowa City puts DXM products behind the counter[221]

Note: See Table 8.1 for abbreviations.

counter status by FDA regulations. Several states have seen legislative efforts to restrict the availability of DXM either fail or become stalled. However, in 2006, legislation passed in Illinois banned the sale of DXM in pure form. Some pharmacists have chosen to keep DXM-containing preparations behind the counter, but this approach has been criticized because it forces recreational users underground rather than giving pharmacists a chance to engage them.[112] (In one newspaper report, a pharmacist stated that he had been able to dissuade two teenagers from buying and abusing DXM-containing cough syrup by warning them of its risks.[113] Whether they obtained the drug elsewhere is not known.) The response of manufacturers has been to discontinue sales of DXM-only cough formulations; this may discourage abuse, but may also increase toxicity from other ingredients such as acetaminophen when abuse does occur.[114]

As mentioned above, outbreaks of DXM abuse seem to have increased with the rise of the Internet. Literature reviews and newspaper articles on DXM have frequently included pejorative or alarmist comments about the abundance and inaccuracy of DXM-related information found on the Internet. Yet the seminal Internet document about DXM, William White's DXM FAQ (Frequently Asked Questions)[115] — first posted to Usenet newsgroups in 1994, and made available on the Web in November of that year — was exhaustive (with scholarly interpretations of hundreds of studies from peer-reviewed journals) and balanced (with the risks of DXM abuse emphasized throughout). If the mid-to-late-1990s upswing in DXM abuse is to be attributed partly to the Internet's ability to spread information widely, perhaps it should also be attributed to the tendency of some readers not to absorb information thoroughly.

8.6 FURTHER READING

To avoid redundancy with several recently published reviews, we have limited our discussion of techniques for abuse-liability assessment. Interested readers are referred to these reviews,[73,74,116–118] which appear in a special issue of the journal *Drug and Alcohol Dependence*.

ACKNOWLEDGMENT

Drs. Preston, Epstein, and Schmittner were supported by the NIH Intramural Research Program, NIDA.

REFERENCES

1. Zacny, J. et al., College on Problems of Drug Dependence taskforce on prescription opioid non-medical use and abuse: position statement, *Drug Alcohol Depend.*, 69, 215, 2003.
2. Abourashed, E.A. et al., Ephedra in perspective — a current review, *Phytother. Res.*, 17, 703, 2003.
3. Cunningham, J.K. and Liu, L.M., Impacts of federal ephedrine and pseudoephedrine regulations on methamphetamine-related hospital admissions, *Addiction*, 98, 1229, 2003.
4. SAMHSA, Nonmedical Use of Prescription-Type Drugs among Youths and Young Adults, http://www.samhsa.gov/oas/2k3/prescription/prescription.htm, 2003. Accessed January 9, 2004.
5. SAMHSA, Overview of Findings from the 2002 National Survey on Drug Use and Health, http://www.samhsa.gov/oas/NHSDA/2k2NSDUH/Results/2k2results.htm, 2003. Accessed January 9, 2004.
6. SAMHSA, The DASIS Report: Treatment Admissions Involving Narcotic Painkillers, http://www.samhsa.gov/oas/2k3/painTX/painTX.htm, 2003. Accessed January 9, 2004.
7. Hockenberg, S.J., American Nurses Association position statement on promotion of comfort and relief of pain in dying patients, *Plast. Surg. Nurs.*, 12, 32, 1992.
8. Kalso, E. et al., Recommendations for using opioids in chronic non-cancer pain, *Eur. J. Pain*, 7, 381, 2003.
9. Jacob, E., Pain management in sickle cell disease, *Pain Manage. Nurs.*, 2, 121, 2001.

10. Nunnelley, P.P., Prosecution or persecution? *Kans. Med. Assoc. J.*, 89, 311, 1991.
11. Gilson, A.M. and Joranson, D.E., U.S. policies relevant to the prescribing of opioid analgesics for the treatment of pain in patients with addictive disease, *Clin. J. Pain*, 18, S91, 2002.
12. Ziegler, S.J. and Lovrich, N.P., Jr., Pain relief, prescription drugs, and prosecution: a four-state survey of chief prosecutors, *J. Law Med. Ethics*, 31, 75, 2003.
13. Reidenberg, M.M., Effect of the requirement for triplicate prescriptions for benzodiazepines in New York State, *Clin. Pharmacol. Ther.*, 50, 129, 1991.
14. Morrison, R.S. et al., "We don't carry that" — failure of pharmacies in predominantly nonwhite neighborhoods to stock opioid analgesics, *New Engl. J. Med.*, 342, 1023, 2000.
15. British National Formulary, Diamorphine, http://bnf.org/bnf/bnf/current/noframes/3521.htm, 2003. Accessed January 12, 2004.
16. DEA, Title 21 USC excerpts, subchapter 1, part C, http://www.deadiversion.usdoj.gov/21cfr/21usc/21icusct.htm, 2003. Accessed January 8, 2004.
17. DEA, 21 USC, Section 811, http://www.deadiversion.usdoj.gov/21cfr/21usc/811.htm, 2003. Accessed January 8, 2004.
18. Meisch, R.A. and Lemaire, G.A., Drug self-administration, in *Methods in Behavioral Pharmacology*, F. van Haaren, Ed., Elsevier, Amsterdam, 1993.
19. Bozarth, M.A., Ed., *Methods of Assessing the Reinforcing Properties of Abused Drugs*, Springer-Verlag, New York, 1987.
20. Brady, J.V. and Lukas, S.E., Testing Drugs for Physical Dependence Potential and Abuse Liability. NIDA Research Monograph 52, 1984.
21. Brady, J.V. and Griffiths, R.R., Behavioral procedures for evaluating the relative abuse potential of CNS drugs in primates, *Fed. Proc.*, 35, 2245, 1976.
22. Woods, J. and Schuster, C.R., Reinforcement properties of morphine, cocaine and SPA as a function of unit dose, *Int. J. Addict.*, 3, 231, 1968.
23. Wilson, M.C., Hitomi, M., and Schuster, C.R., Psychomotor stimulant self-administration as a function of dosage per injection in the rhesus monkey, *Psychopharmacologia*, 22, 271, 1971.
24. Griffiths, R.R., Bigelow, G.E., and Henningfield, J.E., Similarities in animal and human drug-taking behavior, in *Advances in Substance Abuse*, N.K. Mello, Ed., JAI Press, Greenwich, CT, 1980, 1.
25. Woolverton, W. and Nader, M., Experimental evaluation of the reinforcing effects of drugs, *Mod. Meth. Pharmacol.*, 6, 165, 1990.
26. Stolerman, I.P. and Shine, P.J., Trends in drug discrimination research analysed with a cross-indexed bibliography, 1982–1983, *Psychopharmacology*, 86, 1, 1985.
27. Young, A., Discriminative stimulus profiles of psychoactive drugs, in *Advances in Substance Abuse*, N.K. Mello, Ed., Jessica Kingsley Publishers, London, 1991, 140.
28. Overton, D.A., Applications and limitations of the drug discrimination method for the study of drug abuse, in *Methods of Assessing the Reinforcing Properties of Abused Drugs*, M.A. Bozarth, Ed., Springer-Verlag, New York, 1987, 291.
29. Stolerman, I., Measures of stimulus generalization in drug discrimination experiments, *Behav. Pharmacol.*, 2, 265, 1991.
30. Stolerman, I., Drug discrimination, in *Methods in Behavioral Pharmacology*, F. van Harden, Ed., Elsevier Science, Amsterdam, 1993, 217.
31. Balster, R.L., Drug abuse potential evaluation in animals, *Brit. J. Addict.*, 86, 1549, 1991.
32. Holtzman, S.G., Discriminative stimulus effects of drug: relationship to abuse liability, in *Testing and Evaluation of Drugs of Abuse*, M.W. Adler and A. Cowan, Eds., Wiley-Liss, New York, 1990.
33. Kamien, J. et al., Drug discrimination by humans compared to nonhumans: current status and future directions, *Psychopharmacology*, 111, 259, 1993.
34. Bigelow, G.E. and Preston, K.L., Drug discrimination: methods for drug characterization and classification, *NIDA Res. Mon.*, 92, 101, 1989.
35. Preston, K.L. and Bigelow, G.E., Subjective and discriminative effects of drugs, *Behav. Pharmacol.*, 2, 293, 1991.
36. Evans, S.M. and Johanson, C., Amphetamine-like effects of anorectics and related compounds in pigeons, *J. Pharmacol. Exp. Ther.*, 241, 817, 1987.
37. Dykstra, L. et al., Discriminative stimulus properties of cocaine alone and in combination with buprenorphine, morphine and naltrexone, *Drug Alcohol Depend.*, 30, 227, 1992.

38. Garza, R.D. and Johanson, C.E., The discriminative stimulus properties of cocaine in the rhesus monkey, *Pharmacol. Biochem. Behav.*, 19, 145, 1983.
39. Jasinski, D.R., History of abuse liability testing in humans, *Br. J. Addict.*, 86, 1559, 1991.
40. Jasinski, D., Johnson, R., and Henningfield, J., Abuse liability assessment in human subjects, *Trends Pharmacol. Sci.*, 5, 196, 1984.
41. Haertzen, C., Development of scales based on patterns of drug effects, using the addiction research center inventory (ARCI), *Psychol. Rep.*, 18, 163, 1966.
42. Haertzen, C.A. and Hickey, J.E., Addiction Research Center Inventory (ARCI): measurement of euphoria and other drug effects, in *Methods for Assessing the Reinforcing Properties of Abused Drugs*, M.A. Bozarth, Ed., Springer-Verlag, New York, 1987.
43. McNair, D.M., Lorr, M., and Droppleman, L.F., *Manual for the Profile of Mood States,* Educational and Industrial Testing Service, San Diego, 1971.
44. de Wit, H. and Griffiths, R.R., Testing the abuse liability of anxiolytic and hypnotic drugs in humans, *Drug Alcohol Depend.*, 28, 83, 1991.
45. Jasinski, D.R., Assessment of the abuse potentiality of morphinelike drugs (methods used in man), in *Drug Addiction 1: Morphine, Sedative/Hypnotic and Alcohol Dependence*, W.R. Martin, Ed., Springer-Verlag, Berlin, 1977.
46. Johanson, C., Discriminative stimulus effects of buspirone in humans, *Exp. Clin. Psychopharmacol.*, 1, 173, 1993.
47. Zacny, J.P. and Goldman, R.E., Characterizing the subjective, psychomotor, and physiological effects of oral propoxyphene in non-drug-abusing volunteers, *Drug Alcohol Depend.*, 73, 133, 2004.
48. Koob, G.F. and Bloom, F.E., Cellular and molecular mechanisms of drug dependence, *Science*, 242, 715, 1988.
49. Haefely, W., Biological basis of drug-induced tolerance, rebound, and dependence. Contribution of recent research on benzodiazepines, *Pharmacopsychiatry*, 19, 353, 1986.
50. Wise, R.A. and Bozarth, M.A., A psychomotor stimulant theory of addiction, *Psychol. Rev.*, 94, 469, 1987.
51. Branch, M.N., Behavioral factors in drug tolerance, in *Methods in Behavioral Pharmacology*, F. van Haaren, Ed., Elsevier, Amsterdam, 1993.
52. Jasinski, D.B. and Mansky, P.A., Evaluation of nalbuphine for abuse potential, *Clin. Pharmacol. Ther.*, 13, 78, 1972.
53. Mello, N.K. and Mendelson, J.H., Buprenorphine suppresses heroin use by heroin addicts, *Science*, 207, 657, 1980.
54. Preston, K.L., Bigelow, G.E., and Liebson, I.A., Self-administration of clonidine, oxazepam, and hydromorphone by patients undergoing methadone detoxification, *Clin. Pharmacol. Ther.*, 38, 219, 1985.
55. Oldendorf, W.H., Some relationships between addiction and drug delivery to the brain, *NIDA Res. Mon.*, 120, 13, 1992.
56. Gossop, M. et al., Severity of dependence and route of administration of heroin, cocaine and amphetamines, *Br. J. Addict.*, 87, 1527, 1992.
57. Javaid, J.I. et al., Cocaine plasma concentration: relation to physiological and subjective effects in humans, *Science*, 202, 227, 1978.
58. Van Dyke, C. et al., Oral cocaine: plasma concentrations and central effects, *Science*, 14, 211, 1978.
59. Perez-Reyes, M. et al., Free-base cocaine smoking, *Clin. Pharmacol. Ther.*, 32, 459, 1982.
60. Resnick, R.B., Kestenbaum, R.S., and Schwartz, L.K., Acute systemic effects of cocaine in man: a controlled study by intranasal and intravenous routes, *Science*, 195, 696, 1977.
61. Evans, S.M., Cone, E.J., and Henningfield, J.E., Arterial and venous cocaine plasma concentrations in human: relationship to route of administration, cardiovascular effects and subjective effects, *J. Pharmacol. Exp. Ther.*, 279, 1345, 1996.
62. Mayersohn, M. and Perrier, D., Kinetics of pharmacologic response to cocaine, *Res. Commun. Chem. Pathol.*, 22, 465, 1978.
63. de Wit, H., Bodker, B., and Ambre, J., Rate of increase of plasma drug level influences subjective response in humans, *Psychopharmacology*, 107, 352, 1992.
64. de Wit, H., Dudish, S., and Ambre, J., Subjective and behavioral effects of diazepam depend on its rate of onset, *Psychopharmacology*, 112, 324, 1993.

65. Cone, E.J. et al., Oxycodone involvement in drug abuse deaths: a DAWN-based classification scheme applied to an oxycodone postmortem database containing over 1000 cases, *J. Anal. Toxicol.*, 27, 57, 2003.
66. Vidal-Trecan, G. et al., Intravenous use of prescribed sublingual buprenorphine tablets by drug users receiving maintenance therapy in France, *Drug Alcohol Depend.*, 69, 175, 2003.
67. Roberge, R.J., Krenzelok, E.P., and Mrvos, R., Transdermal drug delivery system exposure outcomes, *J. Emerg. Med.*, 18, 147, 2000.
68. Talbott, G.D. et al., The Medical Association of Georgia's Impaired Physicians Program. Review of the first 1000 physicians: analysis of specialty, *J. Am. Med. Assoc.*, 257, 2927, 1987.
69. Gallegos, K.V. et al., Addiction in anesthesiologists: drug access and patterns of substance abuse, *QRB Qual. Rev. Bull.*, 14, 116, 1988.
70. Dose, M. and Tempel, H.D., Abuse potential of anticholinergics, *Pharmacopsychiatry*, 33, S43, 2000.
71. Buhrich, N., Weller, A., and Kevans, P., Misuse of anticholinergic drugs by people with serious mental illness, *Psychiatr. Serv.*, 51, 928, 2000.
72. Cox, D., Ahmed, Z., and McBride, A.J., Diphenhydramine dependence, *Addiction*, 96, 516, 2001.
73. Griffiths, R.R., Bigelow, G.E., and Ator, N.A., Principles of initial experimental drug abuse liability assessment in humans, *Drug Alcohol Depend.*, 70, S41, 2003.
74. Balster, R.L. and Bigelow, G.E., Guidelines and methodological reviews concerning drug abuse liability assessment, *Drug Alcohol Depend.*, 70, S13, 2003.
75. O'Neill, R.T., Biostatistical considerations in pharmacovigilance and pharmacoepidemiology: linking quantitative risk assessment in pre-market licensure application safety data, post-market alert reports and formal epidemiological studies, *Stat. Med.*, 17, 1851, 1998.
76. Hasford, J. and Lamprecht, T., Company observational post-marketing studies: drug risk assessment and drug research in special populations — a study-based analysis, *Eur. J. Clin. Pharmacol.*, 53, 369, 1998.
77. Corrigan, O.P., A risky business: the detection of adverse drug reactions in clinical trials and post-marketing exercises, *Soc. Sci. Med.*, 55, 497, 2002.
78. Ajayi, F.O., Sun, H., and Perry, J., Adverse drug reactions: a review of relevant factors, *J. Clin. Pharmacol.*, 40, 1093, 2000.
79. FDA, Medwatch home page, http://www.fda.gov/medwatch/index.html, 2004. Accessed January 8, 2004.
80. Arfken, C.L. and Cicero, T.J., Postmarketing surveillance for drug abuse, *Drug Alcohol Depend.*, 70, S97, 2003.
81. SAMHSA, DAWN: Drug Abuse Warning Network, http://dawninfo.samhsa.gov, 2004. Accessed January 8, 2004.
82. Roberts, C.D., Data quality of the Drug Abuse Warning Network, *Am. J. Drug Alcohol Abuse*, 22, 389, 1996.
83. SAMHSA, OAS Data Systems for Alcohol, Tobacco, and Illegal Drug Use Treatment, http://www.samhsa.gov/oas/p0000014.htm#NHSDA, 2003. Accessed January 9, 2004.
84. Woody, G.E. et al., An independent assessment of MEDWatch reporting for abuse/dependence and withdrawal from Ultram (tramadol hydrochloride), *Drug Alcohol Depend.*, 72, 163, 2003.
85. Senay, E.C. et al., Physical dependence on Ultram (tramadol hydrochloride): both opioid-like and atypical withdrawal symptoms occur, *Drug Alcohol Depend.*, 69, 233, 2003.
86. Cicero, T. et al., A postmarketing surveillance program to monitor Ultram (tramadol hydrochloride) abuse in the United States, *Drug Alcohol Depend.*, 57, 7, 1999.
87. Arfken, C.L., Schuster, C.R., and Johanson, C.E., Postmarketing surveillance of abuse liability of sibutramine, *Drug Alcohol Depend.*, 69, 169, 2003.
88. Markley, H.G., Chronic headache: appropriate use of opiate analgesics, *Neurology*, 44, S18, 1994.
89. Fisher, M.A. and Glass, S., Butorphanol (Stadol): a study in problems of current drug information and control, *Neurology*, 48, 1156, 1997.
90. Robbins, L., Stadol Nasal Spray — treatment for migraine? *Headache*, 33, 220, 1993.
91. Pachter, I.J. and Evens, R.P., Butorphanol, *Drug Alcohol Depend.*, 14, 325, 1985.
92. Shyu, W.C. et al., Multiple-dose phase I study of transnasal butorphanol, *Clin. Pharmacol. Ther.*, 54, 34, 1993.
93. Abboud, T. et al., Transnasal butorphanol: a new method for pain relief in post-cesarean section pain, *Acta Anaesth. Scand.*, 35, 14, 1991.

94. McCarthy, P.S. and Howlett, G.J., Physical dependence induced by opiate partial agonists in the rat, *Neuropeptides*, 5, 11, 1984.
95. Horan, P. and Ho, I.K., The physical dependence liability of butorphanol: a comparative study with morphine, *Eur. J. Pharmacol.*, 203, 387, 1991.
96. Conley, K.M. et al., Modulating effects of a cold water stimulus on opioid effects in volunteers, *Psychopharmacology*, 131, 313, 1997.
97. Flannagan, L.M., Butts, J.D., and Anderson, W.H., Fentanyl patches left on dead bodies — potential source of drug for abusers, *J. Forensic Sci.*, 41, 320, 1996.
98. Yerasi, A.B. and Butts, J.D., Disposal of used fentanyl patches, *Am. J. Health Syst. Ph.*, 54, 85, 1997.
99. Anderson, D.T. and Muto, J.J., Duragesic transdermal patch: postmortem tissue distribution of fentanyl in 25 cases, *J. Anal. Toxicol.*, 24, 627, 2000.
100. Marquardt, K.A. and Tharratt, R.S., Inhalation abuse of fentanyl patch, *Clin. Toxicol.*, 32, 75, 1994.
101. Arvanitis, M.L. and Satonik, R.C., Transdermal fentanyl abuse and misuse, *Am. J. Emerg. Med.*, 20, 58, 2002.
102. Purucker, M. and Swann, W., Potential for duragesic patch abuse, *Ann. Emerg. Med.*, 35, 314, 2000.
103. DeSio, J.M. et al., Intravenous abuse of transdermal fentanyl therapy in a chronic pain patient, *Anesthesiology*, 79, 1139, 1993.
104. Gorodetzky, C.W. and Martin, W.R., A comparison of fentanyl, droperidol, and morphine, *Clin. Pharmacol. Ther.*, 6, 731, 1965.
105. Shulte, F. and McVicar, N., Deputies investigate doctor in drug case, *Sun-Sentinel*, Fort Lauderdale, FL, p. 1B, March 22, 2003.
106. Zacny, J.P. et al., The effects of a cold-water immersion stressor on the reinforcing and subjective effects of fentanyl in healthy volunteers, *Drug Alcohol Depend.*, 42, 133, 1996.
107. Joranson, D.E. et al., Trends in medical use and abuse of opioid analgesics, *J. Am. Med. Assoc.*, 283, 1710, 2000.
108. Mahony, E., Stalking a "serial killer" narcotic from Boston to Wichita, *Hartford Courant*, Hartford, CT, p. A1, February 23, 1993.
109. Fraser, H. and Isbell, H., Human pharmacology and addictiveness of certain dextroisomers of synthetic analgesics, *B. Narcotics*, 14, 25, 1962.
110. Jasinski, D.R., Martin, W.R., and Mansky, P.A., Progress report on the assessment of the antagonists nalbuphine and GPA-2087 for abuse potential and studies of the effects of dextromethorphan in man, *CPDD*, 33, 143, 1971.
111. Chilcoat, H.D. and Schutz, C.G., Age-specific patterns of hallucinogen use in the U.S. population: an analysis using generalized additive models, *Drug Alcohol Depend.*, 43, 143, 1996.
112. Levy, S., How R.Ph.s can curb teens' abuse of cough and cold products, *Drug Topics*, 146, 31, 2002.
113. Leinwand, D., Latest trend in drug abuse: youths risk death for cough-remedy high, *USA Today*, p. 1A, December 29, 2003.
114. Kirages, T.J., Sule, H.P., and Mycyk, M.B., Severe manifestations of coricidin intoxication, *Am. J. Emerg. Med.*, 21, 473, 2003.
115. White, W.E., The Dextromethorphan FAQ, http://www.erowid.org/chemicals/dxm/faq/, 1994. Accessed January 5, 2003.
116. Ator, N.A. and Griffiths, R.R., Principles of drug abuse liability assessment in laboratory animals, *Drug Alcohol Depend.*, 70, S55, 2003.
117. Mansbach, R.S. et al., Incorporating the assessment of abuse liability into the drug discovery and development process, *Drug Alcohol Depend.*, 70, S73, 2003.
118. Brady, K.T., Lydiard, R.B., and Brady, J.V., Assessing abuse liability in clinical trials, *Drug Alcohol Depend.*, 70, S87, 2003.
119. Jasinski, D.R. et al., Progress report on studies from the clinical pharmacology section of the addiction research center, *CPDD*, 121, 1975.
120. Jasinski, D.R. et al., Progress report on studies from the clinical pharmacology section of the addiction research center, *CPDD*, 112, 1976.
121. Jasinski, D.R. et al., Progress report from the clinical pharmacology section of the NIDA addiction research center, *CPDD*, 39, 133, 1977.
122. Jasinski, D., Pevnick, J., and Griffith, J., Human pharmacology and abuse potential of the analgesic buprenorphine, *Arch. Gen. Psychiatry*, 35, 501, 1978.

123. Howes, J.F., A simple, reliable method for predicting the physical dependence liability of narcotic antagonist analgesics in the rat, *Pharmacol. Biochem. Behav.*, 14, 689, 1981.
124. Lukas, S., Brady, J., and Griffiths, R., Comparison of opioid self-injection and disruption of schedule-controlled performance in the baboon, *J. Pharmacol. Exp. Ther.*, 238, 924, 1986.
125. Austin, R.P., Diversion of butorphanol, *Am. J. Hosp. Pharm.*, 40, 1306, 1983.
126. Smith, S.G. and Davis, W.M., Nonmedical use of butorphanol and diphenhydramine, *J. Am. Med. Assoc.*, 252, 1010, 1984.
127. Hoover, R.C. and Williams, R.B., Survey of butorphanol and nalbuphine diversion in U.S. hospitals, *Am. J. Hosp. Pharm.*, 42, 1111, 1985.
128. Evans, W.S. et al., A case of stadol dependence, *J. Am. Med. Assoc.*, 253, 2191, 1985.
129. Brown, G.R., Stadol dependence: another case, *J. Am. Med. Assoc*, 254, 910, 1985.
130. Preston, K. et al., Drug discrimination in human post-addicts: agonist/antagonist opioids, *NIDA Res. Mon.*, 81, 209, 1988.
131. Preston, K. et al., Drug discrimination in human postaddicts: agonist-antagonist opioids., *J. Pharmacol. Exp. Ther.*, 250, 184, 1989.
132. France, C. and Woods, J., Discriminative stimulus effects of naltrexone in morphine-treated rhesus monkeys, *J. Pharmacol. Exp. Ther.*, 250, 937, 1989.
133. Preston, K.L., Bigelow, G.E., and Liebson, I.A., Discrimination of butorphanol and nalbuphine in opioid-dependent humans, *Pharmacol. Biochem. Behav.*, 37, 511, 1990.
134. Sullivan, J.T. et al., Relative abuse liability and pharmacodynamics of transnasal and intramuscular butorphanol, *NIDA Res. Mon.*, 105, 452, 1991.
135. Preston, K.L. and Jasinski, D.R., Abuse liability studies of opioid agonist-antagonists in humans, *Drug Alcohol Depend.*, 28, 49, 1991.
136. Fukase, H. et al., Effects of morphine, naloxone, buprenorphine, butorphanol, haloperidol and imipramine on morphine withdrawal signs in cynomolgus monkeys, *Psychopharmacology*, 116, 396, 1994.
137. Preston, K.L. and Bigelow, G.E., Drug discrimination assessment of agonist-antagonist opioids in humans: a three-choice saline-hydromorphone-butorphanol procedure, *J. Pharmacol. Exp. Ther.*, 271, 48, 1994.
138. Zacny, J. et al., Comparing the subjective, psychomotor and physiological effects of intravenous butorphanol and morphine in healthy volunteers, *J. Pharmacol. Exp. Ther.*, 270, 579, 1994.
139. Knox, R.A., Complaints mount on migraine drug; nasal spray called highly addictive, *Boston Globe*, p. A1, May 27, 1997.
140. Anstett, P., A migraine drug's relief may come at a high price, *Detroit Free Press*, p. 1A, June 9, 1997.
141. Neergaard, L., Migraine drug Stadol said to be addictive, *Chattanooga Times*, p. A4, June 16, 1997.
142. Greenwald, M. and Stitzer, M., Butorphanol agonist effects and acute physical dependence in opioid abusers: comparison with morphine, *Drug Alcohol Depend.*, 53, 17, 1998.
143. Schlaepfer, T.E. et al., Site of opioid action in the human brain: mu and kappa agonists' subjective and cerebral blood flow effects, *Am. J. Psychiatry*, 155, 470, 1998.
144. Steele, K., Company faces wrongful-death suit, *Augusta Chronicle*, p. B2, April 18, 1998.
145. Preston, K.L. and Bigelow, G.E., Effects of agonist-antagonist opioids in humans trained in a hydromorphone/not hydromorphone discrimination, *J. Pharmacol. Exp. Ther.*, 295, 114, 2000.
146. O'Hara, T., Deputy's pain imperils her job; the school resource officer called in a phony prescription for a painkiller to ease her migraines, *Sarasota Herald-Tribune*, p. B1, September 2, 2000.
147. Walsh, S.L. et al., Enadoline, a selective kappa opioid agonist: comparison with butorphanol and hydromorphone in humans, *Psychopharmacology*, 157, 151, 2001.
148. Vigoda, R., A young life cut short by an overdose, *Philadelphia Inquirer*, p. A1, November 1, 2001.
149. Oliveto, A. et al., Butorphanol and nalbuphine in opioid-dependent humans under a naloxone discrimination procedure, *Pharmacol. Biochem. Behav.*, 71, 85, 2002.
150. Smith, B., District court, *Patriot Ledger*, Quincy, MA, p. 16, April 9, 2002.
151. Poklis, A., Fentanyl: a review for clinical and analytical toxicologists, *Clin. Toxicol.*, 33, 439, 1995.
152. Lohmann, B., Drugged-out doctors find help among their peers, *Los Angeles Times*, p. 2, October 5, 1986.
153. Pekkanen, J., Doctors' horror stories of drug addiction, *Los Angeles Times*, p. 4, December 6, 1988.
154. Lewis, N., Navy lab chemist held in drug case; man linked to powerful heroin substitute, *Washington Post*, p. C1, September 11, 1986.

155. Hilts, P.J., Narcotic lollipop tested as pre-surgical sedative; critics say children get wrong message, *Washington Post*, p. A3, February 23, 1989.
156. Anonymous, Fentanyl patches are new drug on street, *Addict. Lett.*, 8, 3, 1992.
157. Leavitt, P., Potent, deadly heroin surfaces in 3 states, *USA Today*, p. 6A, February 4, 1991.
158. Tyre, P., "Serial Killers" made drug 1,000 times stronger than heroin, *The Gazette*, Montreal, p. A1, March 10, 1993.
159. Anonymous, Rangel bill would equate fentanyl with heroin, *Alcoholism Drug Abuse Week*, 4, 6, 1992.
160. Morris, S., Narcotic lollipop denounced; group urges FDA to block drug, says painkiller endangers kids' lives, *Chicago Tribune*, p. 1, January 26, 1994.
161. Hilts, P.J., A la-la pop for kids leaves a sour taste, *New York Times*, p. 2, January 30, 1994.
162. Braun, R., A special kind of lollipop, *Washington Post*, p. A18, February 12, 1994.
163. McQuillan, A., Drug OD killed med school star, *Daily News*, New York, p. 48, December 14, 1995.
164. Kuhlman, J.J., Jr. et al., Fentanyl use, misuse, and abuse: a summary of 23 postmortem cases, *J. Anal. Toxicol.*, 27, 499, 2003.
165. Anonymous, Woman gets 2-year term in nephew's drug death; man died after ingesting fentanyl, a pain medicine, *Baltimore Sun*, p. 5B, May 29, 2003.
166. Tomlinson, S., Assistant at nursing home accused in medicine thefts, *Oregonian*, p. B2, June 10, 2003.
167. Westmoore, P., Drugs evident in deaths of mother, son, *Buffalo News*, Buffalo, NY, p. B4, November 26, 2003.
168. Magurno, J.A.J. Personal communication to K.L. Preston, January 19, 1990.
169. Degkwitz, R., [Dextromethorphan (Romilar) as an Intoxicating Agent], *Nervenarzt*, 35, 412, 1964.
170. Dodds, A. and Revai, E., Toxic psychosis due to dextromethorphan, *Med. J. Australia*, 2, 231, 1967.
171. Bornstein, S., Czermak, M., and Postel, J., [Apropos of a case of voluntary drug poisoning dextromethorphan hydrobromide], *Ann. Med.-Psychol.*, 1, 447, 1968.
172. Shulgin, A.T., Drugs of abuse in the future, *Clin. Toxicol.*, 8, 405, 1975.
173. Fleming, P.M., Dependence on dextromethorphan hydrobromide, *Br. Med. J.*, 293, 597, 1986.
174. Bem, J.L. and Peck, R., Dextromethorphan. An overview of safety issues, *Drug Saf.*, 7, 190, 1992.
175. Rammer, L., Holmgren, P., and Sandler, H., Fatal intoxication by dextromethorphan: a report on two cases, *Forensic Sci. Int.*, 37, 233, 1988.
176. Helfer, J. and Kim, O.M., Psychoactive abuse potential of Robitussin-DM, *Am. J. Psychiatry*, 147, 672, 1990.
177. FDA, Drug Abuse Advisory Committee, Open Session, Vol. 1, Public Health Service, Washington, D.C., 1990.
178. Szekely, J.I., Sharpe, L.G., and Jaffe, J.H., Induction of phencyclidine-like behavior in rats by dextrorphan but not dextromethorphan, *Pharmacol. Biochem. Behav.*, 40, 381, 1991.
179. Mendez, M.F., Mania self-induced with cough syrup, *J. Clin. Psychiatry*, 53, 173, 1992.
180. Craig, D.F., Psychosis with Vicks Formula 44-D abuse, *CMAJ*, 146, 1199, 1992.
181. Graedon, J. and Graedon, T., Some kids overdose on cough medicine, *St. Louis Post-Dispatch*, p. 3D, January 27, 1992.
182. Walker, J. and Yatham, L.N., Benylin (dextromethorphan) abuse and mania, *Br. Med. J.*, 306, 896, 1993.
183. Murray, S. and Brewerton, T., Abuse of over-the-counter dextromethorphan by teenagers, *South. Med. J.*, 86, 1151, 1993.
184. Hogshire, J., The electric cough-syrup acid test, *Harper's*, p. 24, June, 1993.
185. Holtzman, S., Discriminative stimulus effects of dextromethorphan in the rat, *Psychopharmacology*, 116, 249, 1994.
186. Graedon, J. and Graedon, T., Cough medicine shouldn't be taken for depression, *St. Louis Post-Dispatch*, p. 4E, March 21, 1994.
187. Wolfe, T.R. and Caravati, E.M., Massive dextromethorphan ingestion and abuse, *Am. J. Emerg. Med.*, 13, 174, 1995.
188. Hinderer, J., Teens misusing medicine to get high, *Bismarck Tribune*, North Dakota, p. 12A, February 8, 1995.
189. Graedon, J. and Graedon, T., Cough syrup may heighten delusions, *Austin American-Statesman*, Texas, p. F3, October 3, 1995.
190. Darboe, M.N., Keenan, G.R., Jr., and Richards, T.K., The abuse of dextromethorphan-based cough syrup: a pilot study of the community of Waynesboro, Pennsylvania, *Adolescence*, 31, 633, 1996.

191. Polles, A. and Griffith, J.L., Dextromethorphan-induced mania, *Psychosomatics*, 37, 71, 1996.
192. Dematteis, M., Lallement, G., and Mallaret, M., Dextromethorphan and dextrorphan in rats: common antitussives — different behavioural profiles, *Fund. Clin. Pharmacol.*, 12, 526, 1998.
193. Chung, H.S. et al., Demographic characteristics of zipeprol-associated deaths in Korea, *Arch. Pharm. Res.*, 21, 286, 1998.
194. Chung, H., Drug abuse trends and epidemiological aspects of drug associated deaths in Korea, *J. Toxicol. Sci.*, 23, S197, 1998.
195. Nordt, S.P., "DXM": a new drug of abuse? *Ann. Emerg. Med.*, 31, 794, 1998.
196. Warner, G., Parents credit facilities with saving son's life, *Buffalo News*, New York, p. 4B, April 12, 1997.
197. Anonymous, Homestead teen provided cough syrup ingredient to friend, who passed out, *Milwaukee Journal Sentinel*, p. 2, February 17, 1998.
198. Nicholson, K.L., Hayes, B.A., and Balster, R.L., Evaluation of the reinforcing properties and phencyclidine-like discriminative stimulus effects of dextromethorphan and dextrorphan in rats and rhesus monkeys, *Psychopharmacology*, 146, 49, 1999.
199. Betschart, T. et al., Dose-dependent toxicity of dextromethorphan overdose, *Clin. Toxicol.*, 38, 190, 2000.
200. Baker, S.D. and Borys, D.J., A possible trend suggesting increased abuse from Coricidin exposures reported to the Texas Poison Network: comparing 1998 to 1999, *Vet. Hum. Toxicol.*, 44(3), 169–171, 2002.
201. Fischer, M., Large amounts of a legal drug bought on the Web sickened four teenagers Wednesday, *Philadelphia Inquirer*, p. B1, January 8, 1999.
202. Smith, A.J., We're still losing the "drug war," *Ventura County Star*, California, p. B7, July 26, 1999.
203. Schutz, C.G. and Soyka, M., Dextromethorphan challenge in alcohol-dependent patients and controls, *Arch. Gen. Psychiatry*, 57, 291, 2000.
204. Blum, A., Cough syrup abuse on rise; Internet sites exacerbate problem, *Capital-Gazette*, Annapolis, MD, p. C1, January 6, 2000.
205. Goetz, K., Kids abuse cough pills, *Cincinnati Enquirer*, p. 1D, February 18, 2000.
206. Mangalindian, M., Alleged drug sale on Ebay raises liability issue, *Wall Street Journal*, p. B18, May 30, 2000.
207. Ochs, R., Cough-medicine high: a new worry in teenage drug abuse, *Newsday*, New York, p. C4, November 7, 2000.
208. Schultz, S. and Kleiner, C., Turning to anything, just to get that high, *U.S. News & World Report*, p. 60, June 5, 2000.
209. Branton, J., Police report: overdose of cold pills killed teen, tests say, *The Columbian*, Vancouver, WA, p. C3, January 4, 2001.
210. Parrish, A., DXM, Ritalin become drugs of choice for some BA students, *Tulsa World*, Oklahoma, p. February 3, 2001.
211. Anonymous, Monitoring of cough drug urged, *Wilkes Barre Times Leader*, p. 11A, November 4, 2001.
212. Cornish, J.W. et al., A randomized, double-blind, placebo-controlled safety study of high-dose dextromethorphan in methadone-maintained male inpatients, *Drug Alcohol Depend.*, 67, 177, 2002.
213. Roll, D. and Tsipis, G., "Agent lemon": a new twist on dextromethorphan toxicity, *Clin. Toxicol.*, 40, 655, 2002.
214. Anonymous, Police are alarmed by abuse of cold medication, *Union Leader*, Manchester, NH, p. B3, December 10, 2002.
215. Anonymous, Be alert to new teen drug threat, *Chicago Daily Herald*, p. 8, May 7, 2002.
216. Brown, K., Bill would ban cough medicine sales to minors, *Bismarck Tribune*, North Dakota, p. 7A, February 13, 2003.
217. Hall, S., Teen abuse of cold drug on the rise; many pharmacies relocate Coricidin behind the counter, *Detroit News*, p. 1A, March 14, 2002.
218. Simpson, K., Coroner's jury rules man's death accidental, *Pantagraph*, Bloomington, IL, p. A4, December 13, 2003.
219. Stone, R., Bill targets cough medicine abuse; intoxicant would be denied to teenagers, *San Antonio Express-News*, Texas, p. 4B, January 11, 2003.
220. Seyfer, J. and Wong, N.C., Cold medicine crusade, *San Jose Mercury News*, California, p. B1, February 17, 2003.
221. Fullerton, S., OTC drugs going BTC at pharmacy, *Iowa City Press-Citizen*, p. 11A, September 23, 2003.

Index

A

B

C

D

G

H

I

J

K

L

N

O

P

Q

R

U

V

W